THE LAND
OF NAM

The Vietnam War
in American Film

EBEN J. MUSE

The Scarecrow Press, Inc.
Lanham, Md., & London

SCARECROW PRESS, INC.

Published in the United States of America
by Scarecrow Press, Inc.
4720 Boston Way, Lanham, Maryland 20706

4 Pleydell Gardens, Folkestone
Kent CT20 2DN, England

Copyright © 1995 by Eben J. Muse

British Cataloging in Publication Information Available

Library of Congress Cataloging-in-Publication Data

Muse, Eben J.
The Land of Nam: The Vietnam War in American Film /
by Eben J. Muse.
p. cm.
Filmography: p.
Includes bibliographical references and index.
1. Vietnamese Conflict, 1961–1975—Motion pictures and
the conflict.   2. Motion Pictures—United States—History
and criticism.   I. Title.
DS557.73.M87   1995   959.704'3—dc20   94–34912

ISBN 0–8108–2952–5 (cloth : alk. paper)

Printed in the United States of America

 The paper used in this publication meets the minimum requirements of American National Standard for Information Sciences—Permanence of Paper for Printed Library Materials, ANSI Z39.48–1984.

I fy ferched llygaid las
Eirian ac *Elan Grug*

Contents

Part 4: The Land of Nam

Appendixes

Film Index

Acknowledgments

I am indebted to the people at the State University of New York at Buffalo who encouraged and advised me during the writing of this history. Professors Bruce Jackson, Diane Christian, and Leslie Fiedler were especially helpful in reading the early versions, as was Lydia Fish of the Vietnam Veterans Oral History and Folklore Project. I have presented some of the ideas in this work previously in *Literature/Film Quarterly*, *Durham University Journal*, and *Journal of American Studies*.

Introduction

Viet Nam and Vietnam

I originally intended to title this history *One Epic Narrative,* borrowing a phrase from a review of Susan Fromberg Schaeffer's *Buffalo Afternoons.* The reviewer had enthused that Schaeffer had embodied the war within a single, comprehensive storyline. At the time, the idea that an event as complex and lengthy as the American war in Viet Nam might be contained within one narrative struck me as absurd. Therefore I decided to discover what other stories were being told; to make the project manageable I limited myself to just one medium, the Hollywood film.

My research quickly taught me two things. The first was that I was right: there are a thousand stories about the War. A quick perusal of Gloria Emerson's *Winners and Losers* will show you a hundred of them. Mark Baker's oral folklore collection *Nam* will show a hundred more. There are as many stories as there were participants. The soldiers have their tales, the support personnel have theirs. The antiwar activists can tell some amazing stories, and the mothers of both those who went and those who remained can tell heartrending ones. Most of these people have had their stories retold in some of the more than 250 movies that Hollywood has released about the War and its effects since 1949.

What perhaps I should have realized from the start, however, is that of all the stories, anecdotes, memories, histories, explanations, and excuses that have come out of the War, only a few could succeed in catching the public's imagination; only a few could succeed in telling the public stories that fit in with what they knew about the War and what they knew about themselves,

9

their country, and its history. These are the few that, due to the populist nature of Hollywood film production, would dominate American cinemas and would become the one (sometimes epic) narrative of the Vietnam War.

The purpose of this book eventually became twofold. First, I wanted to explore the various storylines that emerged from the War through Hollywood. I wanted to describe what some of the alternative narratives of the war might have been, and to see if I could understand why they failed to capture or hold the American audiences. Since the United States first entangled itself in Indo-China's politics, several stories have gained popularity with Hollywood. At first, the story was a political one with a violent backdrop, and the films described America's presence in the country as benevolent peacekeepers or freedom fighters. The war story failed to catch on during the War years, and Hollywood concentrated instead on the homefront's story; the youth pictures of the sixties found the antiwar movement to be ideal material for attracting the new, young audiences. For a short time after the War, welcoming the soldier home became popular. These stories shifted in and out of favor with the shifts in the social and political fortunes of the United States, and I have tried to describe these films within this changing context.

To reflect this trait, I changed the title of this history from *One Epic Narrative* to *The Land of Nam.* I also adopted a spelling convention that requires a brief explanation. I refer to the nation in the Indo-Chinese peninsula where the War was fought as "Viet Nam"; but I refer to the land where Hollywood's soldiers go to fight as "Vietnam." The distinction is germane. "Viet Nam" means "the Viet peoples of the South," and has been the name of the country since about the second century BC. "Vietnam" is an American invention, a convenient spelling that has gradually come to be the accepted spelling on maps and histories. As such, it is convenient shorthand for naming a landscape that exists mainly in American imagination and memory. When a Hollywood soldier goes to fight the Viet Cong (an American phrase meaning Vietnamese communists), he frequently goes to Vietnam, a nation similar to Viet Nam, but without its history. Vietnam is a country torn from its past and future. It exists only as a moment of time, seldom more than twelve months, and it ceases to exist once the soldier leaves it behind. If he does not leave it, if he carries it home in his heart or his mind, he suffers from Post-Traumatic Stress Syndrome and will need curing (usually through selfless love, forgiveness, or a chance to refight the War).

The second goal of this book was to examine the narrative that I found increasingly dominated the American cinema where the Vietnam War was concerned. Oddly enough, this turned out to be a romance about a knight who travels for a year and a day in wild and foreign lands before returning to the safety of Camelot's walls. Only the knight was a foot soldier, the wild and foreign land was Viet Nam, and Camelot was the United States. The story was ahistorical and based more on the soldier's twelve-month tour of duty than on the War's history, goals, or outcome. These films described Viet Nam not as a historically, culturally, or geographically distinct location, but as a fantastic landscape where the soldier went to face semi-mythical beasts called "VC." Despite a wealth of period and location detail, the Viet Nam of these films had more in common with the underworlds of myth or with the Land of Oz than any Southeast Asian nation.

The distinction between Viet Nam and Vietnam is shadowy, since one place is a shadow of the other, and frequently it breaks down as filmmakers break through the darkness. But for Hollywood, and America as well, the distinction has been vital. By placing this divisive, destructive war into an imaginary space, the movies have managed to enclose it safely and set it aside. By placing Vietnam outside history, they have removed it from American history's mainstream. They have avoided the need to reimagine America's history as one that can incorporate a costly, destructive failure like the Vietnam War, and allowed it to be summarized as such things as "a noble cause" or a struggle between the good and evil in America's young men.

The War Film before Vietnam

Although the war film appeared before World War I— almost inevitably considering its potential for spectacle and melodrama—it was the War to End All Wars which established the shape that the war film would maintain until the Vietnam era. It was the industry's first opportunity to make films about a war that was actually being fought while the films were being made, and filmmakers were quick to realize the situation required an alteration in the conventions established by films like *The Birth of a Nation* (1915) which had been filmed fifty years after the event. Even before America became directly involved in this European conflict, opposition was rising against the Kaiser and his reported atrocities. Hollywood, like many other American industries, was eager to support the effort and make a profit while doing so. Propaganda films supplied both purposes and, despite President Woodrow Wilson's resistance, quickly became the staple of the industry.

Cecil B. DeMille's *The Little American* (1917) exemplified the theme. Jack Holt portrayed Mary Pickford's German-American suitor who answers Germany's call to arms. Pickford, the "Little American" of the title, willfully chooses to visit an aunt in France, convinced that the Germans will not dare to harm an American. Holt's regiment invades the aunt's home, however, and he nearly rapes America's Sweetheart in the dark! She escapes this fate when the lights come on, but must submit to degradation and torture at the hands of the brutal, dirty Germans. She witnesses the murder of civilians and, after managing to send the British army the position of the German guns, is sentenced to death. Fortunately a bomb arrives in time to kill the firing squad and Pickford escapes, but the lesson is clear. If Americans do not band together to stop the fearful Hun, American women will face the worst horrors imaginable.

The film itself was not a success, but the message—that Germans were subhuman animals against whom America must join to fight or else be ravaged—was. Films of 1918 like *The Prussian Cur*, *My Four Years in Germany*, *The Kaiser: Beast of Berlin*, and *The Eagle's Eye* all treated Germans as amoral, domineering beasts who would stop at nothing to achieve victory, and whose ultimate aims always included the destruction of the United States. No film dramatized this more graphically than *The Battle Cry of Peace*, which narrated the invasion and destruction of the United States by a vaguely Teutonic race that massacres the people and turns the Capital to rubble.

These films addressed two problems facing the American military: the need for soldiers and the consequent need to sell the war to the American people. World War I arrived at the height of a major pacifistic movement in the United States and, even after the sinking of the *Lusitania*, Americans needed a reason for entering a war thousands of miles away over European territorial rights which could not have been very clear to the average American. Defining the issues in terms of race overcame the latter obstacle, and defining that race as an immediate peril to the United States satisfied the former. The war thus proved to be a product that could be sold.

These were wartime exigencies, however, and the war lasted only a relatively short time for Americans. With the Armistice signed in 1918 and the United States still negotiating a separate peace until 1921, Wilson could finally prevail against the anti-Hun films. People had grown sick of the War by now, and the national propaganda interests during treaty negotiations would not be served by reviling America's negotiating partner. The few films left in production at the end of the war were generally altered to accommodate a more forgiving view of the enemy; in a peacetime version of *Hearts of the World*, for instance, one German restrains another from whipping Lillian Gish and explains, "War has made cruel beasts of most of us, but not all of us, thank God" (Brownlow 152). The war film in general fell into disfavor for several years, and when it returned it was a new, cleaner, more romantic model highlighted by the realism and romance of *The Big Parade* (1925), the rambunctious nostalgia of *What Price Glory* (1926), and the gallantry of *Wings* (1927).

Although World War I has generally been envisaged as the great antiwar and the embodiment of modern war's horror, during the postwar years this vision was primarily born out in the literature of the war, in memoirs and novels written by those who served at the front. D.W. Griffith expressed the truth for the movies while he visited the front in preparation for his war film, *Hearts of the World*.

> Viewed as drama, the war is in some ways disappointing.... Everyone is hidden away in ditches. As you look out over No-Man's Land, there is literally nothing that meets the eye but an aching desolation of nothingness. At first you are horribly disappointed. There is nothing but filth and dirt and the most soul-sickening smells. The soldiers are standing sometimes almost to their hips in ice-cold mud (Brownlow 148-49).

These battlefields provided none of the gallantry and spectacle that Griffith had favored in *The Birth of a Nation*; so Griffith resorted to re-staging the war in Britain.

After the war, the popular war films took to the air and behind-the-lines romance. A war of attrition makes poor spectacle, but it supplies splendid opportunity for displaying heroic self-sacrifice or tragically wasted life when the filmmaker focuses on the subjects of that attrition. *The Big Parade* manages the heroic self-sacrifice as its hero returns to the healing of his family after losing a leg. *All Quiet on the Western Front*, perhaps the quintessential antiwar film, presents the tragic aspect when its hero dies moments before the armistice, convinced of the futility and worthlessness of war.

The parallels between the First and Second World Wars encouraged the genre trends established by the first conflict. Both wars began between European nations, both caught America during a period of isolationism, both brought America in through an "unprovoked" attack, and both produced a tremendous shift from isolationism to militarism. As in World War I, the enemy, both Japanese and German, provided useful signs of difference which could be exploited by American film to display their evil. The Germans had their concentration camps and (equally useful to Hollywood) their martial goose-step and salute, while the Japanese had a sneak attack, mistreatment of prisoners, and distinctly non-European racial features.

An important difference between the two wars was the nature of the battlefields. While World War I had been a war of attrition and trenches, World War II provided a variety of battles, troop movements, assaults, and strategic advances to be subjected to the filmmakers' desire for spectacle and drama. Certainly it is the World War II combat film that Vietnam War fiction and memoirs evoke as a referent for what the soldiers expected to see in Vietnam, especially as those films were represented in the figure of John Wayne. According to Kathryne Kane's study of "The World War II Combat Film," Hollywood made twenty-four combat films during the war years and, after 1951, at least one World War II combat film appeared every year until 1970.

Like their World War I counterparts, the wartime films functioned as part of the American war-making apparatus by encouraging enlistment and uniting the country against the common foe. They stressed the importance of duty and unity against implacable, invasive foes and continued the structure of dualities implicit in the racism of World War I films. Ideology is irrelevant in the films because they present the war as a force of history, not ideology, and America is swept up in the tide of events. Roosevelt's decision not to strike the first blow put America in the position of reacting to an act of aggression; it created the impression that America had no choice but to go to war (an impression that may very well have been correct, although its accuracy was inconsequential in the context of its effect).

Pearl Harbor offered American propagandists the key to their justifications of America's war with Japan: the Japanese were a brutal, deceitful race that had already attacked American shores. After December seventh, no *Battle Cry of Peace* was needed to awaken the country to the threat of invasion. Japanese-Americans were quickly rounded up for the internment camps while Hollywood portrayed American soldiers being forced off the Philippines in *Wake Island* (1942) and *Bataan* (1943). History determined that the story in these films would be about retreats. In *Bataan*, for instance, an undisciplined group of American soldiers must guard the retreat of the civilians by defending a strategic bridge from the invading Japanese hordes. Although they know they must die, the men fight on until all the women and children are safe. The last soldier's defiant, final cry, "We're still here! We'll always be here!" echoes MacArthur's famous farewell and affirms America's indefatigable will and courage. Of course, America would return and not leave the Pacific to suffer Japanese brutality, and Hollywood followed that return almost as it happened, with film versions of the early battles arriving as the later battles were fought.

This historical moment dictated many of the genre traits for the combat film that would dominate film making in the latter half of the twentieth century, and which would profoundly influence America's perception of what warfare was and could be. It also determined the type of enemy which the Japanese, and by extension other Asian races, could be. According to these films (and much of American propaganda at the time), the Japanese are deceitful and do not fight by established rules. They are as willing to kill civilians as soldiers. The American mission is therefore justified by a direct threat to women and children. When combat is performed according to decent rules of conduct, it is inherently ennobling. The Americans fight by these rules, and so their noble sacrifice of life provides further justification for the cause. Americans are able to band together to fight a common cause, without at the same time losing any of the valued American individualism. The Asians, on the other hand, have no individuality to lose. They are an invading horde, an unruly mob controlled by an unseen, evil will. In the end, American victory is inevitable: "We're still here! We'll always be here!"

The European combat film came later than the Asian, just as the European war started later, and it utilized a different set of conventions. Until the allies managed to open a second front, the only material for films was the resistance movement (portrayed in films like *Casablanca* [1942] and *Watch on the Rhine* [1943]). Narrating this material required that there be good Germans resisting or being tortured by the Nazis; the sweeping racism of the Asian theater and of World War I was impracticable. The basic theme remained the same, however: America had to unite to meet the challenge destiny had provided.

Just as the end of World War I saw a change in attitudes toward the defeated countries, so V.E. and V.J. days saw changes in attitudes toward Germany and Japan. After World War I, however, America had experienced over twenty years of neutrality and peace. The end of World War II left America as the greatest economic, military, and industrial power on the globe and presented her with a new enemy. The Cold War started before V.E. Day with the race to Berlin and the Yalta Conference, and within five years it would lead to a new, conventional war in Korea. The Cold War was a new kind of war with no battles to depict, no sacrifices to be honored, no enemy to be grasped. It was a war that existed more in theory than in physical fact. It was the first war America had waged as a matter of policy rather than in reaction to another country's aggression.

It also turned out to be one of the most difficult wars to film, in part because of the difficulty of describing an enemy that was distinguished primarily by its indistinguishability. The Communist enemy could be anyone—including a Hollywood filmmaker. Until Korea came along and provided a more conventional frame for the combat narratives, Hollywood resorted to fifth-column intrigues and resistance pictures (which had worked in World War II before America entered the fighting and the second front was established) and science fiction films depicting Americans being taken over by alien forces.

Korea could only have been a relief to Hollywood. At last the enemy was aggressive and looked foreign. Samuel Fuller's *The Steel Helmet* (1951) was the first Korean War combat film and, like its World War II predecessors, it featured a small band of men with nothing but an Asian enemy in common. The enemy is recognizable from the earlier films; little beyond their flags has changed. The Asian remains a savage beast.

America itself, however, had changed. The country had only entered previous wars when our own interests were in immediate danger. Our military then had been composed predominantly of civilians serving for the duration: we had a mission to achieve; we achieved it; we went home. In Korea we went in as a "peacekeeping force" and, because in 1948 we had passed the country's first peacetime selective service act, America had a standing Army with which to achieve an American aim. Although we were part of a multinational force, the nature of that force was overwhelmingly American—right up to its leader, General MacArthur. *The Steel Helmet* reflects this change in its hero, the racist Sergeant Zack (Gene Evans) who refers to every Korean as "Gook."

> In contrast to the grizzled but chivalric GI Joe heroes of the
> earlier war films, Fuller's alienated hero ... is interested only

in survival and is untouched by the slightest hint of humanitarian or sentimental impulses. Thus, gorging himself on a
watermelon, he warns a fellow GI not to touch a dead American's body to get his dogtags. When the soldier is blown up
by the booby-trapped corpse, he sneers contemptuously, "Get
his dogtags, big deal." In addition, Zack wantonly machine
guns an unarmed prisoner (a North Korean officer) to death
in a half-mad frenzy after the death of his South Korean ward
(Auster & Quart, 10).

One of the fundamental assumptions of the World War II
films had changed now that America was a world power. In the
earlier films, America had won because it fought by certain rules.
Americans were the fundamentally decent ones. It was the Japanese who shot prisoners and civilians. Robert Mitchum reverses
these roles when, in *One Minute to Zero* (1952), he orders a band
of refugees bombed because he suspects Communist agents are
hiding among them. The discovery of Communists amongst the
dead justifies the slaughter. In *Battle Hymn* (1957), one Korean
explains the new situation:

What must one do when a choice of two evils is offered? . . .
In order to save, at times we must destroy.... The true answer
is in the Book: "Oh Lord, Thou hast seen my wrong—judge
Thou my cause."

By the time of the Korean War, America's "cause" had been
forced to justify a tremendous amount of "wrong" in the films.
The stakes seemed to have risen above the level of the World
Wars, perhaps because the threats of a fifth column in America
and the paranoia following the "Loss of China" and the McCarthy
era made it seem that, while America had been fighting one enemy
at the gate, another had slipped in through the back window. It
might also have been that America's unaccustomed position as
world power broker now forced the nation to be unusually self-
conscious about its motives. The level of commitment needed in
this new struggle is well illustrated in the POW films of the Korean War that stressed themes of collaboration and the need for
unrelenting commitment to the cause.

The subtleties of the Cold War robbed these men of the absolutes it promised them, however. Later Korean War films question whether this commitment was as historically preordained as it

had at first appeared. These films are set during the peace talks in which the justification for the brutality of the war was being negotiated. In *Pork Chop Hill* (1959) the men are ordered to take a worthless hill to prove a negotiating point to the Chinese. In *The Hook* (1963) an American soldier fails to kill a Korean prisoner on the eve of the armistice, and the morning after must convince his intended victim that today he is no longer the enemy and will not be killed. In *War Hunt* (1962) and *War Is Hell* (1963) American soldiers want to keep on fighting after the war is over just for the joy of it. The questions these films posed appeared as America negotiated peace with Korea and moved on to Indo-China and the Vietnam War.

Part 1
The War Years

Yanks in Vietnam

In 1948, the year Viet Nam first appeared in a Hollywood film, the country was already fighting for its independence. The French, who had lost their colony when the Japanese invaded, were fighting to re-establish their century-old rights to the land. Opposing them were the Viet Nam Doc Lap Dong Minh (Viet Nam Independence League), commonly known as the Viet Minh and led by the Communist Ho Chi Minh. Ho had formed the Viet Minh in 1941 to fight against the Japanese and the collaborating French administration. In 1945, the withdrawing Japanese army transferred power to the Viet Minh, marking the success of Ho's resistance and his pragmatic mix of Communism and nationalism. Ho summarized the history of the struggle in the Vietnamese Declaration of Independence, which he declared in September 1945.

> The truth is that we have wrested our independence from the Japanese and not from the French. The French have fled, the Japanese have surrendered, Emperor Bao-dai has abdicated, our people has (sic) broken the fetters which for almost a century have tied us down; our people has (sic) at the same time overthrown the monarchic constitution that had reigned supreme for so many centuries and instead has established the present Republican Government (Nguyen 478).

Postwar politics and the rising cold war, however, made Ho's declaration too optimistic. With the help of Britain, China, and the United States, France returned to Viet Nam in 1945 and contested the Vietnamese government's control. By December 1946, French warships were bombing Haiphong Harbor, the Viet Minh had fled Hanoi to fight from the countryside, and the Franco-Vietnamese War had begun. It would rage across Viet Nam for another eight years before the Viet Minh, under General Vo Nguyen Giap, won their decisive victory at Dien Bien Phu.

American moviegoers knew little of this history. 1948 was also the year of the Berlin Airlift, and Americans were far more interested in the European Communist menace than the Asian one. China would be an American ally for another year, and Indo-China seemed of marginal and primarily French concern. The American concern with Europe was apparent in one of the two films set in Viet Nam in 1948. In *Rogue's Regiment*, Nazi and Russian weaponry are the dangers. When an American (Dick Powell) joins the French Foreign Legion in Indo-China, it is to track down a leading Nazi rather than to fight the Communist menace. Contemporary reviewers of the film reacted to the Vietnamese enemy with varying degrees of sympathy and condescension. According to *The New Republic*, the film "assumes the Viet Nam nationalists in Indo-China were a group of bloodthirsty brigands," while *Time* declared that "the legion at Saïgon is heroically engaged in beating up some native revolutionists (they appear to want something to eat, or a vote, or some other non-military objective)." These two images of the Vietnamese enemy—brigands or revolutionaries—would define the limits of America's perceptions through most of American Vietnam War cinema.

The violence and eroticism of Asia also attracted Alan Ladd and Veronica Lake for one of their many film noir couplings. This time *Saigon* provided the scene for their love affair and murder mystery. Saigon and Indochina, however, are little more than exotic locales in these films. They are comparable, as Rick Berg notes, to Morocco in *Casablanca*, "exotic and marginal, the end of the earth where criminals and soldiers of fortune retreat, a place without an indigenous population, culture, history, or politics, never a nation, hardly a peninsula, not even a domino, merely a space on a map signifying imperialism's history and its frayed ends" (50).

In 1949, the establishment of the People's Republic of China altered that perception to a degree, though Korea's prominence kept the country on "the frayed ends." During the fifties, five films set in Viet Nam arrived from Hollywood. For the most part these were, like the Korean films of the period, tales of men on a mission. The patrol, squad, or pilots entered the country, achieved an objective or survived an ordeal, and left. In 1952's *A Yank in Indo-China,* for example, a pair of American flyers run bombing raids against Chinese munitions dumps. On one such run the Viet Minh shoot them down and they must escape through the jungle until United Nations forces rescue them. The enemy is, as it was in Korea, the Chinese rather than the native Communists.

Samuel Fuller's *China Gate,* released five years later, may be the most complex of these films. The framework of its conflict remains the same as in the *Yank* film: the French are fighting the Chinese to protect their colony in Viet Nam and the Americans fight as mercenaries. Brock (Gene Barry) and Goldie (Nat King Cole) fight with the French because, as Brock explains, "soldiering is my business—Korea got cold, Indo-China got hot." However, the presence of Lia (Angie Dickinson), a Eurasian saloon owner the French refer to as Lucky Legs, obscures the clarity of this reasoning. She was married to Brock years before, but he deserted her when she bore him an Asian child. Her lover is now the Chinese leader Cham (Lee Van Cleef).

The film opens with documentary footage of an agrarian Viet Nam, while a narrator describes the benefits which French culture brought to the country ("they advanced their way of living and the thriving nation became the rice bowl of Asia") and the danger that Viet Nam faces if Moscow's puppet Ho Chi Minh allows the oppressive Communist influence to replace the benign French. Fuller does not question the facts of this narrative. He does, however, suggest the ambiguities that enter into it when brought to a human level. The depiction of Cham emphasizes the Communist menace. While trying to convince Lia that "it is logical you should marry me," Cham takes her to his arsenal. "This is my garden," the Communist leader tells her and points at the weapons, "those are my revelation." Lia, however, does not immediately reject this slightly sinister marriage proposal. As a Franco-Vietnamese, she symbolizes the culture that France created in the country and for which the Communists and the West are fighting. Her struggle in the film is over whom to trust: the Communist Cham who, although almost religiously bound to destruction, desires her and can care for her son, or the racist American Brock who deserted her but can offer her son America, with all the benefits that place implies. In the end she chooses neither for herself; she dies heroically destroying the munitions dump. Her son, however, will go to America; she exacted that promise from Brock before joining the mission.

From the beginning then, American films described the conflict in Viet Nam as a war for hearts and minds. They compared the benefits of American and Communist intervention and weighted the scales toward America. Ideology exists, but only as an empty piece of rhetoric. Americans must fight communism on a personal level. Thus Lia's mission to destroy a Communist munitions dump is only a way to save her son from war-ravaged Viet Nam. Brock, too, fights ultimately for his Vietnamese son rather than a mercenary's purse or an ideologue's crusade. Americans must stop communism because it breeds men like Cham, who bargains for his lover with weapons and cold-bloodedly proposes marriage as if it were the only logical decision.

The only Vietnam film of the fifties that was not a simple adventure tale, Joseph Mankiewicz' simplification of Graham Greene's *The Quiet American* (1958), defines the conflict upon similar lines of personal loyalty and need. The setting of the story is Viet Nam, 1952, "when the French, the Communists, and assorted other parties were battling for control of the place," as the *New Yorker* review described the situation. The World War II hero-turned-actor Audie Murphy plays Alden Pyle, a youthful American idealist working for an altruistic American organization called Friends of Free Asia. Like Brock, Goldie, and the other American fighters in Hollywood's Viet Nam, Pyle is a free agent. America did not need to call up its young men in the defense of freedom; they saw the need to destroy the threat of Communism and responded. Pyle in particular responds by coming to Viet Nam with plans to develop its economy through a plastics industry. His deeply felt belief that America is Viet Nam's best hope (he even intimates that it is a Vietnamese man who has been to Princeton [as was President Diem] who "if all goes well" will "be its leader") earns him the love of Phuong, the Vietnamese woman he seduces away from the film's other protagonist, the English journalist Fowler (Michael Redgrave).

Like Lucky Legs Lia, Phuong, is played by a white actress (Georgia Moll); and like her predecessor, Phuong offers her love to the man who can best provide for her. At first this is Fowler, but the Englishman is too distant and intellectual; he treats both her and the War as abstractions rather than physical, human facts. Hiding behind a cultivated cynicism, he cannot recognize the value of Phuong, South Viet Nam's struggle, or Pyle's romantic idealism. In the film's conclusion, he learns that the Communists manipulated his cynical egotism and repressed desire for Phuong to make him betray Pyle. According to Mankiewicz, he ends the film "middle-aged, unwashed, unwanted." Like the French police inspector (Claude Dauphin) who reveals Fowler's failure while himself being part of a failed effort in Viet Nam, the Englishman represents the old-world colonialism that America would replace with its panacea of capitalism, democracy and freedom.

Pyle arrives in Viet Nam like a fresh breeze that stirs the hearts of Phuong and her country. He wants Viet Nam to be a healthy, independent nation that can join the United States in a brotherhood of defense against the encroaching Communist evil. While the French fight to maintain Viet Nam's colonial dependence on France, and while the English sit quietly and watch, the American acts to create a "third force" that can liberate the country. He brings economic opportunities for the people. He offers Phuong the security of marriage. Fowler, on the other hand, insists that the Vietnamese must resolve their own problems and merely maintains the woman as his mistress and serving woman. Phuong leaves Fowler for the American's promise of marriage in both the book and the film, but only in the film does she refuse to return to her former protector upon Pyle's death; Mankiewicz has her reject Fowler and go her own way. Pyle has at least liberated her—if not her country—from dependence on the colonial likes of Fowler. In Greene's more cynical novel, she returns to Fowler's care when Pyle's fails.

Pyle's economic aid scheme would have qualified him to be one of the heroes of William J. Lederer and Eugene Burdick's polemic *The Ugly American*. In response to the growing fear of Communist expansion, Lederer and Burdick wrote the book ("fiction ... based on fact") to argue that the responsibility for this growth lay in America's failed response.

> We do not need the horde of 1,500,000 Americans—mostly amateurs—who are now working for the United States overseas. What we need is a small force of well-trained, well-chosen, hard-working, and dedicated professionals. They must be willing to risk their comforts and—in some lands—their health. They must go equipped to apply a positive policy promulgated by a clear-thinking government. They must speak the language of the land of their assignment, and they must be more expert in its problems than are the natives (239–40).

The book presented its message through a series of stories about Americans working in a small, fictional Asian nation named Sarkhan. The characters are examples of good and bad overseas representatives, including a good ambassador, MacWhite, who studies the culture and the politics of the country, and a bad ambassador, Lucky Lou Sears, who comes to Sarkhan as part of his rise to a judgeship and confines his activities to social events. The title refers (ironically since the term has long since developed different connotations) to the good Americans who, although ugly, are hardworking, dedicated professionals with names like "Tex" or "Homer." The book was widely successful when it arrived in 1958 and expressed some of the ideas that soon-to-be President Kennedy would espouse in his Peace Corps and patronage of the Green Berets.

The film maintains the book's dichotomy of good and bad American representatives. In this case the good, "ugly" Americans are MacWhite and Homer and Emma Atkins (Pat Hingle and Jocelyn Brando). Homer is an engineer working on a major road development and Emma operates a small hospital. The bad Americans are the rest of the diplomatic mission and bureaucracy that MacWhite inherits. The Communist forces are represented primarily by two villains who constantly reappear to assassinate fellow Sarkhanese, to foment anti-American riots, or to spy; but their ties are to the Chinese rather than the Sarkhanese. The popular leader of the Sarkhanese, Deong, is a former freedom fighter who distrusts the motives of both the United States and the

Communists since he knows that both have only their own interests at heart. What he does not realize until the end of the film,
primarily because MacWhite fails to convince him, is that American interests are better for the country than Communist interests.

The situation has not altered drastically from *The Quiet
American*'s Viet Nam: the Communists want the country as a
subject-state; the Americans want it as an ally. What has altered
is the dangerously naive character. In Greene's novel, the naive
Westerner had been the American who believed he could change
the country with mere goodwill. Mankiewicz' film transformed
that naiveté into insight. In Englund's *The Ugly American*, lack of
faith in American goodwill has become the dangerous naiveté, and
Deong, who believes he can maneuver between the Communists
and the Americans, dies (like Pyle in '56 and again in '58) at the
hands of the Communists.

The film opens with the confirmation hearing for MacWhite
as Ambassador to Sarkhan. As the appointee enters the room, the
camera shows only his broad, black back walking forward, away
from the camera. This imposing presence reveals itself to be Marlon Brando in his first role as an older, establishment figure, but
he has not shaken off his previous roles as rebel and outsider.
MacWhite is a rebel within the foreign service. He is not a civil
servant but a newspaper mogul who served in Sarkhan during
World War II and feels he can affect successful change. He looks
awkward in the suits and cut-away tuxedos that are the uniform
of the civil servant, like a youth suddenly exalted to the council of
elders. The older establishment figures on the confirmation panel
distrust him because he is an outsider; the president chose him because he is an outsider; he believes he can achieve a free and independent Sarkhan because he is an outsider; because he is an
outsider, he will bring fresh ideas and methods into the fight
against Communism in this small, Asian nation.

America's fight against Communism, however, allows no
third parties, and MacWhite's status alters drastically when, upon
his arrival in Sarkhan, the Communists incite a riot at the airport
and nearly overturn his car. The incident firmly sets him against
the Communists, and, in the either-or logic of the Cold War, on
the side of the establishment. He strides into the council room at

the embassy and takes charge, demanding why his people allowed such an event to take place. That evening he visits his old friend Deong (Akio Wake), formerly an American agent in Sarkhan, now the country's populist leader. When Deong questions American motives, MacWhite labels him Communist and leaves in disgust. The ambassador has failed at being a third force himself and at perceiving the third force when it appears.

The rest of the story follows from this basic flaw. Because MacWhite assumes Deong is a Communist, he blocks any possibility of Deong asking him for aid. Instead he makes deals with the corrupt but anti-Communist Sarkhanese government, deals that serve to increase the unrest among the Sarkhanese people. Deong, spurned by America, makes a pact with the Communists to build a nationalist revolution. The revolution breaks out, but Deong's allies break their pact and kill him. MacWhite, left with a country on the verge of falling to the Communists, sees his error and tries to warn America through the television news. As he makes his speech about the need to treat the country as more than a pawn in the match against Communism, however, the film cuts to the television broadcast in an average American household where a bored husband switches him off.

MacWhite, who begins and ends as an "ugly" American, fails in Sarkhan when he aligns himself with the American foreign service and its dualistic logic. The other ugly Americans in the film, Homer and Emma Atkins, provide a contrasting lesson. They remain aloof from both forces and manage to continue working for Sarkhan's good. They live amongst the Sarkhanese who are building the road Homer engineered. They speak the language and know the people of the country. Most importantly, they do not ally themselves with any government or ideology. They work at projects that will help the Sarkhanese themselves. Emma runs a hospital; Homer uses the road project (which MacWhite usurps to serve the needs of an anti-Communist policy) to teach engineering and construction skills to the Sarkhanese. When the revolution comes, the local people form a human wall between these two Americans and the Communist marauders. They are the only Americans in the film to gain allies amongst the Sarkhanese people.

The lessons of the film are simple and straightforward. The Communists are a duplicitous, determined enemy with goals of domination. The small, Asian countries are vulnerable spots that the Communists are targeting. American policy in these countries is counterproductive because it places too little faith in the people of the countries. Pyle was right: America's revolutionary heritage does make it most suitable to come to the aid of these nations—provided it remains true to that heritage! It is unlikely that in 1963 the film modeled Deong on Ho Chi Minh; it describes him as a leader in South Sarkhan and the Communists are already a force in the North. But the political parallels seen in hindsight are remarkable. Both leaders attempted to negotiate between the Communist nations and the United States, and both leaders eventually allied themselves with the former in part because the latter refused them. Both scenarios also end in success for the Communist parties.

By the time the ugly American arrived in Sarkhan, 15,000 Americans were living in Viet Nam as military advisors and, although they were still in power, both Presidents Diem and Kennedy would be murdered before the film finished its first run in American theaters. By the time of their deaths, Americans had already made the trip to Viet Nam in several films (including *A Yank in Indo-China, Jump into Hell, Five Gates to Hell,* and *Brushfire)* and a pattern had developed that would continue through the in-country films of the war-years. It varied very little from that which Fuller had used in *China Gate* and before that in his Korean War films. The title of *Jump into Hell* suggests the main theme: an elite force entering the hell of Indo-China on a special mission to fight Communism. Like Ambassador MacWhite, the films perceive the Communists as the enemy and the good guys are those who work with the Western power— whether France or America.

Jump into Hell differs from the others mainly in that the elite force are Frenchmen, the special mission is the defense of Dien Bien Phu, and the result is failure. In *Five Gates to Hell,* a warband captures the members of a Red Cross medical team and forces them to treat the band's warlord. When the patient dies, the Vietnamese murder all the team members except for a few nurses who survive, according to *Variety*, by "sheer use of their sexual prowess." In *Brushfire* the Communists capture more Americans who are coming to the aid of anti-Communists in South Viet Nam. *Variety*'s comment about the film was vaguely prophetic: "There is a good story in the current small-scale conflict in South-East Asia. This is not it." In *A Yank in Viet-Nam* (1964), the Chinese shoot down an American advisor, so he joins a guerrilla band in its efforts to save a captured doctor and somehow finds time to romance the doctor's daughter. For the most part these were minor, poorly made films and received little or no notice in the press.

In his autobiography, Tim Page (the photojournalist made notorious in Michael Herr's *Dispatches*) described the making of a French Vietnam war film, *Cinque Gars pour Singapore*, filmed in Viet Nam and starring Sean Flynn, the son of Errol Flynn who died in the War. His description of the production, although from later in the War, sounds like what the production of many of these early, low budget films may have been like. Oddly, in 1992 another film, *Universal Soldier,* would rehash the idea of Vietnam veterans and cryogenically produced super-soldiers.

> And then Flynn turned up with a crew in tow, or vice versa, to shoot a bomb B flick.... The Gay French director had in tow his boyfriend's best friend; Terry Downs, a former Marine and world middleweight boxing champ, was cast as a gunny sergeant on R & R; most of the crew were French hipsters and the starlet a sultry Paris-based American model. Flynn was their leader and the star of the production. A thin plot of dagger derring-do had five grunts out of Eye Corps painting the town, being kidnapped by Red Chinese based on a freighter in the harbor, where they were put into cryogenics and reprogrammed to return to Da Nang and win the war. 'Seen Fleen', as the bar girls chimed, naturally had to save the day. I got paid to sit around various sets as an extra (135).

The first film to present regular American fighting forces in Viet Nam, *To the Shores of Hell* (1965), was also a second-run film with simplistic characters and plot configurations. The story involves an American officer who returns to Viet Nam for a second tour to rescue his brother—another doctor being forced to care for the enemy. This insistence on the Communists' need for

American medical personnel, and on their mistreatment of these doctors and nurses, recalls the racism of the earlier Asian war films that portrayed natives as being too primitive to have developed either medical practices or respect for medical practitioners. Consequently, America's mission in the country appears to be primarily benign and humanitarian. Warfare is only necessary because the Communists reserve this humanitarian aide for the military or for the Communist leaders and deny it to the people. The American military limits its activities to providing humanitarian aide and education or protecting and rescuing those who do.

The Viet Minh (or, as the American military renamed them, the Viet Cong), on the other hand, offer nothing to the country or the people. They are barbarians; they use poison arrows, burn orphanages and kill nurses and children. The first Commie to appear in *To the Shores of Hell* leaps on a young woman washing clothes in a stream; in the nick of time a local Vietnamese boy (named McFinn!) quickly drowns him in the stream while an American priest looks on approvingly. McFinn is an orphan; the Communists hacked his father and pregnant mother to death for refusing to inform for the Viet Cong. As well as barbaric, the communist Vietnamese are also extremely stupid. They must kidnap an American doctor to care for their wounded; he insults them in English as he treats them and they smile ignorantly back. They are poor soldiers who drink on duty and run at any sign of resistance. Their incompetence makes it impossible for them to be an independent force, and the film makes it clear that they are a tool of the North Vietnamese Army.

The South Vietnamese are cut from the same cloth as their Communist enemy in the North. They are, as an admiring American sergeant points out, very efficient in torture and ruthless in their goal of freedom. The difference is their reaction to America's superiority. The North Vietnamese refuse to admit that they need American benevolence, but at the same time they must kidnap American doctors to tend their wounded. The South Vietnamese, in contrast, submit to the American presence gracefully. They respect the doctors and priests who come to their aid, and they appreciate American leadership in the War.

In this film there is no question of ugly Americans or bad Americans; the Americans who go *To the Shores of Hell* are all dedicated professionals. Major Donahue (Marshall Thompson) asks for a second tour in Viet Nam so he can rescue his brother, a doctor whose dedication to his Vietnamese patients got him captured. The "battling padre" in the film refuses to live in the cities where he might be safe because no one needs him there. The battle-hardened non-com, Sergeant Zabriskie, has nothing but admiration for the local ARVN fighting force and, when he discovers an ambush, manages to kill all but one of the enemy before dying (the one he does not kill steals his watch).

The film's final scene confirms the message of American determination, power, and benevolence. A general greets Donahue and his brother upon their return to the States and assures them that, "while you gentlemen were in Viet Nam, we were turning out a product of our own." He pulls aside a curtain to reveal a parade ground covered with recruits marching proudly to the Marine Corp Hymn. In 1965, the year *Jump into Hell* appeared, American troop strength in Viet Nam reached 200,000.

The Failure of the Combat Genre

The claim that the Vietnam War was fundamentally different from other wars America has fought fails to explain the difficulty Hollywood had describing it through the conventions of earlier war films. It was not so very different. It was not the first that Americans had fought in jungles, nor the first to be fought for vague reasons, nor even the first in which Americans had committed atrocities. Americans had fought World War I in what may best be described as a wasteland for a cause that may not easily be described at all, yet Hollywood had managed to glorify and justify it.

In part the wartime combat film was a victim of the times, particularly the social unrest and the growing power of the media. David James argues that the problem for many in aestheticizing the event was that part of the event was the aestheticizing act.

> Michael Herr's claim in *Dispatches* that his attempt to write the war as the soldiers' stories was pre-empted by the fact that it was for them already so artificial and unreal, that it was for them already a movie, is only the most perceptive account of the war as a totally media-ted event, itself made over into the conventions of art. Such a Wildean, mimetic inversion, producing an event always already thoroughly aestheticized, presents a particular problem for a would-be objective documentist, for further transformations of it into language run the risk of merely multiplying the layers of reflexivity (43–44).

The Vietnam War was the first "television war," followed like a football season on the national news, with play-by-play provided by anchormen like Walter Cronkite with his famous, reality-establishing phrase, "that's the way it was," and his maps outlining the terrain and the current strategies. In 1968, during the height of America's involvement, over 600 accredited journalists worked in Viet Nam. The story was a daily staple in newspapers, newsmagazines, and news-shows. And it was not a single story but a mosaic of stories that seemed to describe a myriad of wars.

Michael Herr reports on this chaos in *Dispatches,* explaining that, while the journalists he knew reported their own experience of the War, their journalistic responsibility required that they also report the War as experienced by official sources—the Mission, the American Administration, the Saigon government—whether the two experiences were antithetical or not. He offers the pacification program as an example ("a swollen computerized tit being forced upon an already violated population, a costly, valueless program that worked only in press conferences" [230]). In 1967, he claims, there were more stories on pacification than on combat: "front page, prime time, just as though it was really happening" (230). It was not just the officials that were hamming it up for television, either. Herr describes soldiers reacting to the sight of the cameras as though they were in a war film, "doing little guts-and-glory Leatherneck tap dances under fire, getting their pimples shot off for the networks" (223).

According to Julian Smith, the ambiguities of the conflict caused the dearth of combat films. It is, he writes in *Looking Away: Hollywood and Vietnam,* "impossible to make a war film that does not assume that 'our' side is right" (11). This argument, however, elides the need to assume "our" side, a presupposition that, during the war years, was difficult to make. (Part of the Reagan revolution was the rebuilding of that assumption.) Before Vietnam, the war film had relied on the dichotomy of us versus them, Americans versus a very un-American enemy. By the 1960s, however, America's assumptions about itself were in crisis. In previous wars, Hollywood had been able to present the United States as a predominantly white, technological, male society united by a common goal to stop aggression. By the height of

American troop presence in Viet Nam, however, little of this presentation remained unquestioned. The civil rights struggle had radically altered American society and fractured ideas about the melting pot. To assume that all races melded into one society in America had become a racist attitude. The African, American Indian, and Asian cultures had all gained ground in the United States and claimed a stake in the American dream. The war film had used race as a convenient marker to delineate the enemy in previous conflict; now that marker drew jagged lines at best.

Technology also had defined American strength and benevolence. In World War II films, the American soldier knew he was safe when in the embrace of the American tank, warship, or airplane. As Kathryne Kane has noted in her study of the World War II combat genre:

> Americans rely on their technology to enable them to triumph over their environment and ultimately over the enemy. Their faith is rewarded in the end, but when they are deprived of their technology, they can be destroyed ... ("WWII Combat Film" 90).

By the sixties, however, America had bombed Hiroshima and Nagasaki, entered the cold war, and watched films like *Fail Safe* and *Dr. Strangelove or: How I Learned to Stop Worrying and Love the Bomb* that depicted American technology growing beyond human control. The growing antitechnology movement of hippies and flower-children suggested a developing distrust of the technology being used to process the war.

The government might have overcome these stumbling blocks by providing a cause around which Americans could rally. Instead, it abetted the problem by refusing to define the nation's goals or methods. Johnson built up the commitment gradually and without publicity; the Tonkin Gulf incident provoked America into the War, but it was too petty a skirmish and too dubious an event (the Johnson administration fabricated many of the story's details) to sustain American commitment for long. For his part, Nixon both extended the boundaries of the War and negotiated a settlement in secret. Meanwhile the military and the press measured the progress of the known war in statistics and in abstract—almost surreal—body counts rather than in advances and retreats.

In previous wars, filmmakers and their audiences could take America's mission for granted—Hitler, the Kaiser, Japan, China or some other aggressor had invaded other nations and America was fighting back. This is a narrative that goes to America's heart. It provides the structure for the American gunfighter ritual in which the hero must wait for the villain to draw first and hope to be faster than his hastier opponent. In Viet Nam, America drew first and consequently had to defend that action frequently. The War itself provided no actions, battles, or heroic resistance fighters with which to define a cause. The services had no front line on which to strut their stuff but were forced to prosecute the War against or amid a civilian population; nor did news coverage of soldiers burning peasant homes improve the War's image. Furthermore, America's allies, seemingly childlike and innocent in the early days, were appearing increasingly corrupt and unworthy of the expenditure of so many lives.

Given these circumstances, it is understandable that Hollywood offered the mission films as its view of Vietnam: the brave squad of men or Legionnaires going to Viet Nam to perform a dangerous, vital mission, then returning home with the job well done. This was the ideal behind one of the most popular items of the War as well, the elite Green Beret counterinsurgency outfits —patronized by President Kennedy and popularized both by Robin Moore's fictionalized account of his experiences with them and by Sergeant Barry Sadler's rendition of "The Ballad of the Green Berets."

The men of the Special Forces may have been the one popular (though not military) success of the War. As Alisdair Spark remarks in his study of the Green Beret in popular culture, they were "The Soldier at the Heart of the War." "From the very beginnings of American involvement," he argues, "through withdrawal to post-war self-examination, the myth of the Green Beret has served as a vehicle to express the purpose and experience of Vietnam" (30). When John Wayne decided to "tell the story of our fighting men in Vietnam with reason, emotion, characterization, and action ... in a manner that will inspire a patriotic attitude on the part of fellow Americans—a feeling which we have always had in this country in the past during times of stress and trouble" (Suid, "Hollywood and Vietnam," 20), the Green Berets provided the most likely vehicle for the message.

The Green Berets (1968) was made with the full support of the Department of Defense (DoD) and the Johnson Administration. Lawrence Suid has documented the extent to which Michael Wayne and James Lee Barrett (the film's producer and writer, respectively) worked to secure this support in a dissertation, "The Film Industry and the Vietnam War." Moore's book had found disfavor with the DoD because in it he insisted that the Special Forces conducted clandestine missions into North Viet Nam, an activity the military insisted was outside their current sphere of activity. Michael Wayne's choice of Barrett as scriptwriter was partly an attempt to assure the DoD that Moore would have nothing to do with the film. Barrett was to write "what amounts to an original screenplay using only a few incidents from Moore's book" (Suid "Film Industry," 125). Unfortunately, one of those incidents was the raid into North Viet Nam. The DoD insisted Wayne remove it before they would have any more to do with the film. Wayne, afraid to return to his father without the DoD's support, and wanting the equipment and personnel the DoD could supply, agreed. Barrett replaced the incident and wrote what he considered to be an inferior version of the script.

Financially, the decision was wise. Wayne knew the draw for the film would be his father, not the story. In return for the inferior script, they received approximately $1,000,000 worth of military assistance, including over eighty-five hours of helicopter airtime and 3,800 work days of borrowed military personnel. In addition, the Army gave them the use of Fort Benning, Georgia, sent a platoon of Hawaiian troops from Massachusetts to serve as Asians, and allowed them to film scheduled troop deployments. In return, the government billed the production company $18,623.64 (Cawley 74). The total cost of the film came to $6,100,000 (including John Wayne's reported million dollar salary), and it earned $8,700,000 during its first six months release. *Variety* listed it as the tenth biggest money maker of 1968, above *2001: A Space Odyssey*, *Camelot*, and *In Cold Blood*.

If the reviews can be believed, the Department of Defense got the short end of the deal. Probably the most vitriolic review came from Renata Adler in the *New York Times* who called the film:

> so unspeakable, so stupid, so rotten and false in every detail that it passes through being fun, through being funny, through being camp, through everything and becomes an invitation to grieve, not for our soldiers or for Vietnam (the film could not be more false or do a greater disservice to either of them) but for what has happened to the fantasy-making apparatus in this country. Simplicities of the right, simplicities of the left, but this one is beyond the possible. It is vile and insane. On top of that, it is dull.

But the film was an event even more than an aesthetic artifact, and the reporting in *The New Yorker* may have been more to the point.

> The audience gave the film a warm reception—laughing often, sometimes applauding, and even cheering a little. The applause and cheering were particularly strong at three points in the film: first, when Aldo Ray tells a newsman that you could "fill volumes with what they don't say in the newspapers;" second, when victorious Vietcong soldiers who are attacking a Special Forces camp are caught on the barbed wire of the camp and then set on fire by explosives; and third, when a machine gun in a place, in a few seconds of fire, slaughters hundreds of Vietcong in a Special Forces camp they have just overrun ("Glory" 24).

The film begins "to tell the story of the war" in the first scene as a group of reporters and tourists watch a Green Beret presentation. One by one the members of a special forces unit call out their qualifications, which include weapons specialties, technical specialties, and foreign language proficiency. Afterward, the soldiers allow the reporters and tourists to ask questions that provide opportunities for the soldiers to explain why America must fight in Viet Nam. Sergeant Muldoon (Aldo Ray) clarifies the situation for them.

> Let me put this in terms we can all understand. If this same thing happened in the United States, every mayor in every city would be murdered. Every teacher—every professor—every Senator—every member of the House of Representatives—and their families. But in spite of this, there's always

some little fellow out there willing to stand up and take the place of those who've been decimated. They need us—and they want us.

In response to allegations against the South Vietnamese government, he compares them to America's own founding fathers. Another sergeant pours a boxload of captured Communist weapons on the table before the skeptical journalist Beckworth (David Janssen) as proof that America and the Vietnamese are not just fighting a small guerrilla army but "Communist domination of the world." The sergeant thus justifies the Vietnam War by the same arguments used in World War II films. The Asians are deceitful, their conduct and brutality justify American intervention, and America has a historical mandate to defend liberty. Ultimately, according to these sergeants, America is really fighting to protect its own teachers, legislators, leaders, and families from certain death.

At the end, however, Beckworth complains to Colonel Kirby (John Wayne) that he remains unconvinced.

Beckworth: Your brainwashed sergeant didn't sell me.
Kirby: Didn't sell you what?
Beckworth: Didn't sell me on the idea that we should be in Southeast Asia.
Kirby: You ever been to Southeast Asia?
Beckworth: (looks away) No—I haven't.
Kirby: Huh! (walks away.)

Beckworth is unable to meet the moral force of that "Huh!" Confronted with the fact that he has not experienced the War, that he is not himself a warrior, he averts his eyes from Colonel Kirby. Kirby's reaction suggests more than that the reporter does not know what he is talking about. His obvious disdain for Beckworth, and Beckworth's own embarrassed reaction, suggest that the reporter has not earned a right to discuss the War. Beckworth lacks more than just facts. Until Beckworth arrives in Viet Nam and undergoes some combat experience, he has difficulty looking any of the Green Berets in the eye.

In other wars such a didactic opening might have been redundant, but with the mass of confused rationales for Vietnam, it was necessary to explain what had once been assumed, that

America was the little guy going against the larger foe in defense of liberty. Such an inversion is necessary before the Vietnam War can be incorporated into a John Wayne movie. What Lawrence Suid calls "Waynism" requires that the American side be the disadvantaged one. An attack by someone else always justifies his violence. As David Halberstam described it to Suid, "all the other guys are richer, more powerful and dominate the town, and you are part of the smaller group. You are leading the way for the numerically smaller group, weaker, don't have much ammunition, guns, whatever." In Vietnam, he continues, "you suddenly have to take Waynism and transfer it to a place where you are bringing on the heaviest carnage in the history of mankind, to a peasant nation" (Suid, "Film Industry" 122).

To do this Barrett and the Waynes portrayed the War through the mechanisms of the American Western, the genre in which Hollywood had first defined "Waynism." The film's main action takes place in Dodge City, a Special Forces camp in what an ARVN colonel (Jack Soo) describes as "the heart of VC country. One day it is nothing, next day we are there." The reference to the Western fort narrative is explicit in the camp's name and described location. Dodge City becomes more obviously modeled on the cavalry outposts in America's West when local farmers gather into it for protection. That these farmers and their families have lived on the surrounding farms for centuries does not alter the film's perception of them as helpless settlers who want only to live in freedom.

The enemy of this fort is scarcely discernible from the enemy of the Western. They do not scalp their victims, but they do massacre settlers, mutilate and rob the dead, and rape the women. With one exception during this section, the Viet Cong appear as a mass of figures scurrying through the dark, overrunning the fort en masse, or being exterminated by electrified fences and "Puff the Magic Dragon" (a machine gun in a helicopter that strafes the overrun fort and kills every Viet Cong invader).

The sole individual identified as a Communist is a swarthy, rat-faced spy spotted mapping out the fort. The Berets give him over to Captain Nim (George Takei), the ARVN co-commander of the fort, for questioning. Nim is an honest soldier who cares about his men and the fight against his enemies. His American counterpart describes him as "very active" against the Communists, and the reason becomes clear when he tells the Americans he is from North Viet Nam.

> My home is in Hanoi. I go home too someday. You see. First kill all stinking Cong. Then go home.

Nim defends the spy at first, insisting that none of his men could be a Communist traitor. Suddenly, however, he begins to beat the suspect viciously and Kirby must restrain him—until Nim shows Kirby what he has discovered in the spy's pocket: a lighter belonging to an American soldier the Viet Cong had captured and left mutilated in the jungle. Wayne orders all the Americans out of the room and the screams of the spy follow them out the door. Kirby explains the situation to the outraged Beckworth and concludes: "Out here, due process is a bullet."

As in *To the Shores of Hell*, atrocity is the defining action of the Viet Cong. Beckworth finally adopts Kirby's view when he sees the five-times raped and murdered body of a young Montagnard girl he had befriended; while Beckworth stands in the jungle, his moral stance destroyed, Kirby insists on describing another atrocity involving the rape of a chieftain's wife by forty Viet Cong. There is no logic to these atrocities, no ideology behind them beyond terrorism of the local people. In *Hollywood's Vietnam*, Gilbert Adair cynically wonders about the origins of the stories the writers used.

> Here we are again in the shadowy area of logistics, though the basic problem is ... not how you *film* an atrocity, but how you *invent* one. Why, for instance, forty? Was thirty considered too few? A tentatively suggested sixty laughed out of the writers' room? Or did the calculation proceed along the lines of an auction, with bids steadily rising until forty was settled on as a nice round figure, not so high as to become preposterous but high enough to justify a liberal's conversion to the cause? (1989, 22–23)

Whatever the reasoning, the result is that the Viet Cong appear more like an infestation than an army or a political movement.

The ARVN provide a sharp contrast to the Viet Cong rabble. They have grown into fighting men since *To the Shores of Hell*.

Like their leader, Nim, they are well disciplined and dedicated to the fight. They spend most of their time out on patrols which they leave for and return from in tight formation. During the attack on the fort, they fight side-by-side the Americans; Nim dies when he remains behind to explode the last line of claymores.

These two groups alone represent the Vietnamese: the wild bands of the Viet Cong and the disciplined troops of the ARVN. The only civilians are the Montagnard tribesmen—the helpless innocents the ARVN defend and the Viet Cong abuse. There is no sense that the ARVN share any social, political, national, or even genetic traits with the Viet Cong beyond the fact that they all look alike. The film offers no explanation or sense of where the Viet Cong come from. The reason for this omission may go back to a Pentagon directive against referring to the War as North against South (Suid, "Film Industry," 129), but Michael Wayne's explanation of his film philosophy seems to be more to the point.

> In a motion picture you cannot confuse the audience. The Americans are the good guys and the Viet Cong are the bad guys. It's as simple as that.... When you are making a picture, the Indians are the bad guys (Suid "Film Industry," 137).

The film's recreation of the War as a Western romance eliminated Viet Nam from the context of the film. The war that *The Green Berets* describes bears only the faintest resemblance to even the most hawkish of the contemporary descriptions of the War. Even Moore, who supported the War wholeheartedly, had insisted on including scenes of ARVN incompetence and South Vietnamese corruption. Batjac Productions, however, did not want to "confuse the audience," so they depicted the bad guys as despicable and the good guys as impervious to taint. An early briefing scene locates the "bulk of our problem ... in the northern most areas of the country" and Dodge City is "in the heart of VC country"—implying that the enemy is contained within a specific geographical area. There is, it seems, a front in Vietnam after all. Although both Barrett and John Wayne went to Viet Nam (Wayne came under fire at one point), the film assiduously ignores authenticating detail beyond the proper jargon and technology.

Suid blames the film's failure on the production companies compromises with the Pentagon. He argues that the Waynes traded authenticity and entertainment for military equipment, leaving them with "just another John Wayne adventure story, in fact, one of his lesser efforts" ("Film Industry," 137). The problem, however, was not that the production compromised, but that for John Wayne there was no compromise involved. The Vietnam War was not a John Wayne war; *The Green Berets* war was. Wayne assumed the weaker side were the good guys; the Vietnam War was an inversion of that, so he re-imagined the War. For Wayne, there was no choice.

He re-imagined it, however, in a mold that no longer worked. As Michael Wayne said, "maybe we shouldn't have killed all those Indians." The Western genre had drastically altered by the late sixties. In 1968 filmmakers could no longer make Indians and their iconographic counterparts the enemy without some rationalization. The perception of the white settlers as the weaker, moral party no longer controlled the story. In Westerns like *Soldier Blue* and *Ulzana's Raid*, the white man was not only the more powerful party but often the immoral one. *The Green Berets'* recreation of Viet Nam as a new version of the old West fails not only because it does not resemble the Vietnam War that existed, but because it tries to pattern its recreation on a genre that did not currently function in America. Batjac Productions failed to take the genre's changes into consideration when it applied that genre to Vietnam. The result was "just another John Wayne adventure story."

Other Wars—The Vietnam Allegory

Despite its financial success, *The Green Berets* was nearly Hollywood's last attempt to depict the War until the late seventies. The outraged reviews and the widespread picketing may have convinced the studios that any further attempts would fail without the draw of a star of John Wayne's magnitude. The only exception was a biker film called *The Losers,* in which the government sent a motorcycle gang to rescue an American diplomat being held in Cambodia.

Hollywood could hardly afford to completely ignore an issue that enthralled the American public, so the problem of presentation remained.

> In countless World War II films, the enemy was shown destroying civilians and setting up puppet governments—now *we* were doing it.... In countless earlier films, we first aided struggling nations, then were aided by native undergrounds—now we were interdicting aid to a struggling nation and fighting an underground. For lack of a formula, a way to "handle" the war, Hollywood turned elsewhere (Smith 23).

One place they turned to was the "Vietnam allegory" film that appeared in the late sixties and early seventies. Although set in other wars and other lands, contemporary reviewers and later critics saw them as commenting directly on the war in Viet Nam. Films that critics have identified as allegorical studies of the War include *Ice, Catch-22, M*A*S*H, Soldier Blue, Little Big Man, Johnny Got His Gun, Ulzana's Raid, Slaughterhouse-Five,* and even *Night of the Living Dead.* All of these films told war stories during a war, and audiences could hardly fail to view them as either referring to the current military situation or having their description influenced by it.

They also share a critical view of the machinery (both social and mechanical) of modern warfare, though they may not specifically oppose war itself. *Ulzana's Raid* approves of combat as a method of establishing masculine identity, and the doctors of *M*A*S*H* oppose the war only when it conflicts with their personal plans. But the forces that provoke or conduct wars come under assault in all of them: the officers in *Ulzana's Raid* speak only in phrases from a military manual; *M*A*S*H* officers are inept boozers and womanizers who put more effort into football confrontations than military ones; General Custer in *Little Big Man* is a racist egomaniac. Warfare itself often seems either meaningless (*Catch-22*), imperialist (*Ice*), or juvenile (*M*A*S*H*).

The revisionist Westerns of the late sixties and early seventies (such as *Soldier Blue*, *Little Big Man*, and *Ulzana's Raid*) come closest to matching the Vietnam War in iconography and event; they are also the ones which critics and reviewers most frequently refer to as Vietnam allegories. A contemporary audience could hardly fail to see Vietnam's shadow behind the scenes of American soldiers fighting an inscrutable, technically primitive, guerrilla force of natives. News of the massacre at My Lai was ubiquitous by the time *Soldier Blue* showed the American Cavalry bayoneting children and helpless women, and the Indians who murder the settlers in *Ulzana's Raid* re-enact the brutal atrocities committed by the Viet Cong. The parallels between the wars were recognizably close enough for John Wayne to graft the Indian wars onto the Vietnam War in *The Green Berets*. When that film's reception discouraged further direct representations of the War, filmmakers simply grafted the Vietnam War onto the Indian wars.

The Western was well suited for recreating a war which film production companies were unwilling to show as itself. It had been among the most popular and profitable film genres since the silent years, which meant that the production companies would be willing to risk financing them even if they were controversial. It could also bring many of the era's popular movements together into one narrative: the civil rights, youth, hippie, and antiwar movements all congealed around the story of a young white soldier sent to fight in a brutal, ignoble war against a peaceful or noble race unsullied by modern civilization.

In *Soldier Blue* the young white soldier is Honus Gant (Peter Strauss), the lone military survivor of a cavalry squad attacked by Cheyenne Indians. The only other survivor of the attack is Cresta Lee (Candace Bergen), a white woman whom the Cheyenne had captured two years before but now released. The majority of the film follows the pair's attempts to reach safety and to develop a respect for one another based on some other premise than her role as woman and his as soldier. Bergen portrays the former captive as a thoroughly modern, independent woman who refuses any patronizing from Honus and never seems to consider his masculine role as implying any patriarchal priority. (When she later returns to the Cheyenne, the Indians' attitude toward Cresta suggests that this independence developed from her stay with them, rather than from the generally chauvinistic whites.)

At any rate, Honus's prowess as a warrior and wilderness traveler would not inspire her to any other attitude. He has only been in Indian country for a short time and is still innocently convinced of the masculine warrior ethic; before leaving the site of his platoon's massacre, he pauses to recite "The Charge of the Light Brigade." Honus proves to be too sweet-natured and honest to be a soldier, however. When Indians capture them, Cresta desperately arranges a fight between Honus and the leader which Honus accidentally wins; but as he stands over the defeated Indian, knife in hand, with Cresta shouting to "kill him—finish it," he refuses and steps away. The other Indians quickly leap into his place and stab their leader to death before running off, and Honus walks in disgust away from his foe and from Cresta.

Honus never overcomes his passive inclinations. In the climactic scene, a recreation of the Sand Creek Massacre, he watches as a pompous colonel whips his men into a frenzy and unleashes them against the peaceful Indian village in which Cresta had once lived. The Cheyenne leader comes forward carrying an American flag and a white flag of truce, but the colonel refuses to see it and orders his men to avenge the white man. Honus neither joins the carnage nor fights to stop it. He shouts for Cresta, weeps over the atrocities, and places the body of a young child into the arms of the bemused colonel (who had himself shot the child only a moment before).

At the film's conclusion, Honus is marching in chains behind a wagon, but he appears as childishly happy as he had at the outset. Although the Indians are all dead, he sympathized with their plight and is pleased with himself for that. He has learned not to kill but not to prevent killing. A postscript shows the film's sympathy for this point of view; it dutifully explains that Washington decried the massacre and held those responsible to account. That such official renunciations of the massacre had no effect on the eventual fate of the Indian is ignored. Like Honus, the United States enjoyed a sense of righteousness for having not abetted a wrong, but suffered none of the problems associated with trying to right it. Likewise, the film treats Honus and his behavior at face value while emphasizing his sympathy for the demolished Indians.

Ulzana's Raid follows another young idealist who must confront the brutality of war in Indian Country. Lt. Debuin (Bruce Davison), the son of a preacher who believes that accord is possible between God and the Army, receives his first command when the Apache Ulzana escapes from the reservation and goes on a raiding party toward Mexico. Debuin's orders are to track the Apaches and kill them or bring them back to the reservation. Two guides help him on this mission—a white scout named McIntosh and an Apache scout named Ke-Ni-Tay. The search leads them past several atrocities committed by the Indians against settlers in the area, and for the young Lieutenant, it becomes a quest for understanding. "Why do they do these terrible things," he asks repeatedly, receiving answers that vary from McIntosh's "whims" to Ke-Ni-Tay's "power" to the patrol sergeant's "doesn't matter why."

Both *Soldier Blue* and *Ulzana's Raid* try to resolve a basic problem of the War: how to understand the enemy's motives and methods. The former film relies on the pacifist notion that, if a soldier could only get to know his enemies, he would cease to have enemies. Since the legitimate enemy is unknowable—both the Indians and the Vietnamese are dark, foreign, and savage—the film intercedes with Cresta, a beautiful blonde white woman who acts as the film's Indian figure. Her presence allows Honus to gradually grant legitimacy to a non-European race's concerns and nobility.

At its heart, however, *Soldier Blue* is another of the period's antiestablishment, youth films. The title of *Newsweek*'s review of the film, "U.S. Cav Go Home," recognizes the film's antagonist: the United States government in its cavalry representation. The Indians function as a non-white other with which the youth in the film (Strauss and Bergen are the youngest of the film's main actors) can align themselves against the evil establishment. To do this, the film follows the trend (evident in other Westerns of the period) of mythicizing the Indian into the noble savage, making him a more palatable ally. The antiwar movement was doing the same thing with the North Vietnamese—ignoring or excusing its crimes so that they could support its goals.

In *Soldier Blue*, although the Indians massacre the cavalry escort, they do so in a fair fight; they win largely because an officer failed to prepare for possible attack. Their lovely, blonde spokesperson Cresta provides reasonable explanations for this and other Indian attacks. The U.S. Cavalry, on the other hand, attacks a village filled with civilians after its chief has come forward under a flag of truce. An absurdly maniacal commander leads the soldiers with inanities about glory and vengeance, and they rape and murder women and children with wild, gleeful abandon. In his production notes for the film, Director Ralph Nelson makes the connection between this incident and Vietnam explicit; he describes the Sand Creek Massacre as having "caused a shock comparable to that which has recently followed reports of a massacre by American soldiers at My Lai."

Ulzana's Raid, on the other hand, while still keeping a youth at the film's center, requires him to keep company with Burt Lancaster as the scout McIntosh; and instead of a beautiful white intermediary, the Indians have an Indian spokesman, the patrol's scout Ke-Ni-Tay. While still presenting the army as bureaucratic, the film depicts only Indian atrocities. The result is a diminution of the basic antinomies present in *Soldier Blue*. Understanding the enemy does not lead to peace. The film ends with all of Ulzana's band being killed in a skirmish with the patrol. The film also denies the youth any moral superiority over the older members of the squad. If he believes the Indians are deserving of respect at the film's outset, it is only because he doesn't know the Indians. Once in pursuit of Ulzana, who leaves a bloody trail, the lieutenant quickly learns to hate the Indian for his cruelty.

Lt. Debuin begins the hunt for Ulzana believing that he can remedy the "lack of Christian feeling that's at the heart of the problem." That was *Soldier Blue*'s solution, but in this scenario it does not work. The Indians are not Christian. Spiritual healing for them comes from a source which Christian theology must find appalling. Ke-Ni-Tay explains that a dead man's power goes to the man who killed him. A body releases its power as it dies, and the slower the death the more power it releases. "Fire that burns long time, heat many people," Ke-Ni-Tay explains. The Lieutenant's growing realization of the chasm separating the two cultures leads him to hate his enemy. What a Christian cannot love, it seems, he must hate. Like MacWhite, the ugly American, the Lieutenant thinks in absolutes. Either the natives are future Americans or they are the enemy.

McIntosh, who has an Apache wife, understands the Indian without hating him. "Be like hating the desert for there not being enough water on it," he tells the lieutenant. "Right now I can get by just being plenty scared of them." Less prone than the lieutenant to dichotomous thinking, he sees history at work in the West. The Indian and white cultures could not exist in harmony, so the two races have fought for control of the territory, and the white man has won. He knows that Ulzana can not hope to recapture any territory in his raid and that the Apache's goal is merely to escape the degradation of the reservation.

The story leaves the problem of justice out of the situation because there is no possibility that the white man will draw back from his position. The conquest is history. The white farmers live there now and work the land. Both groups have a right to the land; both have valuable and viable cultures; but one side had to win, and history gave victory to the whites. The film might have treated Ke-Ni-Tay as a traitor to his race, but instead it grants him respect in equal measure to Ulzana or to McIntosh. Both sides deserve loyalty. Ulzana's crime is not that he is an Indian or a brutal murderer; it is that he is a renegade and a threat to the peace. By assuming the inevitability of conflict in the American West, *Ulzana's Raid* implies a similar inevitability in Viet Nam.

Though the pacifism in the films differs to a marked degree, the antiwar attitudes they voice reflect the concerns of the movement opposing the Vietnam War. The atrocities committed by the whites and the Indians in both *Soldier Blue* and *Ulzana's Raid* are reminiscent of the atrocities being reported in Viet Nam, and the genocidal policies they describe resemble the policies that the antiwar movement claimed America was carrying out in Viet Nam. Furthermore, both films rationalize the brutalities that their noble savages commit, just as the liberal antiwar movement frequently idealized the North Vietnamese and their often brutal actions.

Most of the films that critics have considered Vietnam allegories combine some of these traits. *Little Big Man*, for instance, describes the cavalry's genocidal policies toward the noble savages, and the protagonists of *Ice* are Americans fighting a guerrilla war against their own nation to stop its genocidal policies from advancing into yet another technically undeveloped nation (this time Mexico). Other films treated by critics and reviewers as allegories of the War describe a vastly different conflict, however. Sumiko Higashi, for instance, has described a critique of capitalism in *Night of the Living Dead* and pointed out iconographic details that, she believes, provide a link to Vietnam. Films like *M*A*S*H* and *Slaughterhouse-Five* are antiwar films produced during the Vietnam War, and therefore easily linked to America's great antiwar war, but their plots, characters, and iconography seem to have little in common with the other Vietnam depictions of the era. *M*A*S*H* is more concerned with bureaucracy and human weakness than an Asian war; military combat seldom interrupts the activities of the doctors except to provide them with a reason for coming together originally.

That the first combat films to arrive after the War resemble several of these films suggests that both the Western and the other narratives succeeded as representations of the War. *The Boys in Company C*, for instance, has an absurdist philosophy and offers a critique of bureaucracy and officers that might have come straight from *M*A*S*H*. It was the Western, however, that quickly dominated the other forms. John Wayne saw its application when he made *The Green Berets*, and increasingly the most successful films about the War, including *The Deer Hunter, First Blood,* and *Platoon*, would find their truths about the War in its iconography and conflicts.

Welcome Home, Soldier Boys

While combat or actual depiction of Viet Nam might have seemed closed to the non-documentary filmmakers, two other aspects of the Vietnam experience had niches ready for them. The antiwar movement in the States was one of these. Perceived by the public as predominantly a youth movement and having its roots in the general activism of the period, it was tailor-made for the youth films that became a major part of Hollywood's output in the 1960s and '70s. Hollywood also found it profitable to exploit the veteran, the survivor of the War whom television viewers had grown accustomed to seeing burn villages and kill Vietnamese—both military and (especially after My Lai) civilian. The veteran was a valuable commodity for any storyteller in need of a villain defined by traits other than race.

At the end of World War II, Franklin Fearing suggested that, "the meanings with which we clothe the bare facts of demobilization will reveal our basic conceptions of the war itself and the reasons for which it was fought," and popular memory of WWII's demobilization is of parades, welcome home parties and a new national prosperity. The return of the soldiers was a reason to celebrate, and the veteran was the new celebrity. The veterans of Vietnam, in contrast, were unwelcome reminders of a national crisis. These veterans did not arrive on troop ships in large groups; they flew in individually as their tours of duty ended, their arrivals seldom marked except by families or protesters. Nor did any new prosperity welcome them home, as Nixon's Vietnamization brought one million soldiers home the same year that his economic strategy planned for higher unemployment (Dean 61). For the press, the veteran scarcely existed as a story after leaving Viet Nam. He only returned to the front pages when he entered the streets as a criminal or in protest groups like the influential Vietnam Veterans Against the War.

He existed for the public, though. They had watched him on television in the evenings and seen his handiwork. The first televised war had seared images of combat, death and devastation into the public consciousness, but it had done so without providing a satisfying context for the violence. With a couple of minutes to tell a story, the television newsman in Viet Nam could not hope to fully explicate the images that they offered for American consumption. Even in the many longer, thirty- and sixty-minute documentaries American television produced during the War, the nature of the medium severely limited the amount of verbal explication. The result was a Viet Nam that was not a geographical, historical, or political place but a metaphorical one: a warscape instead of a landscape.

If the soldiers were the inhabitants of this warscape, the veterans were its emissaries and immigrants. They wandered through our streets, into our homes and among our families; whereas in the fifties anyone you knew might be a Communist, in the sixties he might be a veteran who could suddenly burst out in uncontrollable violence. Those who doubted the danger the veterans represented were reprimanded by the occasional, and celebrated, outbursts by vets who had failed to adjust to civilian life, who found it impossible to resume their previous lives or who failed to reject the violence they had been forced to embrace (or eagerly embraced) in the War. In 1973's *The Stone Killers*, a doctor diagnoses the problem in a psychotic veteran named Lipper.

> Aggression and violence are part of a learning process. They're habit forming. Now Lipper was a type of addict. We tend to count the victims among the innocent. Now that's not always so Lieutenant. After we've shed our pity for the basketcases and the burned children, we've nothing left for the psychopath we've created. Vietnam doesn't make heroes; it makes a generation of Lippers.

Since this character existed for the public, it was there for Hollywood to use. He showed up in several horror films: a witness to a

Viet Cong rape and murder who now bombs lovers in their cars in
The Ravager (1970); a psychotic killer terrorizing a family in *To
Kill a Clown* (1972); a zombie who injects himself with other
people's blood in the Canadian *Deathdream* (1972); and the victim of a mad scientist's brain transplant experiments *The Blood
of Ghastly Horror* (1972 and also known as *The Fiend with the
Electronic Brain, Psycho a Go-Go,* or *The Love Maniac*).

Such horror stories suggest a powerful mixture of fear and
guilt. *Deathdream*'s ghoul Andy (Richard Backus), a blood-
addict (he shoots it into his veins with a syringe), explains the
situation to one of his victims while stabbing him to death:

> I died for you, Doc. Why shouldn't you have returned the fa-
> vor? You owe me something Doc. You owe me this.

But the guilt was not just over sending boys to die for their country. Films like these evince a growing awareness that America had
failed in its part of the bargain; if you send boys to fight for you,
you return the favor with some sort of honors or preferential
treatment—not with fear and suspicion. In Viet Nam, these men
had killed as soldiers, but that did not make them killers at home.
Tiger by the Tail (1968) and *The Bus Is Coming* (1971) manifested this confusion in veterans falsely accused of murdering
their own brothers.

If, however, being a soldier did not make one a killer, it did
make him a hero—or should. The vampyric veteran Andy in
Deathdream provides an illuminating metaphor. The special horror of the vampire comes not merely from the violence associated
with him but from the fact that he seems to be one of us or, frequently, the best of us. The vampire is commonly an attractive
person with unusual reserves of strength and will. If he was not
interested in feasting on the blood of society, he might be a welcome member. The veteran shares these traits. Andy is attractive
and strong and his family and lover maintain intense devotion to
him; he is able to murder his lover because her love for the remembered Andy overcomes her suspicion at the sight of his de-
composing hands. He remains, however, an evil monster that the
War created and society must destroy.

This doomed devotion to Andy reflects the veteran's social position as the one member of society that has proven his manhood in war. Draft dodgers and conscientious objectors might have shown equal amounts of courage and resolution, but not in the same arena. The sense of war as the last great rite of passage into manhood is deeply rooted in American culture and is apparent in the eighties "Vietnam guilt-chic" noted by Myra MacPherson and others (the reference is to several columnists who described their feelings of having forfeited an important life experience by avoiding military service). During the war years, that sense of emptiness hid under the antiwar rhetoric but surfaced in the film visions of the veteran as being, in the words of one civilian character in *Jud,* "everything that I make myself out to be."

The Vietnam experience poisons this rite of manhood, though. Like Andy, the title character of *Jud* (Joseph Kaufmann) is a newly returned veteran who appears to be strong, confident and supremely sure of himself. Other characters gravitate toward him, and he has to turn the women away. His masculine presence attracts Arness, a weak, young man living off a trust fund who insists they go together to pick-up women. Jud, however, shows little interest in sexual or social intercourse. During sex he suffers from flashbacks to the War and the girl who left him while he was there. Although he has reached his manhood, it is an empty form of masculinity that alienates him from others. When an older woman tries to seduce him, he brutally turns her away. When Arness becomes too insistent, Jud rejects him so coldly that the youth kills himself.

His is a masculinity without patriarchy. There is no social role for this Vietnam-made-man. The other residents of his hotel repulse him and he seeks solitude instead. When asked when he last saw the face of a child, he flashes back to the face of a child he and his squad killed in the War. At the film's end, Jud is a desperate figure. The people who surround him might be weak, vain, even disgusting, but they manage to maintain their place in a community. The veteran has a place chosen for him there as well, but the Vietnam veteran can not fill that place. The film ends with Jud racing his car into the dark night, feeling the weight of his failure—a Christ figure (his initials are J.C.) without a cross.

Vanishing Point (1972) took this image of the Viet vet racing to nowhere and extended it into a complete film. A war-hero (Barry Newman) who opposed the War decides, for no apparent reason, to race from Denver to San Francisco. On the trip he earns the animosity of several state police forces and the advocacy of blind, black disk-jockey Super Soul (Cleavon Little), as well as the support of the counterculture across the Southwest, all of whom are looking for a hero. His death is climactic but without purpose; he crashes into a police blockade and never reaches San Francisco.

The Vietnam War has damned its veterans by denying them the place in society that they have earned. Vietnam unleashed their masculine potential for violence and that violence remains out of control when they return. When, in *Glory Boy* (1971), two veterans accompany a third to his home in the country, the visit ends in rape and murder. Similarly in Elia Kazan's *The Visitors* (1972), a veteran tries to live as a pacifist with his girlfriend and child, but the violence of Vietnam follows him even to Connecticut. Two of his fellow squad members come to pay a visit on their way home from a term in Fort Leavenworth. Mike, the now pacifist veteran, had testified against them at their court martial for the rape and murder of a Vietnamese woman. Back in the States, the pair are quiet and affable, but they rape Mike's girlfriend almost casually before leaving. Both of these films overtly compare the dangerously psychotic version of machismo rising out of the Vietnam War with the less dangerous version encouraged by memories of World War II. Both films show veterans of the older war sympathizing with the violence of their younger fellows, and in both films the community of these veterans foments violence. In *Clay Pigeon,* violence provides the soldier's chief link between the two worlds. In Viet Nam, the hero throws himself on a grenade, but it fails to explode. He returns to the States alive but disillusioned and soon descends into the violence of the drug scene. A fight against pushers climaxes suddenly when he finds himself back in Viet Nam at the moment that the grenade explodes.

Filmmakers could make this homeless, alienated Viet vet sympathetic by giving him some wound that made him harmless. Post-Traumatic Stress Syndrome (PTSS) was already a popular

topic in Vietnam films, although it did not yet go by that name.
Mike, the pacifist veteran in *The Visitors* appears to suffer from
it, though Kazan's film describes it as a loss of masculinity. In
Journey through Rosebud (1972), it is still alcoholism and de-
spair that drive an Indian war-hero to suicide. Frequently the
films dramatized PTSS by alienation, and the Viet vets were
doomed to wander during the War years. In *The Big Bounce*
(1969), Ryan O'Neal has nothing better to do than join a girl on a
crime spree, until even that nihilistic relationship becomes too
much and he wanders off to be a sharecropper. When Johnny
(Martin Landau) comes home in the 1972 television drama *Welcome Home, Johnny Bristol*, he discovers that his home in Charles, Vermont exists only in his imagination; he really comes from
the corners of Charles and Vermont streets in Philadelphia. He
survived life as a POW by learning to believe in a happy home he
never had.

One place where the film-veteran did find comfort was the
nihilistic community of the biker-gangs, and the vet became a staple of the biker film. He appeared there in films with titles like
*Angels from Hell, Satan's Sadists, The Losers, Chrome and Hot
Leather,* and *The Hard Ride.* By 1973 the type was so well established that *Magnum Force* made its band of former-Green Beret
villains rogue traffic cops, patrolling the city in black leather
astride roaring motorcycles. Veterans provided a useful variant on
the biker formula that *The Wild One* had established; their Vietnam experience explained their anti-social behavior. It also added
a skill that the bikers of the fifties had lacked. As a publicity
statement for *Satan's Sadists* expresses it, "he utilizes his combat
training by smashing a mirror in the face of one of the thugs and
drowning another in a toilet bowl" (Adair 1981, 87). A Viet vet's
military training proves useful again in *Angels from Hell*; this
time it allows him to organize his gang as a fighting unit for a
battle against the police.

The Losers, in a plot resembling 1967's *The Dirty Dozen*,
makes the most of this blend of anti-social behavior and Green
Beret training by sending veterans-turned-bikers to Cambodia
with their bikes on a secret mission to rescue an American presidential advisor. According to the press handout, "The result of

their attempt and the mission provide a capsule of what the Vietnam conflict is all about for confused Americans—from fighting an unseen enemy to living with the results of a battle too costly to be called a victory, and too complex and frustrating to result in the human glory that comes from having won" (Adair 1981, 63).

Even amidst the bikers, however, the Viet vet was often a loner. Billy Jack began his hugely successful career as a vigilante by defending his hometown from the ravages of a biker gang, despite the town's ingratitude for his service both against the Viet Cong and the bikers. In *Chrome and Hot Leather,* the Green Berets join a bike gang to destroy it in retribution for the murder of their leader's fiancée. *The Angry Breed* (1968) provides an odd variation on the biker theme when an actor saves a scriptwriter's life in Vietnam, thus earning a starring role in the writer's next film. Unfortunately for the actor, he finds he must fight the leader of a biker gang both for the part and the leading lady. *The Hard Ride* (1971) added race relations to the mix with an Indian biker gang trying to stop a white soldier from burying his black buddy.

Setting the veterans against the gangs channeled the violence that the vets embodied into positive channels; they ceased to be a danger to society and became a source of protection. A shift in their social position accompanies this change. They began to appear alone, apart from any social group and free to act outside the social restraints of community. They became vigilantes or hired killers. Thus in *The Stone Killers* and *Magnum Force* a veteran hires himself out for criminal activity, while in *Clay Pigeon, Slaughter, Black Gunn,* and *Slaughter's Big Rip-Off,* he is a weapon used to protect society from drug pushers.

Often the screenwriters simply tossed service in Vietnam into the story as though that fact alone were enough to explain the developing violence. Other films used military service as a structural element. In *Gordon's War* (1973), for instance, four black veterans apply their military training to the war on drugs in Harlem. They are a disparate group of individuals (a scholar, an athlete, a lady's man, a loner) who band together to fight a common enemy. They immediately collect all the military hardware they can find, establish a command bunker in an abandoned building, and begin operations. Their methods are surprisingly gentle, however. They kill no one until the very end, depending more on intimidation and disruption of business. Their use of non-deadly violence would find a counterpoint in the 1980's television series *The A-Team*, in which a disparate group of veterans made frequent use of explosives and automatic weapons, but never killed anyone.

Veterans seldom worked together, however. Slaughter (Jim Brown) worked alone and for himself. Still, his personal vengeance served a useful social purpose in defeating the pushers. By far the most successful version of this vigilante vet (at least until the rise of Rambo who rescued all of America), was Billy Jack (Tom Laughlin) the hero of a series of films written, directed, produced and created by their stars (the messianic Laughlin and his wife Delores Taylor) under a series of pseudonyms. The saga begins in 1967 with *The Born Losers* and continues through *Billy Jack* (1971), *The Trial of Billy Jack* (1974), and *Billy Jack Goes to Washington* (1977). (Reportedly, Laughlin began another episode in 1986 that never appeared.) The progression of these films leads the veteran from society's margins (in the first film Billy lives alone on the outskirts of his home town) to full integration (in the conclusion he fights corruption in Washington).

His career begins in a small California town. A narrator describes his reputation amongst the local people at the opening of *The Born Losers*.

> He had just returned from the war. One of those Green Beret rangers. A trained killer, people were to say later. Before the war he had hunted and broken wild horses in these mountains. Some said the reason he was so good at those things, and the reason he lived alone in these mountains, was that he had some Indian blood in him. Others said he just didn't like people. All I knew was his name: Billy Jack.

The opening shots highlight his rugged individualism; he showers under a waterfall, spears fish with a stick, and cooks his food under the trees.

The Vietnam War's role in the story is as marginal as Billy's status in the community. Apart from the narrator's opening statement, there is only passing reference to Billy's having been a Green Beret. No one ever mentions the words "Vietnam" or "veteran." His training as a killer shows in his swift dispatch of the bikers when he finally confronts them, but even that is offset by the fact that the gang leader, a childhood friend of Billy, refers to him as having always been tough and wild. The other characters credit his solitary existence to his Indian status; when the gang mocks him, it mocks his Indian roots, not his military service. No one calls him a war-hero or a baby-killer. Vietnam seems to function only as a descriptive detail, an experience an honorable man like Billy Jack would have had.

Billy Jack stands apart as the one member of the community who fulfilled his obligation to serve. In contrast, his childhood friend who stayed home is now the leader of the bikers. It fits into a pattern of actions for Billy. He was the one who went to war. He is the one who helps the gang's first victim. He is the one who finally stands up to the gang. He is the one who takes responsibility for his actions. Like Jud, Billy refuses to help people who will not help themselves. When the bikers' first victim flees to the restaurant where Billy is eating, Billy phones the police but insists the man do the talking. *The Born Losers* is essentially a morality play about the need to take a stand against evil, and Billy Jack's status as a veteran makes him a suitable hero for such a tale.

As the title of the sequel suggests, in *Billy Jack* the veteran has moved from the story's margins. Billy, while still a loner, has associated himself closely with a community, the progressive Friendship School run by Jean (Delores Taylor). He protects the school from the villains, who are no longer outsiders but the people of the nearby town who feel threatened by the alternative community down the road. As Billy comes under the influence of the pacifist Jean and enters further into the Indian culture, Vietnam's role in the story moves further into the margins. The naturalism of the first film becomes almost mystical now; Jean has only to think of Billy for him to appear, and during the film he undergoes an Indian snake ceremony and becomes a "brother to the snake."

Vietnam's role in Billy's life now seems confined to his martial abilities. He is a martial arts master and an expert marksman who protects the school primarily through his reputation. "It's strange how the townspeople fear you," Jean says, "but I guess it's a good thing or they'd hurt the school a whole lot more." On occasion he can make his enemies lay down their arms with the simple threat, "You know me." When he must fight, he can dispatch a gang of thugs or hold off the combined forces of the police and the national guard.

This martial, Vietnam aspect of Billy conflicts with the other, more passive, gentle, Indian side of his nature. The result is a climactic shoot-out in a barn where Billy must defend himself against the forces of law and order, and where it becomes obvious that his martial efforts will only lead to his death. (Twelve years later, another half-Indian veteran would face the same predicament in *First Blood*, the beginning of the Rambo trilogy.) Billy is typical of the American frontier hero: "hard, isolate, and a killer." But in the new world represented by the powerful forces of order (if not of law) and the terrible consequences of force that have led to pacifist movements like that at the Freedom School, the American frontier hero has become outmoded. The frontier has gone, replaced in the present with Euro-American communities and in history with the realization that it was never a frontier to the Indians who inhabited it.

As the crisis at the school develops, only two chances exist for resolving the situation: either Billy dies fighting and the school is left without protection, or he cuts a deal for the school to be protected and hands himself over for a trial in which he can plead his, and the school's, cause. The only obstacle to yielding is the fact of incarceration, the loss of his personal liberty; Jean describes it as "the hardest thing you've ever had to do." The good guys do not abjure violence altogether, however, not even the pacifistic Jean. When the villain rapes her, she refuses to tell Billy because she knows he will kill the rapist. But, when the rapist later kills one of her students, she realizes that the boy would still be alive if Billy had shot the villain. Jean is happy with violence as a useful threat, and sees its usefulness for protecting her School; her attitude toward it is as pragmatic as that of the government's. Unlike the government, however, she knows when to stop and negotiate. At the end, therefore, Billy yields to the passive urgings of Jean and the sheriff.

The character of Billy Jack succeeded fabulously during the seventies, in large part because of the massive advertising campaigns and distribution arrangements orchestrated by Laughlin. By renting theaters in which to show his films ("four walling") instead of renting his films to theaters, he was able to open in a proclaimed thousand theaters on the first night. With the help of marketing strategies like these, *Billy Jack* alone earned $70 million and *The Trial of Billy Jack* brought in $11 million on its first day of release. But his success was equally dependent on Laughlin's ability to bring the vigilante veteran up to a metaphorical, more sublime plain. Vigilantes like Slaughter or Black Gunn defended America from serious physical threats like drug pushers or biker gangs. Billy Jack's enemy was bigotry, racism, and humanity's general cruelty. Where other vigilante veterans were protectors, Billy was a messiah.

In the eighties, the image of the lone man of honor would adapt itself to the rising star of the Vietnam veteran as Hollywood worked to join the post-scripted cheering of the Reagan era. The seventies, however, would see the rise of an alternative veteran figure, almost a mirror image of the vigilante veteran. This figure would be the wounded veteran, the crippled or emotionally unstable soldier who came to be seen as the War's chief victim and most distressing symbol.

Some Mighty Decent, Understanding People

Although (as a sequel to *The Born Loser*), *Billy Jack*'s roots lie in the biker film, its story makes no concessions to those roots; no motorcycles roar through its midwestern town. Instead it belongs to another sixties' film genre, the youth picture. The 1969 success of *Easy Rider* came in a year when the Hollywood studios had gambled heavily on expensive musical productions that had failed financially. In contrast, *Easy Rider* cost $400,000 to produce and was among the most successful films of the year—reflecting that the age of the average moviegoer was between twelve and thirty in 1969. *The Graduate* had been a success in 1967, but after the summer of 1969, which saw *Easy Rider, Alice's Restaurant, Medium Cool,* and *Midnight Cowboy* (all pictures about disenchanted or rebellious youth) become the most successful films of the season, the studios began pouring out films about the radical youth movement, films like *Getting Straight, RPM, The Strawberry Statement, Zabriskie Point,* and *Hail, Hero!*.

The paternalistic attitude of these films is evident in one punning title: *RPM* (Revolutions Per Minute). Perez (Anthony Quinn), the sympathetic college president in *RPM*, explains to a trustee that the protesters "are revolutionaries; but basically they are students, fighting to understand their role in this damn place," and that was essentially the activist's character in Hollywood. The "revolutionaries" in *RPM* take over the administration building and the police must remove them in a brutal raid (called for in desperation by the liberal but practical and—more important—adult president), yet their demands amount to little more than

65

changes in the grading system and a stronger student government. Their demands about the War and racial equality are the first to be forgotten in the negotiations.

Hollywood's traditional economic strategy of appealing to the widest possible market tempered its attempt to pander to the youth market. Instead it attempted the awkward task of describing a radical movement without alienating either side. *The Nation*'s review of *Getting Straight* describes the attitudes expressed by the films that resulted.

> There are some mighty decent, understanding people among the older generation (and, of course, some fearful creeps); the young are beautiful and splendidly idealistic, but willful, meagerly informed, and hedonistic; the police are woefully incapable of restraining themselves, but a certain element among the protesters drives them wild with provocative taunts and dirty words. If both sides would lower their voices, they could hear Harry [the aging liberal hero], the divinely reasonable man, and come to realize that the country is seized by a passion of misunderstanding, not by a crisis of values (Hatch).

Repeatedly these films align the counterculture with sexuality. Simon (Bruce Davison), the young hero of *The Strawberry Statement*, joins the campus riots to meet women and only becomes committed to the cause when the police threaten his lover. In *Getting Straight*, Harry (Elliot Gould) although a veteran of Vietnam and of Selma, Alabama, perceives the protests on his campus in terms of getting laid; the climax of the film has him desert his graduate program, disgusted by the establishment's obsession with sexual innuendo in literature, to make love to Candace Bergen in the midst of a campus riot.

The situation was no better off-campus as far as Hollywood was concerned. Films like *Taking Off*, *The Model Shop*, *Joe*, *Alice's Restaurant*, and *Zabriskie Point* provided what amounted to travelogues of the counterculture world. Typically they assumed that all the radical ideas of youth resulted from sexual repression, promiscuity, and youthful irresponsibility. To summarize the process of radicalization, *The Revolutionary* (1970) placed the movement into a Kafkaesque landscape where the enigmatically named A (John Voight) progresses from being a liberal student to a revolutionary without ever encountering an actual cause. *Newsweek* recognized his story as part of "... the classic radicalization process."

> Bored by the apathy and rhetoric of mildly radical university politics, disillusioned by police brutality, harassed by the army and appalled by its "peacekeeping" missions in the black ghetto, outraged by the indifference of the rich ..., disheartened by the bureaucracy of the old left, he turns to the spontaneity of the extreme left and finds himself sitting on a park bench with a bomb in his lap (Zimmerman).

This populist, defused version of the antiwar and other movements confirmed a notion that would eventually be part of the folk-wisdom about the war years: that the antiwar movement was founded in narcissism and naiveté

As well as being a youth picture, *Easy Rider* was a small, independent production. The implications of this struck the studios as forcefully as did the fact of its target audience—perhaps more so because they went directly to the point of cost and profit. *Easy Rider* cost only $400,000 to produce. For Hollywood studios grown accustomed to million dollar productions and currently going through a period of financial difficulties, the possibility of combining low risk with a successful market was irresistible, and a wave of independent films followed, many of which treated the issue of the War or the protest movement with far less condescension than the big Hollywood pictures managed. Their treatments ranged from Brian DePalma's comic satires of the counterculture in *Greetings* and *Hi, Mom!* to Robert Kramer's activist polemics *The Edge* and *Ice*.

Ice, like *The Revolutionary*, was an allegory of activism, this time told by the independent cinema. Instead of stars like John Voigt and Robert Duvall, *Ice* featured a cast of unnamed people in a story about an underground movement opposing a future imperialist war the United States fights against Mexico. Kramer eschews polished cinema techniques for a *cinema verite* style that borders on being incomprehensible. Like *The Revolutionary*, however, it offers no strong sense of why any of the activists have revolted or what might be the actual purpose of the demonstration they attempt to organize. The activists in both groups seem more concerned with immediate action than any long-term ideas.

The independent films of this period were often highly idiosyncratic and experimental in style. In *Medium Cool* (1969), for instance, Haskell Wexler combined documentary footage with fictional narrative to explore the role of the camera in constructing the reality of events like the antiwar protests outside the Democratic National Convention in Chicago. Documentary footage of the war protests and riots provide the background for a romance between a cameraman and a Vietnam widow, Eileen (Verna Bloom). The latter wanders through the mayhem in search of her lost son like Scarlett wandering through burning Atlanta. The line between fiction and reality becomes so thin that when police throw tear gas canisters into the crowd, a voice on the soundtrack shouts, "Look out Haskell, it's real!"

The soundtrack also catches the protesters crying out to departing television trucks, "Don't leave us NBC"; they fear that once the cameras leave, they will be at the mercy of the Chicago police. Wexler uses this to explore the idea that the camera—NBC's or Wexler's own—defines reality for both news and cinema audiences. The actual release of Wexler's film seemed to bear this out. According to a *Take One* interview with Wexler, Paramount wanted "something to show that the [Chicago] police had more provocation for what they did."

> So they said, "O.K., if you delete 'Let's get the fuckers' [said by the police] and add two 'pigs eat shit' and one 'up against the wall motherfucker' spoken by the anti-war forces, we'll accept the picture." That's a fact (Peary).

Greetings, directed on a shoestring by Brian DePalma and featuring Robert De Niro, was among the biggest successes of the sixties independent cinema. It opens with Lyndon Johnson remarking, "I'm not saying you never had it so good, but its true, isn't it," and proceeds with a white man stepping into a black bar, hoping to be beaten up badly enough to fail his induction physical. The film lampoons the several methods for avoiding induction, including homosexual behavior, fascist rhetoric, and physical disfigurement. It also mocks the culture that created such things as the draft; when one of the protagonists, Jon (De Niro), does go to Vietnam, he fits easily into his new role. In New York, he was a voyeur who talked women into stripping for his camera; in Vietnam, he talks a frightened Vietnamese woman into stripping for a television news camera.

DePalma produced the sequel to *Greetings* the following year. The title of the first film came from the opening address in the Selective Service notification; the title of the second came from the first words of a returning vet: *Hi, Mom!* Now De Niro returns from Viet Nam and continues his voyeuristic pursuits. Like most films about veterans during the war years, it ends in violence—he employs his demolition training to destroy the apartment building he has been filming. He also makes porn films and joins the all-black cast of "Be Black Baby," an alternative theater in which blacks wear white-face and abuse white members of the audience, whom they cover with black-face.

The draft was among the most popular themes for both the studios and the independents. Among the most successful was *Alice's Restaurant*, which retold how Arlo Guthrie (played by himself) escaped conscription only because of a criminal record—on Thanksgiving day he had been arrested for littering. Although this incident was the subject of the song on which the film was based, in the film it as a minor subplot. The draft is only one of the problems Arlo and his friends face—or more often avoid—while staying with Alice (Pat Quinn) and Ray (James Broderick), an older couple who offer their home as a hospice for the youth-culture of New England. The movie's final image shows Alice watching all her young friends drive away in search of new experiences; Ray has just suggested selling their home and moving on, but the lengthy shot of Alice in the falling light suggests that, eventually, even the counterculture must find something worth staying and working for: "You can get everything you want (except Alice!) at Alice's restaurant." Arlo's avoidance of the draft, like the *RPM* students' demand for academic reform, may appear idealistic but finally seems rooted in narcissism and irresponsibility.

The proper reaction to the draft (avoidance, resistance, or serving) featured in a number of independent films of the sixties and seventies, including *Windflowers: The Story of a Draft Dodger, Cowards, Homer, Prism, AWOL, Parades, Outside In,*

and *Journey through Rosebud*. *Outside In* set out the basic conflict that ignites the action in most of these films. A trio of childhood friends gathers for a funeral: a draft dodger who lives in
Canada, a veteran who did not believe in the War, and a conscientious objector who went to prison for resisting the draft. The latter
becomes the film's tragic hero when, after receiving a *second* induction notice, he kills himself.

Of these three options, draft-dodging received the least respect from filmmakers. It was the subject of three Vietnam War
comedies, *Greetings*, *Drive, He Said*, and *The Gay Deceivers*, in
all of which middle-class men went to absurd lengths to fail their
induction physicals. Jack Nicholson's first directorial effort was
Drive, He Said, in which the hero tries to stay awake so long that
the army will consider him too damn tired to fight in a war. *The
Gay Deceivers* offered a more complex ploy: its heroes fail their
physical by acting homosexual. Unfortunately for them, the induction officer smells a rat and follows them around afterward,
forcing them to continue the deception until, desperate to be heterosexual again, they return to the induction office and confess
all. At which point a new induction officer, this one gay and hoping to build an all-gay army, declares them unfit for service.

As well as mocking the extremes to which the privileged
youth of the era went in avoiding service, the films questioned
their motives for not wanting to fight. Primarily, it seemed to be a
question of maintaining their privileged lifestyle, a selfish motive
that led to unkind characterizations of those who dodged. In *Journey through Rosebud*, a dodger betrays the Indian veteran who
hides him on the reservation. When the Indian learns that the
dodger has slept with his wife, he kills himself and the other Indians gather to beat the dodger up. The dodger in the Canadian *Explosion* flees to Canada after his brother dies in Viet Nam, but
when there he can do nothing more constructive than drift into
crime. *Windflowers: The Story of a Draft Dodger* offered one of
the few sympathetic images of the dodger in American cinema;
the police hound him down and a rookie cop shoots him by
mistake.

The acceptable way to avoid military service was not to
dodge it but to resist it. *Cowards* made the point that dodging the

draft may be cowardly (a father accuses his son of cowardice for wanting to flee to Canada) but outright resistance shows firm principle and strength of character. So in *Cowards*, the hero joins a priest in burning draft records (a mostly symbolic and ultimately futile gesture of protest). Likewise, when *Homer*'s brother dies in Viet Nam, the honorable thing for him to do is fight against the War rather than protect himself.

Although *Prism* follows a lawyer who argues the resisters' case, the most ambitious attempt to explain the draft resistance movement was probably *The Trial of the Catonsville Nine* (1972), simply because it eschewed any dramatic storyline. It reconstructs the trial of nine men and women who burned the selective service records at Catonsville, Maryland, offering each of the defendants a chance to repeat their own reasons for the gesture. Father David Berrigan, one of the nine (and the model for a Doonesbury strip character), wrote the original play and the film script from the court records. The nine admit burning the records, but they argue that they had a right to do so, that the raid on the records was an act of civil disobedience to stop the "unnatural, senseless destruction of men, women, and children—a destruction that is wrought in the name of a policy that passes all human understanding."

Unlike most films about the movement, *Trial* is not a "youth picture." Although its message might appeal to the young members of the movement, the characters are not young. Their idealism is not youthful or energetic. The stories they tell of their lives suggest a commitment developed over a lifetime of work, not over a college lifestyle. It gives them the sort of credibility otherwise reserved for veterans, credibility that the students in the films strive for but do not achieve. No one can accuse the Catonsville Nine of opposing the War merely to be fashionable or to keep themselves out of danger.

The third option open to young men who opposed the War was enlistment. Michael Douglas did so twice, in *Hail, Hero!* (his first starring role) and again in *Summertree* (1971). In *Hail, Hero!*, the studios created a wealthy young man who opposes the War but chooses against a college deferment and enlists—in part because of family pressure, but also in the hopes of understanding what he opposes. Carl, the enlistee, has a vague idea that he will be able to go to Viet Nam and love his enemy, thereby disrupting the War. Unlike Arlo and the other filmic draft evaders, he puts his life on the line for his beliefs.

Like *The Green Berets* and *Billy Jack*, *Hail, Hero!* assumes that the soldier has the best right to speak about the War. Furthermore, it strongly suggests that, once in the War, he will change his mind about it. When Carl explains his hopes for loving the enemy to a local girl, she counters with the entirely relevant question, "You can't even make your own brother love you; you expect to make a sixteen-year-old stranger who can't even speak English?" When he realizes that violence can be a reflex action and that he may be able to kill to survive in Viet Nam, the kindly family doctor takes him to an old age home and shows him elderly men fighting to stay alive. This suggests that self-preservation is a legitimate motive for fighting in a war while neatly eliding the question of why a person should go to war in the first place.

Summertree, in which Douglas again enlists due to family pressure, offers the other side of the argument. This time Douglas' father tricks him into leaving music school and going to Viet Nam, where the youth dies. He would have been better off if, once in the Army, he had deserted like the soldiers in *Georgia, Georgia* (scripted by Maya Angelou) or *Two People*. In *Two People*, Peter Fonda spends the war-years traveling in Europe and Asia after deserting in Viet Nam, but eventually tires of life on the run and chooses to come home and face the consequences; an adoring fashion model (Lindsay Wagner) comforts him on the way home. *Parades*, on the other hand, offers an independent filmmaker's description of a deserter's life. Instead of beautiful models, its hero faces brutality and injustice in the military prison. Still, considering the options, it may have been the best choice. Hippies tempt the hero of *Captain Milkshake* to desert, but he remains faithful to the Army and, like Douglas, dies in Viet Nam.

Peter Fonda's return to justice in *Two People* coincided with North Viet Nam's return of American prisoners of war and the beginning of the most controversial legacy of the War: the MIAs who may or may not have remained behind alive. Despite the passionate feeling motivated by the issue since the War, before 1973

American movies barely touched on the question of POWs and MIAs, with two notable exceptions. In *Welcome Home, Johnny Bristol* a soldier relies on idealistic memories of home to survive as a POW, only to find when he escapes that the home town was never more than a fantasy. The other exception was 1972's *Limbo*, in which three women whose husbands have disappeared in Viet Nam meet in a group for the wives of MIAs; one supports the War, one opposes it, and the third does not care as long as her husband comes home.

The American Vietnam War ended in 1973 with the Paris Peace Accords, the departure of the last American servicemen, and the return of American POWs. As it had after other American wars, the subject of the conflict dropped from favor for a short time. The postwar years were, many people felt, a time to put the divisiveness of the Vietnam era behind. Ford pardoned Nixon, offered amnesty to draft dodgers, and declared the end of U.S. involvement in Viet Nam. In 1974 Lt. William Calley's My Lai conviction was overturned. In 1976 the country celebrated its Bicentennial, elected the peaceful, easy-going outsider Jimmy Carter as president, and settled into the Vietnam Syndrome.

Part 2
The Vietnam Syndrome

Nostalgia

The Vietnam War did not end quickly, though America's final departure seemed almost indecently hasty. The peace talks had been going on (covertly and overtly) for over a year when Henry Kissinger and Le Duc Tho initialed the agreement to end the War on 23 January 1973. Four days later both parties officially signed the agreements in Paris and, by the end of March, the last American combat troops had left Viet Nam, followed three days later by the prisoners of war officially held by the North. President Richard Nixon declared that America had won peace with honor. In Viet Nam, however, the War continued until 30 April 1975, when Saigon fell to the Communists and President Gerald Ford declared that the War was "finished."

That presidents Carter, Reagan, Bush, and Clinton have each in their turn announced the War finished suggest that the Paris Accords resolved very little beyond bringing American fighting men home. In Southeast Asia, conflicts caused by the War continue unresolved even into the nineties. The years of the killing fields and Viet Nam's wars with Cambodia and China, the exodus of the boat people, veterans' accusations about Agent Orange, and the controversy over the Vietnam Veterans Memorial all suggest a conflict very much unresolved in the seventies. Yet in 1980, Reagan campaigned on the premise that America wanted to forget the War and its effects, and he won resoundingly by playing to that premise. Carter, who warned Americans that the United States suffered from a crisis of spirit caused in part by the War, lost.

77

While the American public was eagerly forgetting the War, Hollywood was formulating its first efforts to provide a resolution. Having recently completed the successful and acclaimed *The Godfather Part II* in 1974, Francis Coppola was in a financial and artistic position to try a risky subject like Vietnam. He began casting for it in 1975 and began shooting in the Philippines a year later on a schedule that would release the film in May of 1978 (it eventually arrived at theaters in August 1979). The publicity surrounding the project was tremendous—the director of the Godfather Saga to direct the first major Vietnam feature! As difficulties and conflicts arose during the production, publicity grew even greater. Suddenly other major filmmakers began to consider Vietnam film projects. Films and scripts that had been bouncing around the industry for years suddenly saw production, and film projects began enlisting important names like Jane Fonda, Robert De Niro, and Burt Lancaster, as well as television personalities like Henry Winkler and Sally Fields.

The first wave of these films arrived in 1977 and included the first combat film since *The Green Berets*, as well as veterans who were positive, mostly nonviolent characters. But 1978 was the landmark year for Vietnam films, even though *Apocalypse Now* failed to materialize on time. Combat finally appeared in its full fury in *The Deer Hunter*, *Go Tell the Spartans*, and *Who'll Stop the Rain*. Two Vietnam films shared the top honors at the Oscar ceremonies that year, and others remain among the best and most controversial films about the conflict.

The excitement and prospective profit of *Apocalypse Now* were not the only forces that brought Vietnam War films out of hiding at the end of the seventies. By the end of the decade, historians and social scientists were beginning to revise their opinions about events in Viet Nam. The crimes of the Communist governments that succeeded to power after America left, Pol Pot's re-education camps, the boat people, and Viet Nam's invasions of Laos and Cambodia all suggested that America had been fighting a just cause after all. As Lance Morrow wrote in a 1979 article on the sudden outpouring of Vietnam War films, "the psychological effect on Americans of all this criss-cross *realpolitik* is to lift a lot of the moral burden off the American involvement" (27).

Revising the War also provided a useful antidote for the moral and economic depression America suffered in the late seventies when oil prices inflated, Iranian students held Americans hostage, and unemployment rose. Politicians in both parties found it useful to describe the problem as a Vietnam syndrome, a "crisis of the spirit" caused by that divisive conflict. From deep within this slough of despondency, cultural critics desperately rationalized what had happened in Southeast Asia, as though by healing the past they could heal the present. Guenter Lewy's revisionist *America in Vietnam* described the War as both legal and "not immoral," while Leslie Gelb and Richard K. Betts argued in *The Irony of Viet Nam: The System Worked* that America had succeeded in Viet Nam—insofar as we kept Communism out of South Viet Nam until 1975.

These revisionist accounts, however, were coming from the same sources that had provided the original accounts: journalists, the intellectual elite, the military and the government. During the War, these sources had bombarded Americans with information about and explanations for the War, but had managed to lose their credibility through their bitter in-fighting. Since these versions frequently contradicted one another, the various parties would denounce each other's accounts as lies, frauds, or attempts to deceive the American public so as to either prolong or betray America's involvement (depending on whom you were listening to). The press and intellectuals described government as a choice between ineffectual humanitarianism and Nixon's corrupting *realpolitik*; the government portrayed the press as opportunistic and sensationalist; the antiwar movement on college campuses tainted itself with the self-interest inherent in draft dodging. Consequently, no consensus about the War existed; yet, if the American people did, as Ronald Reagan claimed in 1980, want to put the War behind them, they would first have to find a satisfactory explanation for it.

The film industry was a major contributor to this revisionism. Hollywood is in the business of producing consensus narratives—stories that many audiences will find palatable. When the Vietnam War entered the industry's production line, it did so as part of a complex recipe meant to make it easy to digest. This

recipe highlighted the good bits: the music, the idealism, the music, the youth and freedom, the wild styles, the music, the sexual
liberation, the civil rights movement, the sense of unity, and the
music. The actual War itself had to fit into this nostalgic vision,
rather than the other way around.

The 1978 Oscar ceremonies, in which Jon Voigt and the
radical, often hated, Jane (Hanoi Jane) Fonda earned best actor
and actress awards for *Coming Home* while John Wayne presented the best picture award to *The Deer Hunter*, marked the
partial success of Hollywood's recipe; the number of veterans
protesting outside the ceremony, however, marked the limits of
that success. Despite the almost diametrically opposed viewpoints
of these two films (Fonda referred to *The Deer Hunter* as "a racist, Pentagon version of the war" [Morrow 23]), both of them tell
stories of reconciliation between the men who went to war and the
homelands to which they returned. The important difference between them is the relationship they draw between the War and
American society. The War deeply affected the structure of the
working class community *The Deer Hunter's* soldiers come from,
but in *Coming Home*, the War is always off-screen and any
wounds it inflicts harm only the soldiers themselves. Interestingly,
the protesters outside the Academy Awards that year were angry
at *The Deer Hunter*, not Hanoi Jane.

By 1978, sentimental views of the sixties and the antiwar
movement were becoming endemic to the Vietnam War film, and
the war years developed a glow of youthful innocence and idealism. Hence *Coming Home* shows Sally and Luke entering into the
free-spiritedness of the age, flying kites, listening to classic rock-
and-roll and getting involved. *Big Wednesday* (1978, retitled
Summer of Innocence for television release), a coming of
age/surfer film, shows the period as one when boys could surf and
party to great music without concern for the future, and when
wisdom was held chiefly by aging surfers who kept faith in the
Big Wave. The film never shows the War itself, but its role in the
community is clear: going to and avoiding going to Vietnam are
both parts of the process of reaching adulthood. If a man must go
to war, that is too bad; but he will have to get a real job someday
too, and that, also, is too bad. Grow up and accept life's

disappointments; the Big Wave still may come, if you stay true to your youth. *More American Graffiti* (1979), the sequel to George Lucas' 1973 film, keeps the same tone as the original and a similar soundtrack. An end title in *American Graffiti* explained that one of the characters, Terry ("the Toad") later was lost in Vietnam. The sequel tells his adventures there and of his attempts to desert, interweaving his story with those of the other characters living in the states between 1964 and 1967. The War in each of these films functions as the fly in the ointment, the one big bummer in the age of Aquarius.

This nostalgia is especially apparent in the film version of the musical *Hair* (1979), although according to its director, Milos Foreman, "Until the guys on Madison Avenue cut their hair short, *Hair* will not be nostalgia" (McCarthy 18). In this paean to the hippie culture, a young draftee from Oklahoma named Claude (John Savage) falls in with a tribe of hippies in Central Park and quickly learns that life is joyous and evil results from being uptight. War makes people especially uptight and can even depress the tribe—especially when the tribe's leader accidentally trades places with the draftee and dies in Vietnam. The film's final image shows the remaining six tribal members, including the draftee, standing by the dead man's grave in Arlington National Cemetery; the various plot complications have resolved themselves offscreen so that now they stand as three family groups, two of them with children. Despite their attempts to avoid life's complications, the War, symbol of just how complicated life can be, has caught up with them; they are already breaking from tribal to family structure (foreshadowing the roles of their successors in *The Big Chill*).

Hair carefully absolves the soldiers from any guilt for participating in the War. It makes plain that war is the evil, not the soldiers who fight it. Claude, the naive young soldier, has been drafted and Berger, the man who actually goes to the War, is a victim of mistaken identity and fate: although he burns his draft card at the film's opening, he later takes Claude's place for an afternoon—so that Claude can have a last moment with the woman he loves—and is sent to the war before Claude returns. The soldier bears no culpability since this war catches even the resister.

Having the hippies support the draftee's cause and bring him into their fold reverses one of the main charges leveled against the counterculture by the "silent majority." Stories about war protesters greeting the returning soldiers with spit and obscene gestures, or of girls abandoning their soldier-sweethearts after hearing horror stories about them killing babies, are perhaps more metaphorical than experiential, but they form an important part of the War's folklore.

Despite Foreman's protests, *Hair* is a soft-focus, nostalgic vision of the period. *Milestones*, released just three years earlier, throws such nostalgia into sharp relief. Directed by Robert Kramer (who also directed the radical films *The Edge* and *Ice)*, it was a staged documentary that allowed members of the counterculture to review their struggles and achievements of the past ten years. Its characters include activists, deserters, veterans, dropouts, and a baby born in the final scenes. Unlike *Hair* or *Coming Home*, this 1975 film has not yet found the distance to be nostalgic. *The National Review* described it as narcissistic: rather than adore the way they were, the makers of *Milestones* adore the way they are. They must have struck a still-sensitive nerve to elicit *The National Review*'s gloating response in a review titled "Gang Narcissism."

> The wild-throated, oat-sowing young prophets of the 1960s were, in their boom days, famous for publicly parading their parts—ideological, moral, and physical—up and down the highways and the byways of America, singing a song of themselves. Presently, however, they are suffering their Diaspora; they have had little opportunity of late for massive self-celebration, so when I noticed that the New York Film Festival was showing a film of 195 minutes called *Milestones*, a fictional documentary about those lost and witlessly illusioned people slogging about in the badlands of the 1970s, I felt the muscles of my typing forefingers go taut with expectation. The kids would do it all over again for me, I knew (Williamson).

The nostalgia in *Good Guys Wear Black* (the first MIA rescue film and a star vehicle for martial arts champion Chuck Norris) is not for the counterculture but for the military culture.

Norris plays John T. Booker, the former leader of a secret strike force that the peace negotiators betrayed to the Communists. Conrad Morgan (James Franciscus), the chief negotiator, sends the team on a POW rescue mission (probably modeled on an actual, failed attempt to free prisoners from the Son Tay prison camp that occurred near the War's end) that is meant as a trap to deliver Booker's team to the North Vietnamese—a concession insisted upon by the Communists. Most of the team survive, however, and several years after the War Morgan, now about to accept an appointment as Secretary of State and concerned with the possibility of scandal, orders their assassination. Only Booker survives to kill Morgan.

There is nothing in this veteran's evocation of the war years to elicit nostalgia. Booker repeatedly denies any interest in discussing the War except in his classroom where he can analyze it in a semi-objective setting. His interest only revives when his former comrades are in danger, at which point he tries to bring the old gang together. He loves and respects these men with whom he shared combat, and he is deeply bitter that the government never provided them with a clear enemy or a noble cause. His postwar search could remedy that, but his comrades fail again against the enemy, still not recognizing that it is their own government. The future secretary's hitman, a Vietnamese assassin, kills the former soldiers before Booker can reach them, and Booker must fight alone. The film, which begins with the possibility of re-inventing the past, ends in an act of vengeance—destructive rather than constructive violence.

In the eighties, the POW/MIA films would retrieve the hero's honor by allowing him to find POWs and thereby defeat the machinations of the bureaucratic villain. By moving the rescue mission to the end of the film, the story would allow the hero to achieve vengeance against the forces that had abandoned the soldiers through an act of constructive repatriation. The mission would become a symbol of what went wrong in the War and of possible redemption. It would re-invent the possibility of nostalgia for the soldier.

Who'll Stop the Rain (based on Robert Stone's novel *Dog Soldiers*) provides a dark antidote to the nostalgic views of the period. Its plot involves an attempt by a war correspondent, John Converse (Michael Moriarty), to smuggle heroin into the United States from Viet Nam. He convinces Hicks (Nick Nolte), an old army buddy who now sails with the Merchant Marine, to bring the drug to the States and pass it to Converse's wife Marge (Tuesday Weld) in San Francisco. In this film the United States is a corrupt nation and the counterculture is hapless, self-indulgent, and pathetic. The Converses (middle-class intellectuals) are weak and foolish. Marge, already addicted to tranquilizers, begins snorting more and more of the pure heroin. John, who claims that smuggling the drug is "the first real thing" he has ever done, does not actually do it; his chief role in the plot is to instigate it. Even the narcotics agents who trail the heroin are corrupt. Hope, therefore, lies not in a nostalgically envisioned past; it depends instead on current action to salvage the future.

Reviewers like Gilbert Adair who describe the heroin as "the poison of Vietnam" being injected into "the vulnerably fat American forearm" (Adair 1989, 67) have missed the point. Americans themselves invest in the drug, import it, and even inject it into their forearms. Although the deal begins with a Vietnamese official, we are told that he "used to be a very gung-ho soldier. He says it's us came over and corrupted him." The United States degenerated into a corrupt, dependent nation long before the heroin arrives, and it is the United States that has corrupted Viet Nam. From the start of the film, America causes its own problems; the opening sequence shows American planes accidentally napalm an American landing zone. Only Hicks seems to recognize this, and he is constantly reminding Marge that it is the Converses' heroin that caused the couple's problems. Like America, the Converses cause their own fall.

Hicks, a self-made Nietzschien man, embodies that hope. He is a working-class hero—muscular, intense, and devoted to the intellectual Converses who condescend to befriend him. His experience in Viet Nam has honed his skill and will into a dangerous weapon, and John Converse has taught him the Nietzschien philosophy that guides him. Now the weakness of the Converses has provided him with a purpose, that of the American superman who reestablishes community through violent action. The forces of evil—in the guise of the federal agents and nongovernment drug dealers—cannot defeat him, and although he cannot destroy them either, he can hold them off long enough for the Converses to escape.

The film offers no solid hope for the future, but it does suggest that Hicks has redeemed the Converse family. Stripped of the illusions about themselves and American society which they had harbored even while claiming disillusionment, they leave the representatives of America's law and order to fight over the drug. Their future is uncertain. The narcotics agents, although corrupt, were federal agents and the Converses did smuggle drugs. They are outlaws, and can expect arrest if they return home. Their own actions have propelled them past the boundaries of American society, and Hicks gave them the strength to survive the voyage by paying for their mistakes and their crimes with his life. Now they are pioneers driving into the desert. Their daughter is in Canada, beyond the reach of American law, and they too may be heading there to begin a new life.

At the end of the seventies, the Vietnam generation was finally growing up. The last Americans born before the War were preparing to enter college; those who had been in college when the war started were now in their late seventies and had families and responsibilities. These two ages marked either end of the baby boom as well as the War, and what they saw as their adolescence, their numbers allowed them to translate into a turbulent adolescence for America. They were beginning to see their youthful idealism as a bittersweet heritage; their activism as naive youth's free-spiritedness. Now, like the Converses, they were responsible citizens who could respect the sacrifices others had made for the country and who would build on those sacrifices to make a better life for themselves.

Demobilizing

The 1970s was a period of demobilization for the Vietnam soldier. First came Nixon's Vietnamization which brought them all home by 1973. Then followed the longer, slower public relations process of changing the veterans' image from that of crazed killers to impotent victims of a lost cause. As America entered the years of the Vietnam Syndrome, the soldier became first the visible sign of the country's vulnerability and then the hope that would lead it back to moral and physical strength. A made-for-television version of C.D.B. Bryan's *Friendly Fire* neatly summarized the process.

The film tells the story of an Iowa farm couple whose eldest son is killed by "friendly fire" (American artillery) in Viet Nam. He was an obedient son, he worked hard, and he loved his country. He was his father's hope for the farm's future and his mother's golden child. When he dies, the light in Iowa changes from golden- to dirty-brown. The film follows the parents' investigation into the nature of the "friendly fire" that killed their son, an investigation that leads to their growing conviction that a malign influence within the army itself killed him and attempted to cover up the incident. Their investigation of and disillusionment with the United States Army and government convinces the audience that they are right. A reporter, C.D.B. Bryan himself (Sam Waterston), arrives and supports that conviction by believing them as well.

Then Bryan does his own investigation. He talks to the soldiers involved, including the officers and enlisted men who were there. As he listens to their stories, the film flashes back to the war, and for the first time we see what happened. The boy died in an accident of war; someone had miscalculated the height of the trees and the mortar shells had landed short, hitting the platoon. There was no corruption or cover-up involved. The parents' obsession and grief made them misread the facts. The reporter has objectively interviewed the best witnesses available, the men who were there, and resolved the mystery. This small part of the War has successfully been shown. When he returns to the parents to reveal his findings, however, Bryan finds that they do not believe him. He tells them he has found the truth, and they ask him "What truth?" Suddenly the objective reporter is spinning around in the farmers' kitchen, forced to defend his own version of "truth" as the Truth and failing.

The film ends with a visit to the son's grave on the anniversary of his return from the War. The parents are at the graveyard entrance when the reporter arrives. The mother puts her hand out to him, and they visit the grave together, holding the paradox of their contradictory truths in balance or abeyance. What matters finally is the death of the golden child and the need to honor him and his sacrifice. Both sides can unite on that common ground and thus find hope for the future. During the late seventies America, too, began to gather round the memory of its lost sons and to listen to the boys whom they had sent off to war.

During the first years after the United States left Viet Nam, Hollywood continued to concentrate on the youth pictures that had been its staple Vietnam War film during the War, only now they increasingly used veterans as the youthful subject. *Two People*—the story of a returning deserter who encounters a beautiful model on his way home—arrived just as the troops were returning early in 1973. The review it received in *Time* suggests how closely Hollywood remained tied to its paternalistic treatment of the protest movement.

> Once their love is consummated and they are lazying around Paris, the model starts to examine the wisdom of her new-found lover's resolution to turn himself in. She questions the morality of the War in Vietnam and argues that he was right in deserting. Most of the model's arguments are forceful enough, if a little familiar, but the young man never seriously

wavers. "Those statements have all been made," he announces emphatically. "I'm tired of running, Deirdre. I want
my life back." It is because Deirdre wants part of his life too
that all her new-found political indignation becomes the prat-
tling of a spoiled and slightly selfish young woman (Cocks).

In 1974, the Billy Jack series continued with *The Trial of
Billy Jack*, while *Welcome Home, Soldier Boys* continued the
story of psychopathic veterans coming home to do unto America
what they presumably had done unto Viet Nam. Both of these
films offered scenes of nihilistic violence, though they were diametrically opposed in their presentation of who wielded that violence. In *Welcome Home, Soldier Boys*, a group of veterans load
their Cadillac with various weapons and drive into the American
desert; eventually arriving in the town of Hope, they are insulted
and react by annihilating the town. To stop their outburst requires
the power of the National Guard. In *The Trial of Billy Jack*, it is
the government that sponsors and commits the senseless acts of
violence. In the third installment of his story, the half-breed Green
Beret's problems escalate from violent crime to atrocities. First he
witnesses, tries to stop, and finally reports a My Lai-like massacre in Viet Nam, and then back in the midwest he must try to prevent a Kent State-like massacre (though one far more violent and
destructive). Billy has learned to control his outbursts, so that
when he hurts, maims or kills, it is for a good cause. The government, on the other hand, slaughters children. Pauline Kael described *Billy Jack* as a "hip fairy tale," but she saw Laughlin's
new film as "messianic, tent-show movie-making" and "an orgy
of victimization." According to *Time*, "Goebbels would have
loved *The Trial of Billy Jack*. Its moral absolutism, self-
righteousness, grandiosity and incitements to hatred in the name
of love conspire to make it a model for totalitarian filmmaking."
Billy Jack's message had become simple and clear: violence is
evil only when someone else uses it.

Meanwhile the veteran continued his career as a stock villain. Travis Bickle (Robert De Niro) in *Taxi Driver* may be the
most famous example. Obsessed by the filth and depravity he sees
as he drives his cab through the night city, Bickle undertakes to
purge New York through violence. In the film's climax he rescues

a young prostitute (Jody Foster) by shooting everyone from her pimp to her doorman and is nearly shot to death himself. He survives, however, and the press acclaims him as a hero for rescuing the girl. The film is an urban Western and both Martin Scorsese (the director) and Paul Schrader (the writer) have admitted their debt to John Ford's *The Searchers* (with Bickle as the urban Ethan Brand). Although Bickle's status as a veteran is only mentioned briefly near the beginning of the film, critics have latched onto it as a partial explanation for his violent behavior. He provides a link between that Western hero, as embodied in John Wayne, and recent American culture, as embodied in the Vietnam War. According to one of the film's coproducers Julia Phillips, Bickle was "created by American culture and etched in stone by the Vietnam War."

The violently psychopathic veteran became a cliché during the seventies. Detective and police television dramas frequently employed him as a sociopathic villain. Formulaic cop thrillers also found him a useful nemesis for their heroes. Dirty Harry fought a gang of them in *Magnum Force* (1973). The disaster movies that became popular during this decade of American debacles also relied on him as a convenient plot complication or when they needed someone crazy enough to blow up the Superbowl.

The veteran in *Tracks* seems at first to be less dangerous then most, though perhaps just as deranged. Sergeant Jack Falen (Dennis Hopper) escorts a military coffin from Vietnam on a train across the United States. On the way he meets an odd variety of fellow passengers, including an underground radical, a government informer who doubles as a real estate salesman, and a pair of college women traveling to Cape Cod. He attempts to enter their temporary trainboard society, but his sense of alienation and intense paranoia conflict with his desperate need for other people, and he repeatedly fails. At one point Falen believes he sees the other passengers rape a young woman whom he has been trying to seduce, and he draws a gun from his crotch only to have the rape scene dissolve before him into a dream. The violence of his fantasies erupts at the conclusion when no one comes to the soldier's funeral. Falen leaps into the grave and emerges fully armed and raving madly.

> I love. I love. I really do love. And I hate. I hate … Cause I
> love I hate, cause I love I hate.… They sent you to Nam. They
> sent you there. You wanna go to Nam? You wanna go to
> Nam? I'll take you there!

The film's use of a *cinema verite* style suggests an analytic,
objective portrait of Falen, but the fantastic elements repeatedly
disrupt this analysis. In a similar vein, the other passengers respond to him according to their individual inclinations, each of
them seeing in him what they want him to be. He is a co-
conspirator for the radical and the informant, an innocent in need
of love for the college girl, and an object of desire for an older
woman. Falen himself abets the confusion with contradictory
claims about the man whom he is escorting home, seemingly trying to make his explanation pleasing to whomever he speaks;
while talking to a black man the body becomes that of a heroic
black youth, but while talking to a cynical passenger, it becomes
that of a soldier whom Falen never knew. The veteran that
emerges from the multiple and self-serving constructions is a mul-
tifaceted symbol for America to use as it sees fit.

Robert Aldrich's 1977 suspense drama, *Twilight's Last
Gleaming*, demonstrates several of the methods filmmakers would
use to fix this kinetic symbol into a representation of American
honor. The military has framed Air Force General Dell (Burt
Lancaster) for murder because he insists on publicizing the truth
about the War. The general escapes from death row, seizes control of a missile base, and threatens to start World War III unless
the President publicizes the truth about a government conspiracy
to continue the War. Dell's accomplice is Sergeant Powell (Paul
Winfield), an escaped murderer and another veteran of the War.
Casting Lancaster as the deranged general brings a level of integrity to the character that makes the madness sympathetic rather
than frightening. Dell is misguided but well meaning, as the director of the film, Robert Aldrich, points out.

> I think you have to understand that in the Lancaster character
> [Dell] there is a degree of imbalance, because he's willing to
> do an insane thing to prove a point. I don't think you prove a
> point with x millions of lives—you have to be a little crazy
> (Byron 48).

In addition, the point Dell tries to prove is almost banal. The military/government establishment believes that what Dell has to say will devastate the American people, and to protect their nation and themselves from the release of this news, they assassinate the president. Yet when a cabinet member finally reveals the truth, the great government secret is old news: the government prolonged the War to improve American credibility. America already knows that truth and has accepted it as bearable. It is the specter of Vietnam, the suspicion of horrible things, that is dangerous—not the actual truth.

Twilight's Last Gleaming also offers a veteran character that will be increasingly influential in Hollywood Vietnam films. Aldrich splits him into two characters, the noble but weak Dell and the black, cruelly dangerous Powell (Paul Winfield). These two figures are helpless individually, but together they manage to hold the United States government hostage. Powell is a murderer whom Dell brings with him from death row. He is cynical and cold-blooded and he gives Dell the strength to hold fast to his convictions, even though he realizes the truth will set no one free. But he is too self-destructive to act on his own. He needs Dell's idealism to provide him with a cause for which to fight. By splitting these two characters, Aldrich splits the veteran's strength, thereby making him less dangerous—a visionary without strength and a strong man without a purpose. Vietnam film critics Albert Auster and Leonard Quart would define these two characters as the "wounded hero" and "superman," and they, and their gradual recombination, would provide the form of the veteran and his story in the coming years.

Heroes, featuring two television stars, made the psycho-vet even more palatable. It told the love story of Carol Bell (Sally Fields), who leaves New York on a bus for Kansas City three days before her wedding day, and Jack Dunne (Henry Winkler), a veteran and an escapee from a mental ward who is traveling on a quixotic quest to Eureka, California, where he hopes to start a worm farm with his buddies from Vietnam. One of the buddies, Monroe, has already started a worm farm: he died saving Dunne and two other men during the War. Dunne suffers from survivor-guilt and has blocked that memory out, but his trip to Eureka brings it back to him; the journey climaxes when a flashback sequence turns a downtown street into the burning Vietnamese village where Monroe died, and it concludes in the arms of the woman he loves. This veteran is a romantic and this is his love story.

The film begins with a brief quixotic foray by Dunne. The credits roll across images of a Civil War memorial, then the film cuts to Dunne having a computer-generated poster made of himself, like Don Quixote bathetically imitating the older generation of knights. Rolling up the poster, he sights an army recruiting office through it and, like Don Quixote tilting at the windmill, he charges to save several young men from the clutches of the monster-recruiter. The audience takes Sancho's role, seeing a relatively harmless scene where the hero sees evil: the well-dressed, well-spoken recruiter is describing the advantages of an army career. Again like Sancho, the audience is won over by the hero's vision: as the police drag Dunne into a police car, the recruiter is revealed as a bully and a liar, reduced to clutching desperately at the fleeing teens. Through Dunne's eyes the audience sees the recruiter as an evil man, a procurer for death. The sequence ends in the manner of Don Quixote's first escapade, with the battered hero returning to his home (in Dunne's case the hospital) where he will be cared for until he escapes again.

The veterans in this film are marginal figures. The majority of them live with Dunne in the hospital. Dunne and Bell encounter another two on the trip to Eureka. One lives alone on a worn-down farm where he fantasizes about racing his car but never makes it onto the track. The second "went out for a drink and never came back"; his wife lives at home with their children, patiently waiting for his return. For one reason or another, none of these veterans can fit back into the society they left. Dunne differs from them only in his determination to be active even though marginal. He tells the hospitalized veterans to be "positive" and take a bath, he races his friend's car, he commits to the romantic interest, and he determinedly pursues his dream of a worm farm.

The story sends him from the farcical world of the mental institute to the bitter realism waiting for him in Eureka. On the way he grows gradually more rational as his illusions are fractured, eventually he re-assumes a masculine, nonromantic role that is symbolized by his recognition of his role as a soldier. His love interest, Bell, follows an opposite pattern. She is planning to marry in a few days, but has decided to take a bus trip across America first. She refuses to admit that her trip is an intuitive escape from the wrong marriage; instead, she insists she is rationally considering the pros and cons of marriage. Falling under Dunne's influence, she eventually follows her heart and resumes the traditionally female role of the irrational romantic. The film thus reestablishes the traditional gender roles, and the quest results in a partner for a traditional love relationship instead of a partner for a worm farm.

The place of the War in all this is strictly parenthetical, enclosed within the memories of the veterans and harming only them. The War appears on screen only at the climax, when Dunne suffers his vision of Vietnam on the streets of Eureka. Tanks and soldiers appear on the street. Mortar rounds blow up shoppers. A burning monk appears on the sidewalk. Then the town disappears, replaced by the wreckage of a Vietnamese village and the attack in which Monroe died saving Dunne. Like Jack Falen in *Tracks*, Jack Dunne has brought the War home with him. This time, however, the veteran has the love of a beautiful woman to help him beyond the reach of his Vietnam memories. "It's not happening now. It's all over," Bell reassures him. "Listen to me. You're alive—you don't need Monroe. I'm right here and I'm right now."

Just a Little Inconvenience, a television movie that also appeared in 1977, reduces the War to the level of plot device. The film tells the story of a skier who must learn to ski again after becoming a multiple amputee; that he is a veteran explains the lost limbs. Like Jack Dunne, Ken Briggs (James Stacey), the amputee, must learn to move beyond the effects of the War, effects which no one apart from veterans who suffered permanent disabilities feel. To be healed, the film suggests, is to admit that the wounds are "just an inconvenience." As with Dunne, the final proof of his recovery is his success with the girlfriend and the return of male virility which that implies. *Just a Little Inconvenience* ends with the love interest overcoming her immediate shock (not repugnance) at Briggs' condition and agreeing to marry him. Now fully reconstituted through a specially designed ski apparatus, Briggs can race his childhood friend and current ski instructor down the toughest slope of the mountain, "Undertaker's Alley," as described in the novelization.

> From the bottom of the hill Nick watched. She tried to pretend that her fiancé did this all the time, but she was scared for him as the two men schussed in a tight tuck straight for her. A crowd had gathered, awe-struck by the sight of the one-legged man running in a dead heat with the instructor. And that's the way they finished (Brooke).

The War and its effects become just one more challenge for the virile American male to overcome, allowing him once more to strike awe into the hearts of the audience and the woman he loves.

Major Charles Raine (William Devane), the misogynist and former POW in *Rolling Thunder*, abandons the possibility of romantic redemption in favor of homo-erotic power. As a POW he discovered the ability to withstand pain, whether emotional or physical, but at the cost of his own masculinity. He is an emotional castrate who finds fulfillment only through violence and pain; his world is misogynistic, nonromantic, and cruelly violent. His home town honors him with a parade, a car, and a silver dollar for every day he spent in captivity, but his wife greets him with the news that she is leaving him for a local policeman. Raine barely reacts to this news, merely moving out of the house into a shed in the backyard. The woman who had worn his POW bracelet offers herself to him, but he refuses her offer and concentrates instead on his relationship with his son.

Cut off from or uninterested in women, he gains his pleasures in the film through his relations with men. His wife's lover, having replaced him as husband and father, comes by to do the right thing and talk about the affair with the husband. "What kind of man would I be [if I didn't]?" he asks, and explains how he never meant the affair to happen. Raine appears uninterested; he turns the conversation to his torture in Viet Nam. "Do you want to know what they did?" he asks. "Sure you do." Suddenly the lover finds himself torturing the man whose wife he stole, providing a partial answer to his earlier, rhetorical question about what kind of man he is.

The two men—POW and policeman—act out this very physical scene in Raine's dark, confined sleeping quarters. The lover ties a rope around the husband's neck, hands, and ankles, then leans over the victim, pulling back on the rope; Raine, lying face-down on the floor, grimaces in pain while ordering him to pull "harder, harder." While the lover/policeman revolts against it, the husband/POW revels in it. During the torture, Raine seems to come alive for the first time since coming home. "That's how you beat people who torture you. Learn to love them. Then they don't know you're beating them," he explains. For Raine, the exchange of pain has become the erotic act (the one time he engages in heterosexual love, the camera cuts immediately away to a shotgun blast), and he uses eroticism as a weapon against his enemies. After thieves grind off his hand to torture the location of the silver dollars from him, the doctors provide him with a hook; this he sharpens into a spike, making a weapon from a castration symbol. At the film's climax he visits a brothel not to sleep with women but to kill men.

In this way the castrate regains his masculine role. His experience in the POW camps, while depriving him of his masculinity, allows him to appear more masculine than ever. Both his friends and enemies mistake his love of pain for strength and his misogyny for self-control. The one exception is another veteran, one of the thieves who mocks Raine's stoicism as posturing. To the others, Raine appears to be the archetypal hero of the American Western, "cold, isolate, and a killer," while being, in his words, "dead."

> Like my eyes are open and I'm looking at you but I'm dead.
> They pulled out whatever was inside of me. I never hurt at all
> after that, and I never will.

He has paid with his masculinity for this masculine power to withstand pain.

The paraplegic hero of *Coming Home* (1978) has had his masculine prowess destroyed, yet he manages to rejoin peaceful American society. Ostensibly about welcoming the soldiers home, *Coming Home* is actually about which soldiers will be welcome home. The film's warriors must learn that war is a crime against humanity and that it yields only anguish and death. Love—in this case the love of Sally Hyde (Jane Fonda)—is the cure for war's afflictions; wife to one vet and lover to another, Sally offers the chance of salvation to both.

Before her husband leaves for war, Sally is a dependent, passive officer's wife; her husband Bob (Bruce Dern) describes her as "supportive" although, he admits, she doesn't really understand why he is going to Viet Nam. She makes his martinis and his supper, packs his bags, lets him make love to her without complaining, takes him to the station and kisses him goodbye. A friend describes her as "the hole in the donut. When the donut's gone, you disappear." Instead of disappearing completely, however, Sally becomes a feminist. She moves to a house on the beach, buys a sports car, and curls her hair. She disobeys her husband's preference and takes a job working with disabled veterans. She even steps toward being radical and tries to get the base newsletter/gossip sheet to carry a story about the plight of the wounded veterans. (Sally's story in some ways parallels Fonda's own development from her role as a futuristic sex-kitten in Roger Vadim's 1968 *Barbarella* to her activities as an antiwar activist and her visit to Hanoi in 1972, the main difference being, perhaps, that as Sally she champions the veteran instead of the North Vietnamese.)

Throughout this radical leap to freedom, however, she remains essentially naive and passive. The job she takes, she admits in a letter to her husband, is not really a job because it is volunteer work, and the work is essentially what she did for her husband: serving the men and acting as their cheerleader. She can maintain this role and still be independent because these men are incapable of acting without her; she literally stands above them. She can walk and they cannot, consequently she has the power in the relationship—she has the freedom. Still, if these "donuts" left, she would again risk disappearing.

One of the veterans she serves is Luke Martin, a football, basketball, and swimming hero from Sally's high school who replaces the absent husband in Sally's life. He resembles that absent warrior in many essentials: both are male-chauvinists; both volunteer for the War believing in it as an outlet for masculine heroics; both return from the War with physical and mental injuries (though to different degrees). Luke even refers to Bob as his "brother." Their stories differ only in their endings: Luke gets the girl while Bob commits suicide. Luke's eventually passive submission to his physical disability and acceptance of his own culpability in his fate allows him to return, while Bob, still healthy and aggressive, must leave.

The first half of the film describes Sally's growing freedom and Luke's rehabilitation. It opens with a low-angle shot of disabled veterans talking about their thoughts on the War.

> I have to justify being paralyzed, I have to justify killing people, so I say it was okay. But how many guys you know can make the reality and say, "What I did was wrong, man," and still be able to live with themselves 'cause they're crippled for the rest of their life?

The camera rests on the only actor in the group, Jon Voigt playing paraplegic Luke Martin. He lies pensively on a gurney as though studying for his part. The pensive stance turns out to be unusual for Luke at this stage of the film; in his next appearance he is a bitter, angry man who smashes bottles and swings his cane at the nurses and orderlies.

This *cinema verite* presentation of the veterans and their complex dependence on the War suggests that Luke's rehabilitation will involve coming to terms with that dependence, that he will attempt to do what the veterans in the hospital felt incapable of doing, what the real-life crippled veterans like Ron Kovic had done. Kovic's rehabilitation, described in his 1976 book *Born on the Fourth of July* and again in the 1989 movie of the same name, depends on his coming to terms with having crippled himself for a cause in which he no longer believes. *Coming Home*, however, resolves the paradox by minimizing Luke's physical disability. Luke gains mobility and freedom and, through these, power and social status. Although he remains without the use of the lower half of his body, he drives a sportscar, shops, lounges by the pool, makes love, and rescues Sally from her husband. At the end of the film he can say "What I did was wrong, man" because his personal loss has been minimized; he has less at stake.

Luke begins the film angry, but as a cripple he can harm no one but himself. This weakness allows Sally to safely enter his

life and restore his self-esteem, thereby removing the source of his
anger and making him fit for society. Her method is a sort of passive resistance: she tells him he is mean and continues to passively
serve him and the other veterans. The audience watches as he
ceases to abuse the people around him and consequently moves
into social communication. By the end of the film he can cry for
the pain in others and make a radical gesture that is as futile as
Sally's earlier attempt with the base newsletter (he chains himself
to the gate of the local recruiting center). Conversely, the more
passive he becomes, the more he regains the symbols of his masculinity. At the conclusion of his rehabilitation, he has gained his
sportscar, left the hospital, and brought Sally to her first orgasm.

At this point, Bob Hyde returns from Viet Nam after having
shot himself in the foot on the way to a latrine. Faced with pornographic surveillance films the government has made of Luke and
Sally, he manfully goes to warn his wife's lover of the government's spying, then takes his rifle and threatens to kill his wife.
Wanting to talk, Luke comes to the Hyde's home in time to help
diffuse the situation. Rifle in hand, Bob faces the lovers. Sally
holds out her arms to him while Luke calls him brother and urges
him to accept Sally's love. Although he holds the gun, their passive love overpowers him. Unable to kill his wife and "brother,"
he breaks down in sobs instead. Sally holds him in her arms while
Luke removes the bullets from the rifle and clips down the bayo-
net. Bob has succumbed.

The film ends ambiguously after Bob's defeat. Luke
preaches to a group of high school students on the evil of the warrior ethos while Bob, removing his medals, uniform, and wedding
ring, swims into the Pacific Ocean. Luke can preach because he
has fully converted to Sally's pacifism and accepts that what he
did was wrong. Bob, although subdued, is not yet a convert. He
has continued to battle the contradiction between the warrior
ethos he believes in and the warfare he experienced; the day after
his attempt to kill Sally, the Marines decorate him for his foot
wound. To convert he must, like Luke, accept his guilt and deny
the warrior, but he cannot force himself to do so.

Coming Home leaves the resolution of Bob's dilemma
poised between irony and melodrama. Apparently he commits

suicide, but earlier in the film Bob appeared as an athlete; he is probably a strong swimmer as well, making death by drowning an awkward way to go. If it is a suicide, it is curiously absent (like the War itself throughout the film)—more a disappearance than a death. The swim might be a symbolic gesture as easily as a suicide—in his removal of his uniform and wedding ring before entering the waves, he ritualistically abandons two of the institutions that had failed him before diving into the cleansing, embracing ocean. The filmmakers were themselves ambivalent about the ending; producer Jerome Hellman and director Hal Ashby played with several ways of "finishing the husband off," one of which was a violent public blow-up (Dickstein 630).

Jane Fonda originally conceived of the film as an antiwar polemic, but Hal Ashby, the director, persuaded her to play down much of the rhetoric in order to increase the audience appeal (Michael Paris 23). The film thus became a love story with a Vietnam era backdrop. It makes the War palatable to a general audience by sentimentalizing the issues surrounding the conflict while evading the War itself. All we know of the War we learn from Bob—we never see any of it apart from a flash of news footage—and his description is tantalizingly obscure: "I don't know what it's like; I only know what it is. TV shows what it's like." Luke simply refers to it as a bad place to be where he did bad things. It is a place where bad things happen, a place that Luke threatens children with: the Land of Nam.

The story's historical setting compounds the film's ambiguity. A news telecast at the beginning sets it at Tet, 1968, when the issue was ending the War, not mending the rifts the War caused. By 1978 (the year of the film's release), ending the War was no longer a concern—American soldiers had all come home five years earlier—but mending rifts was. "The message came at least ten years too late," according to Lawrence Suid. "No one in the country, even those who most strongly protested the war, really cared about the conflict in 1978, at least as a 'cause'" ("Hollywood and Vietnam," 23). By putting the film in that past, the filmmakers manage to confound the topical issue of veteran status with the historical issue of ending the War. The present becomes another absence in the film, joining the War and Bob Hyde's suicide. *Coming Home* comments on the situation of earlier veterans, yet lays claim from the start—with its semi-documentary opening scene among the actual veterans—to be commenting on current issues. Instead of confronting topical concerns, it confronts issues that are already resolved. It hides in the sentimental past.

The success of *Coming Home* in the 1978 Oscar ceremonies ensured that its formula would reappear in the eighties. Only one additional ingredient would be required to produce the veteran who could lead America forward, and that would be the physical rebuilding of the passive veteran. This would be possible only after the Reagan revolution overcame the Vietnam Syndrome, and it would result in the ultimate Vietnam veteran, John Rambo.

Return to Vietnam

Hollywood's difficulty in producing a successful combat film for Vietnam was unprecedented in the industry. The First World War saw numerous combat films before it ended (as well as several before it began), including Griffith's *Hearts of the World*, Ince's *Civilization*, and Chaplin's *Shoulder Arms*. Even an historical epic like DeMille's *Joan the Woman* managed to incorporate the trenches of the War. Kathryn Kane finds twenty-four films produced during the Second World War that fit her definition of combat film ("uniformed American forces in combat with uniformed enemy forces" ["World War II" 86]). Korea spawned fewer films, but combat continued to play an important role in those that appeared, including Sam Fuller's *The Steel Helmet* and *Fixed Bayonets*. *The Green Berets* was the only major Vietnam War combat film produced during the war years, and not until 1986's *Platoon* would the combat film become a popular form for reproduction of the War.

The missing combat films reflect a missing consensus about the War itself. In previous American wars, the United States government had provided a generally accepted explanation of what the war was about and what was happening overseas. It controlled the source, and therefore the production, of information about the war. Journalists worked with the government and depended on it for their credentials. Filmmakers routinely had their scripts approved by the military and saw themselves as part of the war effort. They worked with government to create a vision of war that would appeal to the American people.

That control waned during the Vietnam War, leaving the filmmakers with a long period of history that had not been predigested by one organization, but by many: press, public, government, military, soldiers, and protesters. Philip Beidler, in describing the task of the Vietnam War writer, describes the position of the filmmakers as well.

> Mainly, Vietnam would always be a place with no real points of reference, then or now. It would become the task of the Vietnam writer to create a landscape that never was, one might say—a landscape of consciousness where it might be possible to accommodate experience remembered within a new kind of imaginative cartography endowing it with large configurings of value and signification. In this way, what facts that could be found might still be made to mean, as they had never done by themselves (16).

The barrage of Vietnam War films that arrived in 1978 shows how difficult this can be. They included sentimental romances, buddy films, nostalgia pieces, a Kung Fu movie, a story of scandal and investigative reporting, and at least one Western. With about two hours to tell their story, filmmakers can not provide very much background material without destroying the momentum. So the filmmakers attempted to graft the War onto well-known stories, allowing the audience to recognize the story's background when they recognized the story's genre. *Big Wednesday*, *More American Graffiti*, and *Our Winning Season*, for instance, graft the War and war resistance onto coming of age stories. General Dell had to be a madman in *Twilight's Last Gleaming* because he was the terrorist in a doomsday thriller, but that he was a witness to Vietnam altered the outcome of that thriller; it highlighted corruption in government and led to the assassination of the president.

Go Tell the Spartans (a small film given only a limited release) provided one of the more successful balances of genre when it combined the war film with the Western. It used the revisionist Western premise that the pioneers were not carving a civilization out of a wilderness but out of another civilization, and it managed thereby to consider the Vietnam War as part of a longer history of Vietnamese struggle. The scenario is similar to that in *The Green*

Berets. An American advisory force leads a group of South Vietnamese "Raiders"—a mixed group of ill-equipped, ill-trained soldiers—and mercenaries to occupy Muc Wa, a village the French had attempted to occupy ten years before. The military's rationale for the occupation is simply that the French failed to hold it and subsequently lost their war. The American military leaders intend to make none of the mistakes the French did—they go so far as to ban "Frenchified" jungle fatigues and question the value of esprit ("a French word," the commanding general notes darkly). The advisory force occupies the ruins of the old village, clears the land around it, rebuilds a watchtower, sends out scouting parties, and provides shelter to women and children. Even without the *nom de guerre* of "Fort Dodge" found in *The Green Berets*, this fort is clearly modeled after the American West version.

The difference between the mythologized American West and Viet Nam appears on a plot of land next door. Three-hundred and four French soldiers who died in the previous defense of Muc Wa are buried there. Corporal Courcey (Craig Wasson), the sympathetic main character, translates the signpost over the cemetery entrance for his Lieutenant. "Stranger, when you find us lying here, go tell the Spartans we obeyed their orders." Amongst the French graves Courcey encounters One-Eyed Charlie, a war-beaten old Vietnamese man with a rifle who leaves him a note demanding "Yanqui go Home" before disappearing into the brush. After the Vietnamese have overrun the fort and slaughtered all its defenders except for the corporal, Charlie reappears. The wounded Courcey, struggling across the ruined cemetery, pauses at the sound of a rifle bolt. One-Eyed Charlie, looking more battered than before, points his rifle toward his enemy for only a moment before losing his strength and dropping it. "Never mind," Courcey tells him, "I'm going home."

The scene, a confrontation between a battered, old Vietnamese soldier and a defeated American advisor/soldier on a French burial ground, suggests a war that was going on long before America became involved, a war that has all but destroyed the land and the people, a war that America did not start but certainly exacerbated. The opening of the film describes the setting as 1964, when the War "was still a little one," hinting darkly at how much more terrible and hopeless it would yet become. References to the French and the length of the Vietnamese struggle point out that the current phase of the War, though modernized through "psy ops" and helicopters, fits into a long history of war.

It goes so far as to define just what type of war this was. The opening of the film offers a brief, two sentence history. The first describes the fall of the French and the division of the country, and the second mentions America's decision to support the South; the War, then, began as a war of liberation that developed into a civil war that the American's interfered in. The presence of Abraham Lincoln (who does not appear in the original novel, *Incident at Muc Wa*) emphasizes this fratricidal aspect of the War. He is a tall, sorrowful looking addict who acts as the fort's medic and speaks in bits and pieces of President Lincoln's speeches. In one scene he stumbles into the fort compound and makes his way up the watch-tower while intoning the Gettysburg Address before a mortar round throws him to the ground.

This sense of history in the film—both the history of the genre and of the War—remains rare in the Vietnam War film. To some extent being ahistorical is characteristic of the war film in general. Katherine Kane notes that the soldiers of World War II combat films "are Everyman swept up by forces of history beyond their understanding, carried into a wasteland to 'slay the dragon,' hoping to survive to return home."

> Why the men fight, then, why they are engaged in this war, what the ideological or political issues or causes might be, are not relevant topics of discourse in the films. For the purposes of the films, the war began when the Japanese attacked Pearl Harbor. To a lesser, and much less clear, extent, America became involved in the war in Europe only after it had to retaliate against the Japanese and in that event, became belligerents in Europe to help its Allies against their enemy (*World War II*, 87).

But at least World War II had a clearly defined starting point and final goal. In Vietnam a soldier did not have to "slay the dragon" before returning home; he merely needed to survive for a year. Consequently the films seldom offer clues about the progress of

the War itself, which tends to set the conflict outside any historical context.

The only other film to concentrate on the combat situation,
The Boys in Company C, suffers badly from trying to combine
World War II genre conventions with Vietnam themes. The film is
overtly antiwar, and like many antiwar films of the early seventies
(*Catch-22*, *M*A*S*H*, or *Slaughterhouse-Five*), it recreates the
theater of war as the theater of the absurd by denying that any in-
telligent purpose guides events. The raw recruits face death for
the first time in defense of a general's food locker. Later, when
more experienced, they order a bombing raid on a nearby, empty
hillside and bathe in a stream while watching the fireworks; afterward the army rewards them for destroying the nonexistent force.
The farce ends in a soccer match between the grunts and a hope-
lessly inept South Vietnamese champion team, a match that the
Americans are ordered to lose.

The film grafts this absurdist scenario onto a traditional
World War II combat film story, following a group of draftees
through boot camp and into combat. Set in 1967, it has many of
the stock characters associated with Second World War features
—the tough, cynical sergeant, the ethnic comic, even the aspiring
novelist who narrates the story, all of whom overcome personal
differences to pull together as a unit. Other stock elements include
a drill instructor (Lee Ermey in the first of several tough-as-nails
Vietnam film roles) with a heart of gold ("It's up to me how they
come back," he explains emotionally), oriental villains with long,
claw-like fingernails, and a simple conflict of good versus evil.

The film tries very hard to satirize all these elements with the
exception of the soldiers themselves. The oriental villains are
America's allies instead of its enemy. The chief conflict is between the soldiers and the officers. The shared values have nothing to do with winning the War, just with survival. The
Vietnamese military is unworthy of American aid, and the American military continues to do battle without any goal except prop-
ping up a corrupt government. None of it, we are repeatedly told,
is worth the lives of the men. The only legitimate purpose the heroes can find is "getting these men out of the bush alive." Yet the
men do fight on. Ordered to lose to the inferior Vietnamese soccer

team, they rebel and are consequently sent to Khe Sahn instead of the promised soccer tour of the Pacific. It seems that they consider their lives more important than winning a meaningless war, but less important than winning a soccer match.

The *Boys* are good soldiers stuck in a bad war. The film spreads the blame around as many groups as possible—the ARVN, officers, the government (American and South Vietnamese) and the civilians back home, to name a few—but purges the American soldier of all guilt. He may appear culpable during the story (as when one of the soldiers tries to smuggle drugs in body bags), but when needed he will defend his country as well as he is allowed. The narrator's final (posthumous) narration recognizes this somewhat wistfully.

> After what happened here today, who's ever going to believe it? We actually had a chance to get out of this god-damned war. All we had to do was throw the game and walk away. But for some reason, we just couldn't. For some reason, winning that stupid game was more important than saving our ass. So I guess we'll just keep on walking into one bloody mess after another, 'till somebody figures out that living has got to be more important than winning.

The Academy Award winner for best picture in 1978, *The Deer Hunter*, also honored the soldier. *The Deer Hunter* was one of the two most important Vietnam combat films of the seventies, and (perhaps inevitably) one of the two most controversial. It went beyond the usual tendency to decontextualize the War. It not only removed the historical context of the conflict, it also radically altered the place and the events. What it claimed to be the Vietnam War, veterans disclaimed as something that bore only the slightest resemblance to their remembered war. The film shows no one in combat; it cuts to Viet Nam immediately after a battle has been fought and then cuts away when battle is likely to start again. Veterans and critics scorned the primary Viet Nam scene in the film, the Russian roulette sequence, as being a total fabrication. Few if any Vietnamese played Russian roulette. The Army rejected the filmmakers' request for production assistance because of the scripts technical and military errors. "In turning down a request for assistance, the Army recommended that the producer 'employ a researcher who either knows or is willing to learn something about the VN war'" (Suid "Film Industry," 217).

A second criticism was that the film relied on racist stereotypes of the enemy. The Vietnamese have two roles in the film: as refugees (tramping down a road or fighting for room on departing planes) and as Russian roulette players. The film offers them no sympathy or history. The refugees at the gate, part of the hellish landscape the heroes descend into, are fleeing from an invading army, but the films pays no attention to this fact nor to the lives they have left behind. By removing the historical context of the War, Cimino removed the plight of the people; neither they nor their cause has a history. The film effectively reduces the Vietnamese to one of the archetypal anti-American villains: the inscrutable, barbaric, Asian horde. One critic called it "xenophobic to an extreme that not even the conservative John Ford ... ever ventured" (Fox 24). When the film was entered in the Berlin Film Festival, the Soviet Bloc walked out, calling the film "an affront to the struggle of the Vietnamese people."

The War and the enemy are not the only decontextualized elements of the film, however. Cimino stylizes reality throughout. The fictional Pennsylvania mining town of Clairton is an idealized town created out of pieces of five other Pennsylvania towns. When the men of this town go for a day's hunting, the film shows them in the dramatic Rocky Mountains instead of the older, lower Appalachian Mountains that are in Pennsylvania. The church in this working-class town is fabulously rich and exists in the city of Cleveland. The main character, Michael, shares the mythical stature of a Natty Bumppo or Daniel Boone, yet he lives within the social confines of this small town. Everything, including the War, is decontextualized by the film and reset into a new context with a new meaning. Cimino has re-imagined the American working class, the American wilderness, the American hero, and American history to place them in a nonspecific, almost metaphorical, war.

Russian roulette certainly works as a metaphor for combat, if not as an image of the Vietnam War. De Niro, referring to the Russian roulette during a 1989 *American Film* interview, notes

the metaphorical nature of the sequences as well as its weakness
as used by Cimino.

> The Russian-roulette thing was a metaphor.... It shocked peo-
> ple in a way they wouldn't've felt if they just saw another bat-
> tle.... I had been reading a book during this period about
> POWs over there, and they were always told to recant—to say
> they were wrong for invading Vietnam. It wasn't about
> money. That clutters it; it gets in the way. It was about *ideas*
> (Barry Paris 36).

The film makes the places, people, and events archetypal,
and as such they have a new context that can give their roles a
meaning the Vietnam War could not. Fox describes how this con-
textualizing works within the diagesis of the film.

> Yet the moment the people of this town enter the church, they
> are transformed: the formless routine of factory, housing, bar-
> room is suddenly connected to a tradition in which fat old
> ladies have a formative and important place, in which there is
> a traditional community that could never be sustained without
> a historically powerful outside influence. The church's out-
> landish, oversized presence in the film is as necessary here as
> the overheroic posture of DeNiro in the mountains. An over-
> riding influence, it must override the audience (23).

The idealized versions of place and character in the film connect
the story to an ahistorical structure based on symbol and arche-
type, instead of *Go Tell the Spartans'* historical one.

Not only the iconography, but also the film's narrative refers
to this ahistorical structure. The romantic triangle suits the Vietnam War's divisive nature. In this triangle, two men fight for the
same social position regarding a woman, or do not fight but try to
live peacefully balanced in their awkward social positions. That
frequently only one of the men remains alive at the end hints at the
difficulty of maintaining this balance. Several of the postwar
Vietnam films used it, including *Rolling Thunder, Who'll Stop
the Rain,* and *Coming Home.* In *The Deer Hunter*'s scenario Michael (Robert De Niro), the deer hunter, loves his best friend's
sweetheart but is bound by loyalty to remain chaste towards her.
Linda (Meryl Streep), the sweetheart, loves Michael, but is also
bound by loyalties toward her lover Nick (Christopher Walken).

Nick, the friend and lover, sees signs of the love between his friend and his lover early in the film, but he either fails to or refuses to understand them. Linda's loyalty finally falters when Nick goes MIA, and she seduces Michael.

This structure resembles one of the structures in the Arthurian Romance: the betrayal of Arthur by Lancelot and Gueneviere. Mike, in the Lancelot role, is the perfect knight who discovers his humanity in the illicit love he feels for his friend's lover; Nick is the Arthur character, trusting his lover and his friend instead of his instincts. The film develops the comparison with its opening images of the men wearing shiny silver coats of asbestos and visored helmets which look very like medieval suits of armor. And they live in an oversized world where great heroism, sacrifice, and nobility are possible.

The actors' characterizations add to the similarity. De Niro concentrates on near, physical surroundings: his gun, his drink, his friend's face. Walken, a thinner, more fragile physique than De Niro, frequently shifts the focus of his eyes. His preferred gaze is into the distance. He loves the mountains for their peace; Mike loves them for their isolation—they provide a suitable climate for his concentration on the "one shot." As portrayed by De Niro, Mike personifies the American, masculine virtues (strength, skill, isolation, control) as well as the virtues valued in the Arthurian knight—chastity and loyalty.

Mike is not a leader, however; that role falls to Nick, who settles quarrels, unites friends, and inspires loyalty. Steven chooses Nick, not Mike, to stand up for him at the wedding, and Mike says of Nick, "I hunt with you or I hunt alone." When Nick disappears in Vietnam, the community of friends begins to disintegrate; the oversize grandeur of the first half of the film is gone, there are hints that Linda has been unfaithful, and the bonding between the men has weakened—when they fight there is no one to heal the breach as Nick had done. Mike is unable to rebuild the community, and he aggravates the situation with his isolation, his affair with Linda, and his impossible personal standards.

Linda, although the third point in the triangle, has only a supporting role: the prize to be won by one or the other of the men. The film presents her as a medieval-style damsel in distress.

She appears first in an upper room serving her father, an ogre who beats her in a drunken fit of anger. The scene stands out in the opening half of the film as the single overtly unpleasant event. Her life appears small and petty. She comes to Nick for protection, and he grants it to her. Later, when Nick is MIA, she goes to Mike for warmth, and he, in turn, grants that to her.

After they sleep together and Mike's chastity ends, he leaves his over-controlled, isolated world and fully enters the community. During the next hunt, he comes to an agreement with the Noble Stag in the mountains (his "Okay" echoes through the mountains). He brings the crippled Steven home from the Veterans hospital and returns to Vietnam in search of Nick. At the beginning of the film, he had promised to bring Nick home, and the return to Viet Nam fulfills that promise. But his rescue efforts offer more than personal redemption; they redeem the community. Mike has begun to assume Nick's power of binding the community together.

The Western, a narrative concerned with the need to build or maintain a civilization in the midst of a barbaric world, also uses this triangular structure. Through it, the Western balances the need to establish order through violence against the paradoxical need for civilized men to eschew violence. The Arthurian romance (also a story about the birth of a civilization) attempts the same balancing act but fails: the king dies and the civilization dies with him. The Western version saves the king and the civilization by allowing the wilderness hero to perform the necessary violence for the civilization and then nobly depart. The gunfighter in the Western seldom remains in the society he establishes or defends. He is part of the old order and must depart with it. He either recognizes the change and leaves gracefully, or the society finds some way of controlling his violence, often by making him sheriff, the town's official protector from the wilderness. This way the community can be built out of violence but without sin.

The Deer Hunter contrives a compromise between these two narratives. The civilization hero dies. Nick attempts to break away from the violent wilderness, but discovers an aptitude, if not a taste, for the violence as symbolized in the Russian roulette. He shoots himself, turning the violence back at his own temple. His death thrusts responsibility for the community on the one member strong enough to fulfill it, the wilderness hero. Mike is "cold, isolate, and a killer," but he is also a part of the community that cannot be disowned. He maintains his place through the symbolic gesture of bringing Nick home to rest. The end of the film shows the community reunited. The wilderness hero sits with them all, neither at the head nor the foot of the table. When they break into "God Bless America" (not the national anthem), they celebrate a community that has altered since the film's beginning, that has faced some truth about its creation, and which continues. It is a scene of communal bonding, even to the inclusion of an oblique reference to the Christian communion, the beer and toast replacing the wine and wafer (Beck 14).

These parallels with other, more romantic narratives put the Vietnam soldier of *The Deer Hunter* amongst a company more noble than that provided by America's only defeat. As the knight/king, settler/gunfighter, he ceases to be among the war-criminals and becomes one of the war-nobles. He enters a tradition of men who go to war for a high cause, who are working to build a civilization out of chaos and wilderness. In so redefining its warriors, the film also enters into the tradition of military re-writing that turned a small Welsh barbarian king into the Champion of Christianity and a mercenary gunfighter into the Knight of the West. The process of re-contextualization is not unique to the Vietnam War.

In some ways *The Deer Hunter*'s plot harkens back to the first American films set in Viet Nam, to *China Gate* and *The Quiet American*, in which two men fight for the heart of Viet Nam in the form of a Vietnamese woman. The difference is that the heart being contested now belongs to an American woman and the contestants are also both Americans. The triangle has become a domestic struggle fought in the Vietnamese wilderness. *The Deer Hunter* can be seen as another film about returning veterans, but one that roots the veteran's postwar trauma and alienation deeply within the context of his world before and during his combat duty. The structure of the film—the lengthy first section's elaborate celebration of community and masculine society, the second section's shocking evocation of war's brutality, and the final, bittersweet third when the young men come home from war—bound together the War and the society that made war.

Part of the Vietnam War film's allure is its claim to share some previously unrevealed or unacknowledged truth—to cut through the government and press mediations and offer a view of the thing itself. Critics, often quoting veterans, raged against *The Deer Hunter* for distorting the War, criticized *Coming Home* for refusing to show it at all, and praised *Go Tell the Spartans* and to a lesser extent *The Boys in Company C* and *Heroes* for daring to present a view of the actual combat. Audiences used the touch-stones of "accuracy" and "truth" to measure the films, though their judgment of that accuracy and truth was often highly subjective. In a 1983 reappraisal of *Go Tell the Spartans*, Rob Edelman quoted from many of the film's less enthusiastic and negative reviews which criticized the similarity of this version of the War to other wars; they complain that the story is mired in war film or Western genre conventions. Edelman makes the point, however, that the film was so concerned with accuracy that the filmmakers enlisted a South Vietnamese infantry major as a consultant on the battle scenes and Vietnamese boat people as extras, and he goes on to quote a veteran's approval of the film's detail.

> The filmmaker got the hootches down right; the sets re-minded me of an actual base camp. The film captures the futility of American military posturing in a very real way. It eloquently sums up the sentiments of vets who saw the ab-surdity of the conflict, the fact that the war was unwinnable and ridiculous—and some of these were regular army people (Edelman 54).

The point made by the negative reviews reflects a notion that the Vietnam War had to be different from other wars, and so any film that used war film conventions must be inaccurate. The com-bat situation, which was only one of the social, political, and his-torical events that comprised "the Vietnam Experience," was developing into the symbol for the entirety of that experience. It represented America's commitment to the effort against North Viet Nam. When it ended, most America's saw it as the end of the War, and many critics, authors, and filmmakers have sought the truth about Vietnam there. On the other hand, the veterans would dismiss the resulting representations, "puzzled and appalled at the need for inventing a metaphor for the Vietnam War" (Just 1979, 65)

When Coppola's recreation of the War finally arrived in 1979, the director claimed it did more than merely show the War: "My film is not about Vietnam," his film notes declared, "it is Vietnam." The protracted, costly, secretive, remote, and highly publicized production of the film did resemble America's handling of the Vietnam War. In addition, both the War and this cinematic reproduction ended ambiguously and suffered accusations that they lacked purpose or vision. *Apocalypse Now* was also the only one of the triumvirate of controversial Vietnam War films at the end of the seventies (with *The Deer Hunter* and *Coming Home*) accused of being a failure. While critics might describe the other two films as racist, fascistic, sentimental, or oversimplistic, they are generally recognized as being, within their limits, artistically successful. Critics often accuse Coppola's epic, on the other hand, of a failure of vision. In this way it reflects America's sense of the War as being a meaningless conflict. However, both the film and the War demanded too much of their audiences for people to reject them easily—hence the revisionist attitudes to the War and the insistent defenses of the film.

Much of Coppola's film is easily defended. Colonel Kilgore's Air Cavalry attack on a Vietnamese village—with the helicopters charging at dawn on the quiet village, Wagner blasting from speakers affixed to the machines, and Kilgore striding through the wreckage of the aftermath, oblivious to the mortars landing around him while he inhales "the smell of napalm in the morning" and orders his men to surf—stands as a classic piece of combat film; the audience might be tempted to believe that, if the War was not really like this, it should have been. The film's other set pieces—Willard "getting softer" between assassination missions, the Playboy bunnies arriving on helicopters from the darkness and disappearing again while soldiers drip from their landing skids, the Do-Long Bridge at "the asshole of the world"—succeed in evoking a world where, once seduced into it by scenes like Kilgore's attack, America could not help losing its way.

The idea for the film began as a topical semi-documentary about a war that America was currently fighting. Milius wrote the script for George Lucas to direct in 1969. The idea was to keep the budget low and use a lot of documentary footage. Milius based the screenplay on the *Odyssey*.

> Willard's whole trip is like the Odyssey, penetrating further into himself. In essence, he meets the Cyclops—the surfing Colonel, Robert Duvall ... and he meets sirens, these playboy bunnies (Thompson 15).

Coppola removed the documentary aspect of the original script (though his own presence as a cameraman during the beach assault may refer to it) and decided that the Milius screenplay was too much like a comic book. He restructured it to fit Conrad's *Heart of Darkness*, making Willard penetrate further into the heart of the War and less deeply into himself.

Notes, Eleanor Coppola's journal of the filming, and *Hearts of Darkness*, the 1991 documentary based on Eleanor Coppola's notes, tapes, and film of the production, make clear how much her husband defined the film's vision during the production. Brando arrived for his one month stint before the cameras far too fat to fit into the active role which Coppola and Milius had scripted for Kurtz, so he added his own perceptions to the film's vision, leaving Coppola to hastily rewrite the ending at night and film with Brando during the day, desperate to complete the climax of the film before the actor left. He eventually shot three different endings in which Willard alternately kills Kurtz, joins Kurtz, and dies with Kurtz in an American bombing attack.

The script that eventually appeared borrows from a variety of sources, including the *Odyssey*, *Heart of Darkness*, Raymond Chandler's private eye Philip Marlowe, and Sir James Frazer's *The Golden Bough*. Willard's mission—to travel up-river into Cambodia and "terminate with extreme prejudice" Colonel Walter Kurtz, a military wonder-boy who has "quite obviously gone insane" and begun "acting without any decent restraint"—is a quest in which Willard takes on the various characters of Odysseus, Marlow, Marlowe, and rejuvenated god at different times, only to find that none of them is quite suitable to his task.

Odysseus wanted to return home; Willard went home and "realized it didn't exist anymore." More importantly, he lacks the old Greek's wit and guile. As Kurtz notes, Willard is "an errand boy—sent by grocery clerks—to collect a bill." Willard remains a pair of eyes, observing the War but scarcely participating in it. Coppola certainly intended some such passive role for Willard; he fired Harvey Keitel because that actor came across as too strong. Martin Sheen as Willard barely comes across at all; he is a dreamer who allows himself to be carried along the dream without trying to wake up. The audience must depend on Michael Herr's post-filming narration for any access it has to the character. The camera's subjectivity also interferes with Willard's ability to filter our experience. The image on the screen often overwhelms Willard's mediation. This passivity should not be confused with the cool detachment of Conrad's Marlow either. Willard is deeply implicated in all he sees. The military sends Willard to kill an American officer who has gone beyond the bounds of acceptable behavior, but with six assassinations to his credit, Willard has himself gone beyond those bounds. As he travels up the river, he discovers that he respects, admires and identifies with the man he must kill.

If Willard does not fit the roles suggested by the film's acknowledged sources, his alienation, his insistence on a type of personal integrity, the often repeated image of his eyes, the voice-over commentary, and his role as an un-official soldier suggest another role for him, that of the American hard-boiled private eye. This genre subtext helps explain what are otherwise illogicalities in the story. As an assassin, Willard would probably have been helicoptered into position with a team of men and would have known nothing about Kurtz beyond the facts he needed to complete his mission. Instead, he goes alone on a river voyage that takes him through a landscape as decayed and corrupt as Marlowe's southern California. He receives Kurtz's dossier so that he may study his target, but an assassin doesn't study his target, he shoots it; a detective studies his target. Kurtz is a suspect whom Willard must "terminate with extreme prejudice."

As John Hellman has noted, however, Willard is not the equal of this progenitor either. Marlowe's loyalty to his personal code of justice allowed him to judge others and defend humanity. Willard's code, in contrast, leads him to murder a young woman. In a scene Coppola once described as the most important in the film, a sudden movement in a boatload of natives causes the Americans to fire on them, killing all except one young girl whom they badly wound. Before they can load her onto Willard's boat for transport to "friendlies," Willard shoots her and his voice-over narration explains:

> It was a way we had over here. We'd cut 'em in half with machine guns and give them a band-aid. It was a lie; and the more I saw of them, the more I hated lies.

In the scene, Willard acts as both judge and executioner, but he does not execute the people he judges—he executes their victim. This is Willard's personal code, an insistence on truth even above humanity.

The episode prefigures one Kurtz will relate to Willard in the story of the inoculations. According to Kurtz, his men went to a village and inoculated all the children. Afterward, the Viet Cong came to the village and cut-off all the inoculated arms. "I cried, I wept," Kurtz explains. "If I had ten divisions of those men than our problems would be over." Willard, the Viet Cong, and Kurtz all punish the innocent to prevent the guilty from assuaging their guilt. This code of truth finds its ultimate expression in Kurtz's compound, a chiaroscuro landscape strewn with hanging bodies and heads mounted on stakes. "Slow death; malaria; nightmare," Willard says. "This was the end of the river alright." In Kurtz' notebook he finds a recommendation: "Drop the bomb. Exterminate them all."

In the Cambodian temple where Kurtz has established his headquarters, a world has grown from the ideal with which, through constant loyalty to it, Willard has maintained his own sense of self. The creator of the world is Kurtz, who has obviously come to be regarded by the Montagnards as a near thing to a god (though less explicitly than in the earlier Milius script), and he has made his world not in his image but in that of his ideal. Marlowe had always survived the disillusionment his investigation caused by returning to the certainty of his ideal; Willard finds that his ideal has been part of the illusion.

Willard—detective, assassin, voyager, idealist—having reached his destination, must now fulfill his mission. The Army's euphemism "terminate his command" gains new resonances in the Kurtz compound. "They were going to make me a major for this," Willard reflects, "and I wasn't even in their fucking army anymore." In Cambodia he finds new commanders. His orders now come from Kurtz and from the jungle, "who [Kurtz] really took his orders from anyway." The mission begins again, therefore, this time without the military trappings. No military hardware transports or protects the assassin. He rises out of the swamp and stalks through the firelit night. The ritual slaughter of a beast counterpoints his movements. His weapon is a machete; four blows suffice to slaughter both beast and man, and Willard walks forth on the temple steps, stained with the blood of his victim and receiving the venerations of the multitude. The camera gazes up at Willard, the new god, as he passes through the crowd to his boat and sails away. Willard's face fades in over an image of the temple idol, remaining superimposed over it until both fade away and are replaced by a brief fade-in of the helicopters from the film's opening napalm attack (this time the Doors do not inform us that "this is the end").

To the list of Willard's roles has been added that of rejuvenated god in a cycle of death and rebirth. The slow pans across volumes of *The Golden Bough* and Jesse Weston's *From Ritual to Romance* that preceded the ritualized slaughter insist on this motif. They suggest that this was Kurtz's hope, that he wanted Willard to kill him so he could be reborn and the cycle begin again. A new cycle would cleans the decay at the heart of his world. If so, then the books are part of a message to Willard (as much as to the audience). Again, however, Willard will take on a role without fulfilling it. Not Odysseus, Marlow, or Marlowe, he is finally not even the rejuvenated god. Willard walks down the temple steps, returns to his boat, and departs. "It was a real choice mission," he commented at the beginning of his tale, "and when it was over I'd never want another." The Montagnards, Kurtz' fighting force, are left to fend for themselves in the Cambodian jungle, outside the legitimate confines of the War.

It did not have to end this way, of course, and very nearly did not. Coppola filmed three different endings before the film crew left the Philippines, including one involving the biggest explosion of the film when the air raid razes the compound. The ending finally chosen for the film's distribution was selected after audience test screenings selected it as the most popular. It is also the only one of the three (in which Willard kills Kurtz, joins Kurtz, and is killed with Kurtz in an American bombing attack) in which superimposition of one culture upon another finally happens. No American air strike eradicates this Vietnamese-American hybrid by punishing the survivors. As Willard floats back down the river, the "slow death; malaria; nightmare" remains accusingly behind him. It is not a positive ending, it signifies no absolution for the Americans by suggestions that we could or would repair the damage; but it is not a denial of the damage either.

In the seventies, *Go Tell the Spartans* and *The Boys in Company C* tried to describe the Vietnam War as though it had been essentially just like World War II or Korea. Cimino showed an imagined Vietnam that no one recognized. Coppola attempted to show what Vietnam was really like but ended by denying that it was possible. In the eighties, Oliver Stone would take up the challenge and show "Vietnam. The way it really was. On film."

Part 3
Recovery and Rehabilitation

Looking Back

The 1987, low-budget comedy-horror film *House* features a spiritless Vietnam veteran, Cobb (William Katt), who has lost his son to kidnappers and wife to divorce. Amidst the shambles of his life, he moves into the house from which his son disappeared to write a war memoir. He soon discovers that the ghost of an MIA army buddy (Richard Moll) haunts the house. The ghost now holds Cobb's son captive in a Vietnamese tiger-pit, and the father must rescue his son and destroy the MIA ghoul. Cobb places a grenade in the spirit's festering belly, grabs his son, and runs out to the waiting arms of his returning wife. The house explodes, but the patriarchal family is restored.

This fantasy embodies a belief that President Ronald Reagan espoused and that lay near the heart of the Reagan Revolution in the eighties, a revolution that began in the late seventies, even before Ronald Reagan took control. Carter's foreign policy began benignly enough with human rights and the Camp David Accords, but became increasingly martial in the second half of his presidency as he confronted America's "crisis of spirit" by renewing draft registration, boycotting the Olympics, and daring a commando raid on Tehran to rescue the American hostages. The Great Communicator, however, was the man who recognized the changing attitudes in America and inspired a cultural revolution that finally overthrew the Vietnam Syndrome's proclaimed grip on American society. His patriarchal vision of the American mission to civilize and defend the free world had the same effect on the Vietnam Syndrome as Cobb's grenade had in the MIA's belly. Reagan insisted America was crippling itself through obsessive fear of Vietnam. He believed that the War had been "noble" and that "we didn't lose that war," and he was willing to say so. He accused those opposed to his foreign policy efforts, especially in Central America and Grenada, of the same failure of nerve that lost the Vietnam War. His defense secretary summarized the lesson Vietnam now taught: "We should never again ask our men and women to serve in a war that we don't intend to win."

Fear of Vietnam had made this nation feel impotent and susceptible to incidents like the Iranian hostage crisis; only if America could overcome this fear would it again find itself patriarch to the world (the invasion of Grenada provided an example of this hope). A 1985 ABC News/Washington Post poll, taken while Viet Nam celebrated the tenth anniversary of the fall of Saigon, highlighted the American public's short memory about what the "cause" (noble or not) had been. This poll claimed that already one-fifth of Americans could not remember whether the United States had supported North or South Viet Nam.

The status of the veteran in American society was a major factor in America's recovery from the Vietnam Syndrome. Groups like the Vietnam Veterans Association gave them a concerted voice with which to protest the abuses they felt they had received. They made Agent Orange a national issue and forced Veterans hospitals to investigate its effects. In 1981, four VVA members were the first Americans to visit the new Viet Nam by invitation. The MIA issue also empowered the veterans as they became the spokesmen for a group that has reached near-mythic status in America. Presidents Carter, Reagan, and Bush have all had to confirm their governments' commitments to account for every one of the 2,273 officially unaccounted for soldiers. In 1983 Reagan granted it "the highest national priority," and the POW/MIA flag has the distinction of being the only flag other than the stars and stripes to fly over the White House; it has flown there once a year since 1982 (Franklin 45).

The growth of the veterans as a public pressure group also made it possible for America to memorialize the war. The Vietnam Veterans memorial was dedicated in 1982 with a week of ceremonies that included a three-day vigil and the reading of every fallen soldier's name. The following year the remains of an unknown soldier were buried in Arlington National Cemetery. At the ceremony, the president confirmed the importance of identifying all the MIAs (somewhat paradoxically since the records of the Unknown Soldier were destroyed so his identity could never be known). Reagan also took advantage of the occasion to reiterate his version of the War and of the soldier.

> He saw the horrors of war but bravely faced them, certain his own cause and his country's cause was a noble one, that he was fighting for human dignity for free men everywhere.

The veteran's status had risen so high that non-veterans now pretended they had been there, and politicians listed their Vietnam service in their campaign literature; by the end of the decade, Dan Quayle's avoidance of service had become a black mark against him in the vice-presidential race. Those who had not gone to Viet Nam now envied those who had, as Myra MacPherson describes in *Long Time Passing: Vietnam and the Haunted Generation.*

> A new current of thinking that can only be called "Viet Guilt Chic" comes from some of yesterday's draft dodgers and avoiders. If not a trend, it seems nonetheless to have become a staple of columnists or writers having a bad day. From the sanctity of fast approaching middle age, they write of their guilt for avoiding the war, making money off these *mea culpas* appearing on the "Donahue" and "Today" shows to confess all (159).

The symptoms of this "guilt chic" include a sense of personal loss at having missed the masculine experience of warfare and favoring a draft for the current younger generation (as though to save them from the same loss). MacPherson quotes Christopher Buckley (a speech writer for Vice-President George Bush and a draft dodger) as feeling that the veterans he knows "seem as though they would be head and shoulders above us in a crisis" (159). This envious view would become a vital factor in action movies of the eighties, as the Vietnam veteran increasingly became the action hero, or villain, of choice. Thus in the conclusion of *Lethal Weapon*, the police stand back to let two veteran supermen struggle for final supremacy, and in *Blue Thunder* the skies belong to the two veterans as they engage in a final duel for the skies.

The aging of the baby-boom generation contributed to the Reagan Revolution. The ending of *Hair* with the tribe of hippies and their young children gathered around a soldier's grave, hinted at what was to come. The counterculture was entering the establishment and had to accept the associated responsibility. The paraplegic veterans in *Coming Home* had to find a way to accept that they had sacrificed their bodies for a cause in which they no longer believed; the anti-establishment radicals now faced a similar dilemma: accepting that they were now part of an establishment that they had once forcefully reviled. Hollywood would help them justify this in such nostalgia films of the eighties as *Fandango, Return of the Secaucus Seven, Four Friends, 1969,* and especially *The Big Chill.*

The Big Chill (1983) begins with the burial of a radical who killed himself, unable to accept that the days of revolt and commitment had ended. His college friends come for the funeral and spend the weekend burying their anxieties with their friend. Despite the occasion that brings them together, the film is seldom somber and no conflicts mar the friendships for long. Everyone seems to have all they could ask for, or if not they get it by the end of the film. One woman, a successful executive but unmarried, longs for a child to make her life complete; another longs to make amends to her husband for an old infidelity. To resolve both desires, the wife loans her husband to the executive for a night. This is a happy, wholesome group almost unaware of how generously life has blessed them.

The one misfit is a drug dealer left impotent by the War. Like the suicide victim, he continues to dwell on the past and drifts aimlessly through life. His backwardness causes the one conflict that erupts in the film when he insults a policeman and nearly brings the law down on his host, a local businessman. This running-shoe maker had once been a successful and committed activist; now he is a successful and committed businessman. He sees no contradiction between the two, and neither does the film. The movie implies that being in the protest movement had been worthwhile in the sixties, but it never bothers to explain what the point of the protests had been. We learn that they had been enjoyable, well-motivated and well-executed, but not why anyone had bothered. Like the shoe business, it was a living. Certainly it was not worth suicide or ruining one's life. The film ends with the drug dealer reformed and taking the room and girlfriend left vacant by the suicide. There is talk of his helping the shoe sales-man develop some property and possibly living there one day. Everyone else departs happily. They had been facing various minor crises, but regaining contact with their youth had reinvigor-ated them, and reassured them of their special status in America.

Their right to this status is confirmed in a number of coming of age films in which the danger of Vietnam is the impulse for confronting maturity. Twenty years after the landmark year 1968, *'68* and *1969* collected anecdotes about the period and hung them on a simple, heartwarming plot: a pair of young men encounter all the elements of the sixties (drugs, hippies, free love, classic rock 'n roll, racial conflict, the generation gap, Vietnam, and the draft, to name a few), discover the generation gap is not as wide as they assumed, and try to avoid induction—one draftee tries to steal his draft records, but the other more imaginatively kisses his induc-tion officer. In both films, the anti-draft efforts arise from pure idealism rather than more selfish reasons. When in *1969* the hero escapes to Canada to avoid the draft, he could only be making a symbolic gesture, since he is a freshman in college at the time and hence would have qualified for an exemption until the end of the War. Perhaps he realizes this, because he changes his mind at the last moment and returns to fight against the War instead.

Complex portrayals of the movement and the issues Vietnam raised could provide a degree of balance to these elegiac visions, but Hollywood did not provide them. A television movie of *Kent State* (1981) showed just how high the stakes could be, but the victims at that college were mostly innocent bystanders. One film that provides a less nobly remembered draft dodger, though one no less sympathetic for not being a martyr to an unspecified cause, was *Fandango* (1985, starring the still undiscovered Kevin Costner). A small film that received only a limited run, *Fandango* hearkened back to road movies of the period like *Easy Rider* and *Zabriskie Point*. It told the story of five college friends, the "Groovers," who leave their graduation party for a joy ride across Texas, supposedly to recover a bottle of champagne they had buried on a similar excursion years before. The proximity of the Mexican border, however, suggests a more serious purpose for a group who have just found themselves eligible for the draft.

As in the other nostalgia films, the recent graduates experience most of the sights and sounds of the period (at least those that could be found in the Texas backcountry). Amongst these is a psychedelic experience in a graveyard (reminiscent of a scene in *Easy Rider*, but without the drugs) and a frenetically painted airplane that might have been left from *Zabriskie Point*. The graveyard scene provides a foretaste of combat as the boys chase local girls around the tombstones with fireworks left over from the Fourth of July. These boys are neither pro- nor antiwar, nor are they imbued with any false idealism. The ROTC graduate talks about serving his country although the thought obviously frightens him. Another groover fears going to war and uses it as an excuse to call off his wedding, while Gardner (Kevin Costner), who has no intention of going to war, simply assumes that if you don't have to risk dying in a foreign country, you don't.

These nostalgic glances at the war years, unfortunately, did the antiwar movement's reputation a great deal of harm. By dwelling on the good fellowship, music and drugs of the period and ignoring the dedication and effort of many people, these films make protesting the War seem merely populist and self-serving. In *1969,* the young hero sums up Hollywood's conception of counterculture idealism: "We don't need jobs," he tells his friend when they join a picnic at a nude beach. "We've got naked people giving us free food!" Campaigners who had a great time at the rallies replaced those who suffered for their beliefs. It is noteworthy, for example, that no serious film has appeared about the protest movement in the eighties apart from Oliver Stone's biography of Ron Kovic, *Born on the Fourth of July*, in 1989.

Kovic begins his story as a gung-ho patriot and ends as a paraplegic leader of the Vietnam Veterans Against the War. His service and sacrifice in Viet Nam endow his protest with a weight denied to civilians. The film shows campus activism through Kovic's eyes, and on his authority it can admit that the students took risks and dedicated themselves to a cause. Stone even puts them into battle with police during the riots at the Republican

National Convention. In the final, climactic scene when Kovic disrupts the Republican National Convention, the activists again enter battle as Kovic leads an assault and calls on his men to "take back the hall." Stone films the scene to match the earlier one in Viet Nam when Kovic was wounded. He is luckier this time, however, and gains fame and political power; in the next scene he is signing copies of his war memoir.

The civilian antiwar movement received even less respect from the soldiers fighting overseas in the combat films of the eighties. A key element in the developing formula for Vietnam combat films were the letters from girlfriends seduced by the self-righteous protest movement, or tales of soldiers who went home and were insulted by college kids. In these scenes the protesters become another enemy for the soldiers to face. Rather than ending the War, the protests only managed to discourage the soldiers, playing unwittingly into the hands of the enemy. Not only are the protests discouraging, they are infuriating as well because their leaders do not understand the situation in Viet Nam. The Vietnam Veterans Against the War organization is one of many antiwar groups that were based off the campuses, but it and the others are conveniently forgotten in these films that group the protesters to-gether as liberal college students or their teachers. As a sergeant in *Hamburger Hill* explains it, "you have to show up. You don't necessarily have to fight, but you have to show up."

As well as producing only one serious film about the antiwar movement, the Vietnam War cinema has produced very few films that condemn war itself. There have been several opposing the Vietnam War, but as that particular conflict is long since over, that target is hardly topical (as long as the Vietnam soldier him-self is omitted from the denunciations). *Gardens of Stone*, set in Arlington National Cemetery where they bury the war dead, might have seemed a logical prospect for a antiwar story, but the film is almost slavishly devoted to the army and its rituals. Ron Kovic's story was another opportunity, but in the end Stone celebrated Kovic as a war hero.

One of the few films that does manage to protest war is *Birdy,* based on William Wharton's novel. When the story opens, Birdy (Matthew Modine) is an a psychiatric ward, suffering from a PTSS induced psychosis; he perches in his hospital cell, staring up at the barred windows. His boyhood friend, Al (Nicolas Cage), badly disfigured by a burn wound in Viet Nam, talks to him about their childhood in the hopes of bringing him back to reality, and the film flashes back from the grim hospital setting to the more idyllic scenes of their youthful adventures in Philadelphia. Although their childhood was often tough, the two managed to survive through their friendship and Birdy's idealistic visions of the aviary world.

Their prewar lives were healthy and often exhilarating. Birdy's obsession with birds was antisocial, but the film shows it as also being wonderful and life-affirming. At one point he seems to become a bird himself, as the camera takes a bird's point of view and flies out of the room and across the Philadelphia sky. In sharp contrast, their postwar lives are trapped behind the barred windows of the hospital and Birdy's love has become a psychosis. Al's therapy for Birdy eventually leads them to memories of the War, where Birdy suffered the trauma that locked him away from the world and his birds and where Al's face was burned. War ended their childhood in death and violence instead of maturity. The story disregards the issues and details of the particular war that did this to them; it could have been any war (William Wharton used World War II in the original novel).

The Stunt Man also contrasts another war with Vietnam to probe the nature of warfare itself. After Vietnam veteran Cameron (Steve Railsback) runs from the police he finds sanctuary as a stuntman in a World War I film. Cameron's crime is unspecified through much of the film, and his character depends on the well-established image of the psychotic veteran. Railsback's edgy, paranoid performance adds to the effect, as do memories of his 1976 role as Charles Manson in *Helter Skelter*. The director, Eli Cross (Peter O'Toole), hides him amongst his crew because he hopes that the veteran will provide inspiration for his antiwar epic, as well as providing a litmus test for the film's success. If he can't convince one half-crazy veteran, he reasons, whom can he convince?

From what *The Stunt Man* shows of it, Cross' film is an often slapstick satire of warfare; the Huns fall over themselves like

Keystone Cops in the chase scenes and a war widow sets an indecent Victorian toy on her beloved's grave. Cross calls war a "symptom," like "whistling in the dark, inventing enemies"; the real curse is man's propensity for "tilting at windmills," for seeing enemies everywhere. Before Cameron realizes he is on the set of a film, he sees a car that appears to be running him off the road, so he throws a stone at the windshield and the car crashes in a river. Later, Cross asks him why he expected the driver to run him down and he replies:

> I didn't get the chance to ask him. He was coming at me too goddamn fast. You want to get home for Thanksgiving, you better figure the guy coming at you is trying to kill you. Learned that from the gooks.

Cross's goal is to show that there has to be "a better way to get home for Thanksgiving."

A classic problem for filmmakers wanting to make antiwar films has always been how to make war films without making warfare appear exciting. War films wonderfully. The solution, perhaps, is to reduce the war's presence and concentrate on the before and after, as do *Born on the Fourth of July, Birdy, and The Stunt Man*. Focusing on the price paid, however, begs the question raised in *Coming Home*: how to condemn something that cost so much. It can't always be done, and many would argue that the cost is what makes the event so important. Certainly that is part of the message the Vietnam Veterans Memorial offers.

The Boys Are Back

The importance of the Vietnam War Memorial to Americans is difficult to overstate. Its unveiling in November 1982 was part of a week-long ceremony attended by President Reagan that included a three-day vigil while the names of every soldier listed on the memorial were read. For the rest of the decade, it was the most popular monument in Washington DC and a smaller version toured the country. President Reagan's address to the vigil expressed the sentiments of many there

> These are men who died for freedom, just as sure as any men who ever fought for this country. The tragedy was they were asked to fight and die for a cause their country was unwilling to win. I think we're beginning to understand how much we were led astray at that time. We are beginning to appreciate that they were fighting for a just cause.

The controversial dark slabs of the memorial, however, express no such assurances. They list only the dead with neither explanation nor apology; it might almost be a memorial to the victims of a natural disaster, a plane wreck or a landslide. Their suffering has alone sufficed to bring them honor. Hollywood's treatment of the soldiers who survived the suffering and returned to America has followed a similar theme. In the eighties, with the War over and becoming a distant memory—and for a new generation history—the veteran could be welcomed home without the concern that he might, somehow, bring the stain of the War with him, since no one seemed certain what that stain might be.

The psycho-vet still rampaged through thrillers like *House, Fear* (1988), and *Don't Answer the Phone* (1986), but now a more sympathetic veteran was there to oppose him. In *Fear*, for instance, the veterans are prison inmates on a violence spree, but they have the misfortune of choosing another veteran for their victim, and his mixture of natural nobility and Vietnam-taught fighting ability are no match for the wilder group. The hero is a good soldier who abjured the excess violence and the villains are the bad soldier who reveled in it, a dichotomy insisted on in combat films of the eighties like *Platoon, Casualties of War, Leathernecks* or *The Lost Idol.*

By and large, Vietnam was no longer a specter to haunt Americans. Now it haunted only the veterans. The psycho-vets in the horror films turned their violence against other vets more often than they did against innocent civilians. When they didn't, when they struck out against other Americans, the films managed to excuse their behavior with the catch-all phrase Post Traumatic Stress Syndrome [PTSS], the eighties' version of battle-fatigue now given wider recognition and treatment. Hollywood latched on to it as the ideal symbol of the American soldier's martyrdom in Vietnam.

The best known example of a cinematic veteran suffering from PTSS is undoubtedly Sylvester Stallone as John Rambo. He first made his appearance in the 1982 film *First Blood* (based on a novel by David Morrell) as a friendless wanderer who has been run out of one too many towns. In Vietnam he was the finest member of an elite group, the Green Berets, and received the Congressional Medal of Honor for his heroism. In the United States he has no use for the skills he learned in the War, and he wanders around the Pacific Northwest searching for his old army buddies. All his friends have died, however—suicides, addicts, or victims of Agent Orange. Their country used them to fight its war, then discarded them like rusty nails.

First Blood takes pains to make this veteran a Christ figure, albeit a violent one. He is crucified by a sadistic cop in the police station, "killed" by weekend warriors in the National Guard, survives a hellish tour through a mine shaft, and emerges into the light to bring not peace but vengeance. At first he tries passively to resist the police persecution, but when the town refuses to leave him in peace, he returns to burn it down. He captures the sheriff who led the hunt (a veteran of Korea) and prepares to kill him; again he has proven his ability at combat, but again he is in a battle that cannot be won. The sheriff is at his mercy, but they are both trapped in the police station, surrounded by National Guard warriors. If he takes his revenge and kills his tormentor, the guardsmen will overwhelm him through strength of numbers and he will die. He beat them all, but in the end he stands alone and must yield; he leaves the building wrapped in the arms of his former colonel. Although he will re-emerge from prison four years later, for the present he remains a victim.

Filmmakers found PTSS to be a useful explanation for alienation or personal failure in their film characters. In *Eyewitness*(1981), William Hurt played a well-educated, heroic veteran who is now content to work as a janitor. Liam Neeson's deaf-mute homeless man in 1987's *Suspect* was a decorated veteran. In *Graveyard Shift* (1990) the crazy exterminator killed by a giant rat is a veteran. Typically a stress-induced flashback to a Vietnam firefight or atrocity signaled PTSS in a film. The spark that sets off Rambo's course of destruction is a flashback to Viet Cong torture that overwhelms him when the police beat him. Don Johnson nearly shoots his family while hallucinating that he's back in the jungle in *Cease Fire* (1985), and Clint Eastwood nearly crashes a stolen Russian fighter plane when a flashback overtakes him in flight during *Firefox* (1982).

A useful corollary to PTSS was survivor's guilt. Many veterans have found difficulty in accepting that they were lucky, smart, cowardly, or quick enough to escape from Viet Nam alive while equally deserving soldiers returned in coffins or wheelchairs. An extreme case was Ron Kovic, who did return in a wheelchair, but blamed himself anyway; in particular he blamed himself for the death of another grunt during a firefight. In his mind he rationalizes his paralysis as punishment for his crime, and it is only when he can see both himself and the dead soldier as victims that he can be a productive member of society again.

Jacknife (1989, based on Stephen Metcalf's play *Strange Snow*) simplified the psychology of survivor's guilt by reversing Kovic's situation. Veterans Megs and David owe their survival to Bobby, who died rescuing them in a firefight. The film treats the

War's effects as an incurable disease; like alcoholism, it is a weakness from which the ex-soldier never fully recovers. Veterans attend a support group that operates like a Alcoholics Anonymous meeting, with each veteran testifying to Vietnam's hold on his life. When Megs races from a meeting to help David, the group leader warns, "Don't let him drag you back down," as though Vietnam were a disease he could catch again or a fatal allergy to which Megs should be wary of exposing himself.

David Flanagan (Ed Harris) does not attend groups like this because he still lives in denial. He believes he has put the War behind him although he lives a sterile, empty life at home with his maiden sister. In High School he was a star athlete, but after receiving a knee wound in Viet Nam he cannot even join a pick-up basketball game. He drives a truck for a living, drinks heavily, and occasionally offers to do chores for a neighbor couple that lost a son in the War. In contrast, Megs (Robert De Niro) energetically embraces life and loves to talk about his tour of duty. He intrudes madly into David's life and forces him to face the truth about the War and Bobby's heroic death. Megs' embrace of life—which soon includes David's sister Martha (Kathy Baker)—forces David to confront both his own sterile existence and his guilt about the War. At the film's climax he can retell the story of his own failure to his sister, to Megs, to himself, and to the veterans support group.

The sister is a conduit between Megs and David. She has been caring for her brother since his return, and by attaching himself to her, Megs eventually manages to replace her as David's support when the crisis breaks. "How can she understand? She wasn't there," Megs reassures David during the latter's confession; as he cradles his buddy's head in his hands, Martha watches helplessly from a doorway across the room. After David's breakthrough they leave her: Megs leaves town, his work finished with David firmly on the road to recovery, and David turns not to her but to the men at the veterans support group.

At the last moment, however, the film has a change of heart. While Megs drives away, David tells the support group about Bobby.

Bobby said that certain girls glowed. When they touched you, you weren't scared or tired. When they'd just sit next to you, you weren't confused. Bobby said someday we'd all find girls like that and then finally things would make sense, just because you were with them. Bobby said that would happen to us because we—we all of us—we deserved it.

As David speaks, Megs suddenly turns the car around and returns to Martha, who welcomes him back with open, glowing arms. Megs is rescued from the feminine role of nurturer to other veterans; as a reward for services rendered (to his country? to David? to Bobby?) he receives the masculine role of lover.

If the role of woman in combat films is often that of salvific light—the hope of the combat soldier and the source of nurturing for the wounded—in *Jacknife* she becomes an award for services rendered. "We will get her because we deserve her" is Bobby's message to his friends, and Megs gets what he deserves (despite having dumped her the night before). The shift marks a movement away from dependence on women and the feminine that marked films like *Heroes* and *Coming Home* in the seventies, toward a more independent masculine stance. The men no longer need the women. Women are a useful commodity, but the brotherhoods of soldiers and veterans offers the primary source of nurturing and companionship. The roles have reversed so far that it is again the women who need the men. The best of the men went to war and either never returned or came back feminized by the experience, and the result has been a dearth of men. Since Megs has regained his own masculinity, he can demand a woman and deserve to be obeyed. Without Megs, Martha would likely remain a lonely spinster, her life as empty as her feminized brother's.

The films of the seventies offered two methods for overcoming the War's debilitating effects. The veteran's potential for violence could either be eliminated through some form of physical disability or diverted into a nonviolent form of emotion. Luke, the most successfully reintegrated veteran of the seventies, succeeded through both methods as his paraplegia eliminated his potential for violence and his relationship with Sally Hyde offered a nonviolent release for his anger and guilt. Major Charles Raine, on the other hand, was an emotional cripple who could only find release for his feelings through physical violence. Both men received offers of salvation from women, but Luke accepted it while Raine declined; consequently, Luke reentered society and Raine left it.

Susan Jeffords describes the re-integrated veteran of these films as "feminized"; Auster and Quart describe him as "wounded." Both descriptions imply a denigration of the character-type. Their suggestions of passivity and weakness echo Reagan's rhetoric about the Vietnam Syndrome and America's need to stand proudly again. The cure became the disease as America perceived the effect of the War as being to feminize American might. The vet again became a symbol, this time of the War's castrating effect on America. And again, the movies sought a cure through the veteran. A process of re-masculinization took place for the veteran during the 1980s as the wounded veterans of the seventies returned to their positions of responsibility as patriarchs and defenders of the home.

This meant that the wounded vet continued to be a staple character in family dramas. In *Cease Fire* PTSS overwhelms a father when he losses his job and can no longer care for his family. In *Distant Thunder* (1988) John Lithgow has abandoned his family and lives with other unstable veterans in the Oregon mountains. These vets are treated with sympathy but also with the firm understanding that their weakness is hurting the people who depend on them. These vets must finish with their self-pity and memories so that they can reassume their responsibilities at home. Both these veterans manage to confront the harm their self-pity or weakness has done to their families reassume their roles as husbands or fathers.

A community of wounded vets is at the heart of *In Country* (1989), the story of a teenage girl, Sam (Emily Lloyd), who was born after her father died in Viet Nam. She now lives with her Uncle Emmett (Bruce Willis), an unemployed veteran who spends his days watching television or hanging out with other vets at the local Dairy Queen. *In Country* provides an possible sequel to *Gardens of Stone*; eighteen years later, the soldier's grieving widow, who barely had time to know he husband before he left for war, has practically forgotten him; she has moved on to a new

husband and a new home. Her daughter, however, cannot do the
same. She never knew her father or the War, and so for her they
cannot be memories—they are already history and part of her pat-
rimony. Yet it is an inheritance she can not claim; the adult members of the town of Hopewell—her mother, Emmett, the veterans
in the town, her father's family—refuse to talk to her about the
War. They argue that she had to live through the war years to understand what happened, or they insist that the past is gone and
she should not try to reclaim it.

Like the veterans in *Cease Fire* and *Distant Thunder*, the
War has led Uncle Emmett and his friends to opt-out of their social roles. Emmett, jobless and aimless, resists even Sam's efforts
to force him to see a doctor about possible Agent Orange contamination. Sam begins an affair with one member of the group
that slows to a halt when he reveals that the War left him impotent. The other members of the group cling to their memories of
the War as the matrix for their community. Their ties to the people of the town—including their families and friends—are subor-
dinate to their ties to the veteran community. As one local says,
"Those guys are still back in Vietnam. Ain't none of them come
to nothing." He says it without rancor, however. He and the rest
of the town of Hopewell treat their veterans with bemused
tolerance.

It is Sam's insistent quest for her own past that leads
Emmett, at least, to break his silence and offer some sense of the
War to the next generation. She forces the issue when she finds
her father's diary and letters home. Her mother abandoned these
papers when she remarried, and Sam finds them accidentally.
These documents are an independent, primary source about the
War and as such they provide her with a direct link to the past.
Her father's voice narrates the diary as the film flashes back to
Vietnamese swamps.

> July 12. Face to face with a V.C. I won. Clean head shot.
> Back of his head gone. Picture of his babies in a pocket. Eas-
> ier than I thought.

The experience is too direct and sudden for her, and she tries to
deny the diary, her father and the War. "The way he talked about
the gooks and that killing. I hated it. I don't like him anymore,"

she tells her uncle. It is the capricious response of a child, and Emmett tells her so. "Who are you to say that about him?" he demands. She was not there. She does not know what they experienced in the Nam. She can not judge them. Then he immediately tries to explain what she cannot understand, speaking both to her and to himself.

> They're all still alive, you know that? They're all sittin' around a village that's all burned out having ham'n'mutherfuckers waiting for the huey to come and evacuate us. They got a dead VC propped up in a hootch with a cowboy hat on and a cigarette stuck in his mouth. They're all wondering where is old Emmett. How's he doing back in Hopewell. And they're wondering why I ain't out there with them. They're just waiting for me.... Like there's this hole in my heart. Just there's something missing and I can't get it back. Out there with them. I'm already half dead.

The film culminates in a pilgrimage by Emmett, Sam, and Sam's grandmother Mamaw to the Vietnam Veterans Memorial. All three touch the name of the one man who links them together: Daryl Hughes—friend, father, and son. The overweight, aging mother climbs a ladder to touch her son's name; the daughter kisses the name and leaves her graduation photo at the foot of the wall; the war buddy squeezes a medal into a crack by the name. The Wall allows them to honor their shared past, but it also helps them to move on to the future. They walk away from the wall not reminiscing about the dead but contemplating lunch.

Few movies treat the wounded vet as other than a family issue. Usually the lost veteran is a father who abandons—figuratively or literally—his family, but sometimes he has dropped out of society altogether. In *Americana* (1983), David Carradine's army captain wanders across the midwest like a hobo until he finds an abandoned carousel in a small, dirty town. Only his quiet seriousness hints that he is not an ordinary tramp but a man of rare ability. This is not another Rambo, however. When he pauses for a few weeks in the town to repair the carousel, he meets cruelty and bigotry but never betrays his anger. He simply continues to work on the carousel amidst the abuse he suffers. When he is finished, he quietly walks on down the road while the townspeople who had opposed his efforts ride the merry-go-round.

The director in Richard Rush's movie about a war film, *The Stunt Man* (1980), blackmails another wandering veteran (Steve Railsback) into working as a stunt-double for the star of an anti-war movie, and then uses him both for stunts and for inspiration. Again the vet acts as a catalyst that allows a society to achieve a form of cohesion. Along the same vein is *The Ninth Configuration* (1980), in which a veteran takes command of a military asylum for mentally disturbed Vietnam veterans. Eventually the commander's actual status as the asylum's chief inmate is revealed. The army had given him command of the hospital in the hope that serving others would heal his own Vietnam trauma.

The veteran's wounds are not always mental, although that is the more popular form of injury in Hollywood. In *Modern Problems* the veteran is in a wheelchair and works as an air traffic controller; it is a job for which he must be very well adjusted, and indeed he is. He provides a counterpoint to the main character (Chevy Chase) who, although physically whole, is far less able to cope with his life. Cutter (John Heard), the title character in *Cutter's Way* (1981), is far from adjusted to postwar life. The loss of a leg and an eye in Viet Nam left him deeply embittered. He is a self-destructive Ahab searching for a great white symbol on which to pin the guilt for his misery. He finds that symbol when a friend witnesses a local industrialist disposing of a woman's body in a trash can. The industrialist's arrogance and power convince Cutter that he has found at least one of the power-brokers responsible wrecking his body.

A television movie, *My Father, My Son* (1988) picks up on another curse of the veterans, fear of Agent Orange contamination. The military made wide-ranging use of this chemical defoliant in Viet Nam with little regard to its cancerous side-effects on the civilian population or the American soldiers. The movie tells the story of Admiral Elmo Zumwalt, who ordered the use of Agent Orange, and his son, Elmo Zumwalt III, who swam through a river coated with it to attack the Viet Cong and later died of cancer. A more metaphorical examination of this toxic chemical's use was *Jacob's Ladder* (1990), in which a veteran discovers the military used his squad to experiment with a new nerve gas during the War. Supposed to make them more aggressive fighters, the gas turned the men against each other and the squad destroyed itself. Twenty years later, either the effect of the gas seems to be reasserting itself or the survivor's are discovering that they did not, after all, live through the experience.

These portrayals of wounded veterans were strongly counterbalanced by the developing image of the superman vet, a masculine figure that first returned home as a vigilante. His roots go back to Billy Jack's defense of the Friendship School and *Taxi Driver*'s Travis Bickle. This figure is closely related to the psycho-vet, but he has learned to control his violence or at least to channel it against generally acceptable enemies of the people. The popular appeal of the character—a man who could combine the skills he learned in Vietnam with his aptitude for heroic action—is apparent in the number of television series based on him that appeared in the early eighties: *Magnum, P.I.* (1980), *The A-Team* (1982), *Riptide,* and *Air Wolf* (1983).

He does not always operate from outside the law, however. *Blue Thunder* (1983), *Above the Law* (1988), *Lethal Weapon* (1987), and *The Year of the Dragon* (1985) all have veterans who now work for the police, and in *Firefox* (1982) the veteran is an Air Force pilot. But his methods always take him beyond the limits proscribed by law. Corruption within the government or the police force frequently provides an excuse for the veteran to take violent, personal action. His right to do so originates in his integrity (proven by his service) and his ability to shoot straighter than the official forces—in a memorable scene in *Blue Thunder*, when the corrupt government officials send two jet fighters after the maverick Vietnam veteran, the jets accidentally bomb a skyscraper!

The A-Team television series that began in 1982 provided a popular format for the character. In the series pilot, a group of veterans are unjustly accused of robbing the Bank of Hanoi and become the object of an obsessive, but futile, search by the United States Army. They wander about the country as outlaws, helping oppressed Americans by fighting injustice with plastic explosive and automatic weapons fire (neither of which ever kills). *The*

Annihilators (1985) provides a less-benign version of this squad, with a band of veterans hired to protect a neighborhood from youth gangs, while the Army finally takes the hint in *American Commandos* (1984) and enlists a gang of veterans to destroy the opium trade in Southeast Asia.

Frequently the vigilante vet would be self-employed. *The Exterminator* (1980) went to work clearing the streets after a friend was murdered, and he returned to the task when more acquaintances die in *The Exterminator II* (1981). Similarly the hero of *Eye of the Tiger* enters crime prevention after a biker gang kills his wife, and *The GI Executioner* works at bar in Singapore until he catches his big chance to kill bad guys. *Soldier's Revenge* altered the formula slightly when its veteran, a deserter, is saved from an angry hometown mob by the chance to thwart a South American revolution.

The action of the vigilante movie does not have to occur in the United States or even after the War. Two cop-as-vigilante movies take place in Saigon during the War: *Off Limits* (1988) and *Saigon Commandos* (1987). Both detail the adventures of military police who find themselves fighting their own people or their supposed allies. In the latter movie, an MP wages a personal war against the Vietnamese heroin cartel. His commanding officer, upon finally tracking him down, allows him to murder the leader of the cartel before arresting him. In *Off Limits*, two officers from the Criminal Investigations Detachment (CID) in Saigon (Willem Dafoe and Gregory Hines) suspect the Vietnamese of corruption but find it in the American military command. Their own commanding officer has been murdering Vietnamese whores who have born Amerasian children.

The vigilante role offers the veteran the opportunity to complete a job many saw as unfinished. The veteran could finally serve the American people against a recognizable enemy. In fact, in several of these movies that enemy is the Indo-Chinese and the drug trade. Mickey Rourke's Detective White battles the China Town opium trade in *The Year of the Dragon*. In *Steele Justice* (1987) the vigilante veteran traces the murder of a Vietnamese friend back to a former Vietnamese general who is now a drug lord in America. The hero of *Vietnam, Texas* is now a priest, but

he reverts to his military training to protect his illegitimate Vietnamese son from the Vietnamese mafia in Texas. *Search and Destroy* turned the tables as the former Vietnamese official searches
and destroys veterans.

Alamo Bay (1985), Louis Malle's movie about shrimp-
fishing wars on the Texas coast, studies the paradox of American
soldier's proving their worth by fighting against the South Vietnamese, America's former allies. In an actual incident that provided the basis of the story, Vietnamese refugees joined the
fishing fleet and sparked Ku Klux Klan violence by cutting into
the white fishermen's take. In Malle's movie, the Vietnamese are
inheritors of the American dream and work ethic. They work
longer hours and for less pay than the white fishermen, and in return receive not their expected slice of American pie but enmity
and violence from the whites who must now work harder for less
pay themselves. The white fishermen are poor already and feel the
government has mistreated them. Now they face further economic
hardship at the hands of a people they once fought to protect.

The racial issues raised by the War were a popular film subject during the war years, but in the eighties it received scant attention in cinema. For many blacks and other minority soldiers,
however, the problem of having fought in what many saw as a
racist war plagued their consciences, even if they had had little
choice but to go to Vietnam. The fact that they came home to a
racist and ungrateful nation aggravated their feelings. A few film
have touched on the issue from this angle, including *Some Kind of
Hero* (1982), in which a black veteran (Richard Pryor) receives
only abuse and apathy from the institutions he turns to. Although
he was a POW, he made a statement in support of Hanoi and the
army condemns him as a collaborator. Cut off from all benefits
and unable to find employment, he finally becomes successful at
crime. Likewise *Ashes and Embers* (1982) had a black vet returning to the States but finding nothing there that he could label
home. The latter movie especially brings the War into a historical
continuum. It does not attempt to resolve the issues signified by
"Vietnam" through one man's reintegration. The fact that the protagonist in *Ashes and Embers* is black, and that he wanders
through black society, means that he must face more than what he

did to the Vietnamese and what the War did to his fellow soldiers; he must also face that what he did there, he did in support of a society that will not accept his people as equal members. He, the victim of American racism, fought for America in a racist war. Haskell Wexler's plays the same theme in *Latino* (1985), having a Latin-American Vietnam veteran train Contras in Honduras for the United States Army.

Behind both the wounded and superman veterans lies the theme of reconciliation and recovery. Films like *Alamo Bay* and *In Country* shifted the emphasis from the veteran to the American society and treated Vietnam not as a syndrome but as a part of America's history and culture—to be accepted and understood rather than denied as a foreign disease. Emphasizing the veteran—either as victim or redeemed patriarch—emphasizes the need to heal the rifts caused by the War. These stories climax with the father or husband returning to his social role or responsibilities and putting his Vietnam-inspired guilt or fears behind him. The films suggest that the divisions and conflicts aroused by the War have healed with time, and that to dwell on them is to be self-pitying. In the early eighties, while the Vietnam Veterans Memorial was still only an inconvenient bit of construction by the Lincoln Memorial and the Unknown Soldier of Vietnam just unidentified human remains, coming home movies could still show veterans returning and finding no place they might call home.

The Memorial, the Unknown Soldier, and the parades of the mid-eighties, on the other hand, used the soldier as a symbol for the War and its issues, and by claiming to welcome them home, tried to conclude the episode of the Vietnam War. This was also the theme of the bulk of films about veterans released during the Reagan era. The Vietnam Syndrome, like Post-Traumatic Stress Syndrome, had to be (and could be) overcome. Americans must heal the breach. Thus the television movie about the construction of the Memorial is titled *To Heal a Nation* (1988).

Veterans Betrayed

Although the America public has grown increasingly unsure of the War's details (such as whom America fought, who won, who were the allies, and why we fought there), they generally accept that something went wrong during the war years. It was not the success America usually expects its wars to be, and so the search has continued for a culprit, someone on whom to pin the blame. A cursory glance at the titles in the Vietnam War section of the library show that this is neither a recent nor a one-sided effort: *The Ugly American* (1958), *The Bitter Heritage* (1966), *Winners and Losers* (1976), *The Irony of Vietnam: The System Worked* (1979), *The March of Folly* (1984), *No More Vietnams* (1985), *Lost Victory* (1989), *A Great Shining Lie* (1989), or *Kiss the Boys Goodby: How America Betrayed Its Own POWs in Vietnam* (1990). These books balance between trying to establish who the real victims are and denying responsibility for the failures. Nixon's book *No More Vietnams* goes so far as to warn America how to avoid making the same mistake twice, while at the same time casually claiming credit to Nixon for getting us out the first time.

By the eighties, the soldier and veteran had been established in the minds of many Americans as the War's chief, or certainly most visible, victim. Hollywood, as is its wont, followed suit and made the soldier and veteran the victim in films. The one-shot ending that sacrificed young Nick in *The Deer Hunter* echoed through the eighties in films like *Full Metal Jacket, The Siege of Firebase Gloria, Platoon, Casualties of War,* and even *JFK*. The central image of *The Deer Hunter* is the "one shot"; it recurs in the hunting scenes, the POW sequence, and especially in the Russian roulette sequences. By the end, when Nick turns the gun barrel against his own temple, it has become one more of the ritual actions that obsess Cimino throughout the movie. Nick's death is a sacrifice, and although Mike does not pull the trigger, it is his mania for the masculine control of the one shot that Nick evokes before firing.

The Siege of Firebase Gloria ends with a similar sacrifice. DiNardo (Wings Hauser), "one of those gung-ho soldiers the marines are famous for," dies at the hand of his friend and mentor, Sergeant Hafner (Lee Ermey). Hafner shoots his friend to fulfill a pact the two made years before, that one would never leave the other paralyzed. So he reminds his friend of a recent experience in a whore house, caresses him lightly, then fires the bullet. *Platoon's* narrative revolves around two sacrificial murders. First the brutal Barnes kills the peaceable Elias in the forest, and later Chris shoots the helpless Barnes after the fire-bombing. In *Born on the Fourth of July*, Ron Kovic's confession to the parents of an American boy he accidentally shot signals his recovery from the War's trauma.

The list goes on, and while it may seem banal to insist on the soldier's death as the highlight of a war film, it is not always so. Combat films from other wars highlight the sacrifice of American soldiers but do not mark them out as victims; rather, their deaths tend to make them heroic. When John Wayne died on *The Sands of Iwo Jima*, it was clear that his death would help pave the way for victory against the Imperialist Japanese. The frequently ritualistic murders in Vietnam War films—most of them by "friendly fire"— identify the soldier as victim; heroism and noble causes are seldom an issue.

Consider some of the other films that have an orchestrated act of violence or a one-shot killing as their central image. Brian DePalma's signature scene in *Casualties of War* is a dance of death for a young Vietnamese girl, mowed down by four American grunts with automatic weapons. So too in the climax of *Full Metal Jacket*'s first section, a draftee shoots his drill instructor (DI) and then himself, and in the second section the anti-hero Joker (Matthew Modine) fires a single bullet into a the body of a female Vietnamese sniper. Willard in *Apocalypse Now* coldly but cleanly shoots a wounded Vietnamese girl while on his way up-river, but at Kurtz's compound the final murder, though ritualized by Coppola, is committed clumsily with a machete. None of these killings suggest any heroism on the part of either victim or killer. All are cold, brutal acts of violence that identify a victim—in these cases the Vietnamese as well as the soldiers.

Even those films that attempt the old-style, heroic action, war film minimize the heroism and accentuate the lack of honor the soldiers receive. The boys who fight to conquer *Hamburger Hill* die for a useless objective and the people back home insult them. In *BAT-21* Colonel Hambleton's heroic, true-life struggle to escape from enemy territory is demeaned by his frightened, self-defensive killing of a peasant farmer in front of the farmer's family. These films repeatedly identify victims rather than heroes. There are exceptions, of course. The squad in *Platoon Leader* defends a Vietnamese village and the Viet Cong soldier Ho in *The Iron Triangle* (Liam Whatley) dies heroically defending his commander's retreat. But such films were rare and seldom appeared for long in theaters before being consigned to videotape.

Hollywood's most literal attempt to assign guilt for the War has to be Oliver Stone's *JFK*. In a tour-de-force of montage and pacing, Stone attempts to persuade the audience that the military/industrial complex, in collusion with the CIA and Lyndon Johnson, assassinated John Kennedy to prolong the War in Southeast Asia. According to a mysterious informant from military intelligence identified only as X (Donald Sutherland), Kennedy planned to end the cold war and remove all American military personnel from Viet Nam by 1965. He had already signed National Security Action Memo 263, ordering the first thousand troops home by Christmas 1963. The generals who wanted their war, the industrialists who wanted their war profits (Vietnam saved Bell Helicopter from bankruptcy, X explains), the CIA who wanted to be needed, and Lyndon Johnson who wanted to be president conspired, therefore, to kill Kennedy.

Stone recreates Lyndon Johnson's first meeting with the military and industrial leaders after being sworn in as president. X narrates the scene.

X: [voice-over] Tuesday 20th of November, the day
                after they buried Kennedy.
LBJ: Gentlemen, I want you to know I'm not going to
                let Vietnam go like China did. I'm personally
                committed. I'm not going to take one soldier out
                of there till they know we mean business in Asia.
X: [voice-over] Lyndon Johnson signs National
                Security Memo 273 which essentially reverses
                Kennedy's new withdrawal policy and gives a
                green light to covert action against North Viet-
                nam which provoked the Gulf of Tonkin Incident.
LBJ: Just get me elected. I'll give you your damn war.
X: In that document lay the Vietnam War.
Garrison: I can't believe they killed him because he wanted
                to change things.

There are problems with this argument. It is not clear to many historians that Kennedy was soft on Communism or that he planned to withdraw from Viet Nam. He was, in fact, responsible for one of America's first military build-ups in Indochina, and he colluded (to a degree) in the assassination (twenty days before his own) of Vietnamese president Diem. Arguably Kennedy needed Vietnam and the cold war to rebuild his image after the Bay of Pigs fiasco. In any event he could hardly have threatened the military/industrial complex to any great extent; he lacked the po-litical support after his narrow election victory. Stone himself al-lows X to admit that Kennedy's National Security Action orders were never implemented due to "bureaucratic resistance." LBJ's motivation is also doubtful. The cornerstone of his administration was to be the domestic Great Society, not a foreign war. He esca-lated the Vietnam War to terrible heights, but it destroyed both his presidency and his Great Society.

It is useful to look at Stone's conspiracy theory in the light of his earlier work, especially *Platoon*. The young soldier there must choose between two father-figures: the brutal, cruel Sgt. Barnes or the gentle, noble Elias. The hero suggests at the end that we were in Vietnam because of this paternity conflict within our-selves and within America. *Wall Street* was another Stone story with a young man torn between two fathers, one noble and the other decadent. Likewise *Born on the Fourth of July*'s Ron Kovic struggles within himself between the aggression that sent him to Viet Nam and the self-respect that allows him to fight against the War. This time Stone replaces the dark father-figure with Kovic's ambitious mother, while the good father's patience and strength imbue his commonplace life as a grocery clerk with a nobility that his son cannot understand. JFK and LBJ are simply the latest incarnations of this duality for Stone. He has linked his obsession with good and evil to the characters who have been iconized in America as the hero and villain of the sixties.

Of course, LBJ had to contest with Nixon for chief villain, but Nixon comes at the end of the Vietnam tale, and he makes his defense in Robert Altman's *Secret Honor* (1984). According to the screenplay by Donald Freed and Arnold Stone, the secret structures of power that run DC had Richard Nixon in their control. The Committee of 100 was forcing him to extend the War, just as the military/industrial complex forced Kennedy and Johnson. To escape their power and save the nation, Nixon sacrificed himself on the sword of Watergate, a scandal he arranged specifically to force himself out of office.

There is an obsessive quality about this search for guilt, a need for justice that is nicely illustrated in *Cutter's Way*. Alex Cutter (John Heard) is a cynical, furiously angry veteran who lost an eye and a leg in the War. His best friend is the handsome Richard Bone (Jeff Bridges), a yacht salesman and gigolo who avoided going to the War and is constantly chided for this by Cutter who calls him a girl and an Ishmael. Cutter himself would be an Ahab, except that he cannot name the whale that took his leg. Bone solves that problem when he witnesses a murderer dispose of a body. Cutter seizes on the murder as a clue to his own fate. He uses the draft evader's guilt to force him to identify the killer and to bring him to justice. "On point. Only place to be," he insists. "Purple Heart land. That's where I was."

The pursuit leads them to J.J. Cord, a wealthy industrialist whose businesses profited from the War. Here at last Cutter has a place to lay the blame, although they never establish any proof that Cord killed the woman. Like Johnson for Oliver Stone or the White Whale for Ahab, Cord fits the description Cutter is looking for. In the pursuit, Cutter loses the little that he had, including

wife, home, friends, and finally his life. Security officers shoot
him down in a final attack on the majestic, white-suited Cord
while Bone watches helplessly. It is only the veteran's death that
convinces this Ishmael. "It was you," he finally realizes. "What if
it was," Cord arrogantly replies before he replaces his dark
glasses and Bone shoots him.

The need to assign guilt for the War is a driving force behind
many of the war films. It is what Rambo's adventures lead to. It
is what the soldiers discuss in the bush. It is what the veterans
worry about after their return. The films attempt to set the record
straight: to bring those responsible to public account and to praise
those who suffered. Justice is therefore the driving force behind
many of the Vietnam films. When Chris shoots Barnes in *Platoon*'s climax, the audience feels less pity for the helpless victim
than jubilation at his death. Chris has meted out justice on a
small, physical scale, and the audience recognizes this. The event
is a recognition of the justice of Chris' actions. He has identified a
legitimate victim and sacrificed him to a morality that the film and
the audience recognize as absolute. In sharp contrast, when Barnes kills Elias, he is condemned by the audience and by Chris for
having committed a gross injustice. Barnes' actions conform to a
morality with which America does not sympathize. In recognizing
Chris' right to murder Barnes (even while criticizing him for
adopting Barnes' methods), America recognizes that Barnes and
the moral code he represents are guilty for what happened in the
Vietnam of *Platoon.* "We were fighting ourselves," Chris needlessly notes at the end.

Platoon was a morality tale, a sometimes too simplistic story
of good versus evil. Stone's next Vietnam War film, *Born on the
Fourth of July,* would be far more realistic, far grimmer, and far
more condemnatory of America's complicity in the Vietnam
nightmare. The film seeks explanations and justice for two
wrongs: Ron Kovic's paraplegia and Ron Kovic's killing of a fellow American soldier. The two are linked because, for much of
the film, Kovic seems to believe that his crippling wounds are di-
vine justice for his accidentally shooting a young soldier in his
squad. Kovic's punishment makes him physically and emotionally
unfit to fill the masculine ideal in which he believes. The supreme

irony of this lies in the fact that he went to Viet Nam attempting to fulfill that ideal. The film's opening scenes establish prewar America as an idyllic land of parades, home runs at baseball games, parental adoration ("Ain't he a little firecracker in that hat"; "Yeah, he's my yankee doodle dandy"), Kennedy's rhetoric, and young, innocent love. As the young Kovic plays at war near his home, the older Kovic remembers, "We turned the woods into a battlefield, and dreamed that someday, we would become men." His struggles for manhood lead him to sports and to war, but also away from the girl he loves, who watches him wrestle and hit home runs from the arms of other boys.

The film insists on war as a natural consequence of American life and culture, a culture that depends on the sort of self-delusions that Cimino showed in *The Deer Hunter*. Like Mike Vronsky in that film, Ron Kovic is a chaste knight who longs for the woman he cannot have. But Kovic, a real person, lacks the semi-mythical Mike's strength and control, so he fails in the feats of strength he insists on attempting. As a young athlete he fails to win the conference championship; the camera looms down on him from above as he lies sobbing on the mat while the home crowd boos his conqueror. As a young soldier, he fails to win glory or honor; instead he accidentally kills women, children, and a fellow soldier.

Kovic's vision of the world is romantic, articulated best in Kennedy's stirring rhetoric and personified in John Wayne. In Viet Nam, however, Kovic must struggle with an experiential reality that contradicts the assumptions behind Kennedy's vision. As in the other struggles of his life, he fails at this one and the cost is his physical manhood. To a friend back in the States, he describes how he was wounded, how he did "the John Wayne thing," still fighting even though wounded in the foot, until a bullet caused the more serious wound in his spine. Afterward, Kovic continues to struggle with his old faith. He participates in the Fourth of July parade as he had watched other veterans do in his youth, but his address to the crowds is interrupted when a crying baby causes an aural flashback to the crying of the Vietnamese baby his squad had killed. Later he travels to a Mexican resort that features brothels that cater to disabled veterans. There he finally finds a woman to love him, only to return the next day and find her serving another customer.

His companion in Mexico is played by Willem Dafoe, no longer the conscience-stricken warrior of *Platoon* but a bitter, wheelchair-bound cynic. When the two of them find themselves deserted on the side of a Mexican country road accusing one another of *not* having killed babies, Kovic finally begins to see the light. He has exchanged his dream of masculine prowess and virility for the sham provided by whores who laugh behind his back "because he can't move his dick." He is being tricked into the same machismo that sent him to Viet Nam.

His redemption begins when he visits the family of the man whom he had killed. Kovic is a Catholic, and his visit has overtones of the confessional as he tells the family, who are unaware of the circumstances of their boy's death, that he, Kovic, killed him by accident. But this home is not a confessional; the dead boy was an only son, a husband, and a father. The camera shows the face of the dead boy's mother gradually collapse as she hears that her son died at the hands of an American. The family cannot forgive Kovic for what he has done, though they sympathize with his pain.

By finally confessing what he did in the Viet Nam, Kovic also discovers the truth that he was as much a victim as the boy he shot. A lie sent both of them to Viet Nam. The war he experienced ended only in death (of both Vietnamese and Americans) and pain, not the honor offered by the army recruiters, John Wayne or the American masculine ideal, the ideal that seduced Ron Kovic away from his young love, Donna, and into Viet Nam. Stone and Kovic denounce this ideal as a principal contributor to warfare. In Kovic's book, he describes the start of his antiwar activism, a speech he made at a high school, and compares it to the marine recruiters' visit to his high school.

> What if I had seen someone like me that day, a guy in a wheelchair, just sitting there in front of the senior class not saying a word? Maybe things would have been different. Maybe that's all it would have taken.... I am glad he has brought me here and that all of them are looking at us, seeing

the war firsthand—the dead while still living, the living reminders, two young men who had the shit shot out of them.

If *Platoon* showed men having the moral "shit shot out of
them," Kovic's story shows men having the physical shit shot out
of them. Stone emphasizes the scenes of carnage and degrading
treatment that follow combat as though he were putting two para-
plegics before a high school class. That these scenes disgusted
audiences is evident in some of the reviews the film received. A
critic in *The Spectator* raves, "not since Jane Fonda went to Hanoi, put on a pith helmet and posed next to a downed American
fighter plane have the Yankee-haters had such an opportunity to
rejoice. Stone's anti-American propaganda makes poor old Dr.
Goebbels sound like Hamlet" (Taki).

The film is not anti-American, however, nor ultimately
opposed to the aggressive masculine ideal. The hospital scenes
condemn the treatment veterans received after the War, and they
cut into the military idealism that makes Kovic a castrate and a
cripple, but they are not anti-American because they appear in a
pro-American context. At the 1968 Republican National Convention in Miami, Kovic, again in uniform but now an antiwar activist, leads a sortie into the convention hall to shout down Nixon.
The FBI forcibly expel them from the hall and nearly arrest Kovic
in the ensuing scuffle. He escapes, however, and leads the activists on a second assault: "We're gonna' take the hall back. We're
gonna' go to the gate and take the fucking hall back! Move out."
The camera soars up and away to display the battlefield that the
street has become as the sound of helicopters mingles with the
shouting.

When the film cuts to the Democratic National Convention
four years later, Kovic has become a war-hero and a politician.
Fans, guards, and assistants surround him; a woman asks him to
sign his war-memoir; reporters push and shove to hear him as he
disappears into the great white light of the applauding convention
hall. Possibly another Donna waits for him, seduced more easily
by politically correct military action than by any of his other se-
ductions. "Just lately I've felt like I'm home. Maybe we're home,"
he tells the reporters. With the moral victory over the evil Repub-
licans at one convention and the soldier's triumph at another, the

audience has witnessed justice being reaffirmed and the guilty party made visible by its victim.

That Kovic remains implicated in the events of the War, a victim of his own delusions, provides a far more complex examination of the forces that led to the Vietnam War than many films managed. It was rare for any film to make the soldier responsible for the result of the War. When DePalma tried to bring the soldier to justice in *Casualties of War*, he was roundly criticized, especially by the increasingly powerful veterans groups in the United States. The soldier was, at least on the immediate level, responsible for the violence; however his violence was directed primarily against the Vietnamese enemy and the justice of this violence is assumed. In *Platoon* it is almost irrelevant, just part of the day-to-day life in the Nam. To describe it as a persecution might be comparable to calling Chris' beating of the ants from about his neck a persecution. The films seldom need to justify their attacks on the designated enemy. Thus the absolute righteousness of the squad that drops a handful of grenades on an unsuspecting Viet Cong squad (in *Platoon Leader*) obscures the brutality of their justice; after all this Viet Cong squad, or one very much like it, had just murdered a woman whom the American squad knew.

The true victims in these films are the soldier and the Vietnamese peasant, both of whom appear to be at the mercy of forces over which they have no control. The peasants are victims of the armies that march across their lands, especially the Vietnamese army that brutalizes them almost casually (when the Americans victimize civilians, it is because the Vietnamese army has used the civilians as hostages or camouflage). The soldiers are most noticeably victims of the enemy, a natural enough scenario in a war film. However, in Vietnam films the soldiers are also victims of the social forces that rebelled against the War in America and of the military/government establishment that used them as pawns in its game of *realpolitik*. The films recognize both of these forces as persecutors of the soldier. America's defeat at the hands of an insignificant Asian people and the atrocities committed by American soldier are the two inexplicables of the Vietnam War. During the war years, they were linked as clues to a mystery that led to the soldier-as-suspect. Later, the re-estimation of the Vietnam soldier gave him a voice to explain his actions and allowed him to transfer the blame. The obvious choices for that blame were the antiwar factions at home—including the "college-types" and journalists—for withholding the moral support the men needed, and the military/government forces for refusing to make sufficient use of the sacrifices the men made. *JFK* and *Rambo* ("Do we get to win this time?") exemplify the latter. Since the American soldier in Viet Nam was the equal of the American soldier in every other war, the argument goes, it could not be his fault that America failed so miserably in Viet Nam. Notably the problem has been simplified to merely losing the War, instead of the complex of moral questions that had once been at issue.

The other culprit was the antiwar movement. As Americans increasingly perceived the soldier as the War's primary victim, films portrayed protests against the War as protests against the soldier and a part of his victimization. Thus letters and tales from home demoralize the boys in *Hamburger Hill* more than the desperation of their plight. One young grunt eagerly plays a tape his girlfriend sent from home, only to hear her repeat the lies and half-truths her fellow college students have been telling her. She is more than half-convinced that he is a sadistic war-mongering baby-killer, when in fact he is simply a young man trying to stay alive. The antiwar journalist in *The Siege of Firebase Gloria* is weak, drugged, and cowardly. The protester in *Gardens of Stone* apologizes when a soldier breaks his jaw.

If Coppola tried to show Vietnam they way it was in *Apocalypse Now*, in *Gardens of Stone* he showed the way it should have been. This film's warriors are brave and true, the protesters pompous fools, the women selfless and loyal, and the military is a man's true family. To create this world, it stays out of the Viet Nam entirely, and out of American society almost completely, secluding itself within the military community at Arlington National Cemetery. This is a securely masculine world ordered by military rites of male bonding, including fights in bars, getting drunk together, and sharing the grief of bad news from home. Women are mostly unnecessary. The army barracks provides family enough for any man, complete with both paternal and fraternal mates. The men exhibit many maternal qualities as well—love for men, concern for the finer things in life (like fine food, literature, and Persian carpets), sensitivity—balanced with positive masculine traits. Both of the main female characters take on masculine characteristics as they become involved in the lives of the men; Clell's girlfriend Sam (Anjelica Houston) announces that she cannot have children, and Rachel, Willow's wife (Mary Stuart Masterson), cuts her hair short and is welcomed into the army at her wedding.

Both these women are fully supportive of their warriors. Although they clearly cannot understand why their lovers and husbands need to join the army and fight, they do realize that as women they must acquiesce in that need. Sam, who works for the *Washington Post* and supports the antiwar movement, never explains her opposition and finally supports Clell's desire to go to Viet Nam. "You've got your job to do. I've got mine." Rachel resigns herself to the same attitude in her soldier. Her first response to his belief that "a soldier at the right place at the right time can change the world" is a tired, "I'd hoped you'd outgrown that," but during the same dinner conversation she agrees to renew their love affair. She finally stands up to her father, a profiteering colonel, and marries Willow although he is just a non-com. Willow addresses his letters from the front to Clell, not Rachel, and describes her as a beacon of hope for a lonely, frightened warrior with no remark on the lonely, frightened wife she is.

Although Willow dies in Viet Nam, he does not suffer a victim's death. He goes willingly to the War, convinced of the necessity of his sacrifice even though he questions the ends it serves in this particular instance. No one forces him to become a soldier; he enlists and begs his commander to send him to the fighting. His death is off screen, as though it were not a bullet but the War itself that killed him. His funeral is a military ritual—employing the signifiers of nation, of sacrifice, and of a noble cause—that reaffirms the military tradition and the value of a young man's death.

This death confirms the value of the military culture in the face of its greatest crisis. It provides the best defense of the system possible and insists on the value of the military culture, even though in this instance that culture is working for a losing cause. "There are no fronts in Vietnam," the older and wiser Sgt. Clell

Hazard tells the eager, young Willow. Hazard insists that the
United States should stop the War because it is impossible to
fight a soldier who can "march a hundred miles with no food
through jungle you would not believe, slaughter his own people—
babies if he has to," a soldier who would "fight a helicopter with
bows and arrows." He is questioning America's ability, however,
not its cause. To question America's cause would be to suggest
that Willow's death (and the sacrifice of the thousands of others
buried in Arlington) was meaningless. He faces the same problem
expressed by the paraplegic veterans in the opening of *Coming
Home*: how to condemn a war that cost so much pain, anguish,
and death. Hazard's response is a faith in the military to endow a
young man's death with meaning.

   Further confirmation of the military order comes from a fellow soldier at the barracks, Wildman, who begins as an inept private and ends with the Medal of Honor. He seems out of place in
the military and repeatedly offends the drill sergeants. He drops
his weapon, trips, arrives late, and hides pornography under his
mattress. Willow must take him under his tutelage to save him
from disgrace, but what Wildman truly needs is described in a
conversation with Clell while on maneuvers.

   Clell: Did you ever stick your neck out for anything?
   Wildman: No sir, it's not my way sir. Does that mean I'm
              not a man?
   Clell: You're as much a man as anybody. It's just that a
              man has to feel good about himself.

This, then, is the purpose of the military for the soldiers. It is the
means by which they can develop the self-esteem that will elevate
them from a dependence on pornography to a mature relationship
with an adoring, loyal, and beautiful woman. The true crime the
protesters commit is to smear this self-image. Likewise it is the
soldier's duty to uphold the honor of the military. Thus Willow's
death is not a waste because Sgt. Hazard can describe him as
having made a noble sacrifice for his country. (Ronald Bass'
screenplay of the story deletes the actual death in Viet Nam,
which Proffitt's book describes in detail as a pitiful waste: Willow
falls victim of a Vietnamese atrocity.) In the same honorable vein,
the hapless Wildman earns the Congressional Medal of Honor,

the highest decoration awarded to a soldier and returns to Arlington to assume the role of honoring the dead soldier. The reverence Coppola shows to the dead in the film may have been influenced by his own son's death during the production. Whatever the reason, the film was successful enough as a homage to the military that the Army presented Coppola with a "Certificate of Appreciation for Patriotic Civilian Service" (Cowie 204).

The Vietnam War provided blame and to spare partly because many different groups offered many different views about what, exactly, was wrong with it. By the eighties, the controversy had settled down a bit and a few issues came to the fore. The point that America had committed atrocities there became the issue of the effect these atrocities had on the young American men. The question of whether we should have been there became irrelevent—we sent our boys there, and we should have supported them. The role of the protesters became one of disloyal or irresponsible citizens who betrayed the soldiers. Who was to blame might still be an open question, but at least America now knew who the victim was.

Part 4
The Land of Nam

"The Way It Really Was"

With the rise in the veterans' status, experiential accuracy (the aspect of the War that the veterans were most authoritative on) became the touchstone for describing the war years. *The Deer Hunter* and *Apocalypse Now* had used metaphors to describe their versions of the War, but *Platoon,* a film about soldiers made by a veteran, came from a soldier's experience, and it thereby broke the film barrier that released the next flood of wartime films. *Platoon* showed "Viet Nam, the way it really was, on film."

Walter Hill's 1981 film *Southern Comfort* provides a useful reference for the generally accepted details of the narrative before *Platoon.* Although set in the swamps of Louisiana, many critics identified it as an allegory of the Vietnam War (in the tradition of *Ulzana's Raid* and *Soldier Blue* but using Cajun-as-VC instead of Indian-as-VC). A squad of National Guardsmen, weekend-warriors training in the swamps of Louisiana, foolishly initiate a conflict with local Cajun fishermen. The conflict quickly escalates and the Cajuns kill all but two of the guardsmen. Their deaths result equally from personal dissensions within the squad and the superior skills of the Cajuns whom they have made into an enemy. Among the details that identified it as a Vietnam allegory for the critics were the jungle location and the date (1973), the dissension among the men, the mostly lower-class origins of the guardsmen, the generally hapless way the Guards instigate and carry-out the conflict (contrasted by the cohesion and competence of their enemy) and images of a burning hut, a dope-smoking soldier and a village that appears friendly but might be hiding the enemy.

How radically this perception of the War changed during the Reagan years is evident in a 1987 film also identified as an allegory of the War. In *Predator* the soldiers are a tightly knit band of professionals who can defeat any enemy they encounter. They follow their leader, the cigar-chomping, supra-macho Dutch (Arnold Schwarzenegger), on a mission to rescue Americans captured by rebels in a Central American jungle. Dissension among the men and hapless soldiers are no longer Vietnam signifiers: these are replaced by a CIA that treats soldiers as expendable tools, by soldiers who must be enraged by enemy atrocities before they start into action, by Communist involvement in the conflict, and by the soldiers' eventual success once they escape the confines of the bureaucrats and the false-security of high technology. In the end, Schwarzenegger stands alone and triumphant, stripped of weapons and clothing, in a land wasted by an enemy that resorted in defeat to nuclear weapons.

The differences between these two films are emblematic of the changes that occurred in the 1980s. In the 1981 film we see what went wrong: the bumbling incompetence, the sacrifice of lower-class Americans, and the unexpected strength and dedication of the enemy. By 1987 the allegory is repairing all these problems and showing how we could have won had we not been betrayed. For one thing, it changed the focus from means to ends. It was also a change from reality—what was—to fantasy—what might have been. It is no accident that *Predator* was a science fiction film set in a generic jungle country, or that its heroes were the overbuilt Schwarzenegger and Carl Weathers. It was a trend that would continue in films like *Universal Soldier* (1992), with Jean-Claude Van Damme and Dolph Lundgren converted into cybernetic soldiers, and *The Lost Platoon* (1989), with a squad of vampires fighting through the century. Both these fantasies remove the humanity from their heroes to make them perfect fighters. In the early eighties, however, the Vietnam soldier was still human and fallible, and he went to a real war in real country. The first combat film of the eighties, in fact, dramatized Philip Caputo's war memoir, *A Rumor of War* (1980). Caputo was a gung-ho second lieutenant with the first U.S. combat unit sent to Viet Nam in 1965. He left in 1966 under the shadow of a murder charge that the marines dropped to avoid a scandal. In the book Caputo describes the naiveté of the American arrival.

> War is always attractive to young men who know nothing about it, but we had also been seduced into uniform by Kennedy's challenge to "ask what you can do for your country" and by the missionary idealism he had awakened in us.... So, when we marched into the rice paddies on that damp march afternoon, we carried, along with our packs and rifles, the implicit convictions that the Viet Cong would be quickly beaten and that we were doing something noble and good. We kept the packs and rifles; the convictions, we lost (xiv).

The book describes Westmoreland's strategy of attrition replacing Kennedy's "missionary idealism" as the soldiers face the hard reality of warfare against a "lethal, determined enemy." It is this gradual loss of conviction that gives the memoir its power.

The film acknowledges this original idealism, but the emphasis is on Caputo's desire for excitement. Brad Davis portrays him as a tense twenty-two-year old, tired of living at home and eager to make a mark with his life. Kennedy's death—rather than his ideals—is the stimulus for his enlistment; the purpose is to escape the confines of home. Rather than losing his convictions, his character seems to develop its violent potential as the brutality of the War releases his personal demons. He appears far more in character leading his men on a rampage to burn a village than he does apologizing to a farm woman whose hut he has just searched.

A Rumor of War was originally produced in the seventies and intended as a cinema release, but it did not appear until September 1980 (just two months after Carter signed the bill authorizing the Vietnam War Memorial) and then as a two-part television film; so it raised the question of the soldiers' culpability at a time when they were finally receiving recognition for their sacrifice. It portrays Caputo as slightly unbalanced from the start and compares him to other second lieutenants who behave more nobly than he manages to do. It also provides two sergeants who act as father figures to the lieutenants, and who, from their paternal perspective, provide further moral recriminations. After Caputo abets the murder of two Vietnamese civilians, and while he waits for trial on murder charges, one comes to scold him:

"What went on out there—you should never have let that happen." At the same time, however, the film shows the extenuating circumstances of Caputo's actions—especially the deaths of one of the sergeants and of a fellow lieutenant, two of the film's moral voices. Caputo thus appears as a man predisposed to violence, in a situation that fosters violence, yielding to that violence.

He eventually pleads guilty to lying under oath, receives a reprimand, and returns to the United States. That no one holds him accountable for the murder becomes the film's—and the book's—chief accusation regarding what was truly wrong over there. America's culpability lay not in its men but in its military command. Self-image is the primary concern of the American military officers; the court martial covers up Caputo's guilt to keep its own name clean. In another sequence, Caputo works as assistant to Adjutant Major Ball (Stacy Keach). Ball's chief amusement is the helicopters on his operations map board; he makes whooshing sounds as he flies them over his little Viet Nam. When a general comes to visit, Ball insists that Caputo display four Viet Cong bodies killed the night before although Caputo has already thrown them into a pit for burial and they have begun to decompose. When the general arrives, he pays more attention to the Major's map—he likes the colors, he says—than to the bodies.

The men receive no sense of mission, no purpose or goal. The officers prod them with the cliché that they are here to help the local people, but their training is to kill. This they do when they have a chance. They are told to kill for enjoyment (part of Caputo's training consists of a hatchet tossing officer who chants "ambush is killing and killing is fun") or to kill to survive; for a time Caputo is even in charge of Major Ball's scoreboard listing killed, wounded, and kill ratios for the day, adding competitive spirit to the list of reasons to kill.

Vietnam films in the eighties repeatedly faced this challenge of condemning what happened there without condemning the men who fought there. The problem was not inherent in the material since the soldiers should be viable candidates for guilt. They are the ones who did the actual killing—committed atrocities that were, if not more frequent than in other wars, more publicized—and it was the soldiers whom much of the wartime rhetoric held accountable. Their innocence was now one of the assumptions about the War, however, and only few films have dared to hold them accountable for their actions; Brian DePalma tried in *Casualties of War* and faced a fury of protest in response (despite an ending that takes the force out of its moral rhetoric). These perceived scapegoats of American military strategy and *realpolitik* were thus able to dictate what was and was not the truth of the War. Oliver Stone, a Vietnam veteran who wrote, directed, and took a bit part in a movie about his experiences in Viet Nam, gave cinematic voice to this authority.

The genesis of his film began in the seventies. Stone wrote the original script during the bicentennial celebrations in post-Watergate America. The Watergate experience, Stone felt, had been like "peeling an onion."

> There was a sense of liberation, of an oppressive burden being lifted off .... I'd say that, maybe in the same spirit, I was probably saying to myself, "Let's peel the onion, let's get to the truth of Vietnam" (McGilligan 20).

Unfortunately, the time was not as ripe as Stone seemed to think, either for *Platoon* or Stone's other Vietnam project, Ron Kovic's *Born on the Fourth of July*. *Platoon* was, Stone thought, "too 'depressing' and 'grim'" (Corliss 61). The latter film—which would eventually be the grimmer of the two—came closer to production in the seventies, perhaps because, as Stone noted in 1987 "That was really a story of the Seventies, Ron's story, very angry" (McGilligan 18). The story of wounded veterans returning home did arrive in the seventies when Jane Fonda made *Coming Home*, but with the anger dissolved. Kovic's story failed to appear because the money fell through.

> We were three days from shooting. I had spent a year on the screenplay, working with Ron Kovic, who had written a terrific book, poetic, a wonderful piece. I saw the whole movie in rehearsals. We changed what we had to change. Pacino [in the role of Ron Kovic] was white heat. Friedkin, the director, had dropped out, which was a real shame, but he had been very ably replaced by Dan Petrie. But then the money fell out.

> It was one of those crazy half-German, half-U.S. deals—three
> days before shooting (McGilligan 18).

This experience, and what he describes as the death of liberalism
("Watergate was over, Carter lost, Iraq had taken the hostages,
liberalism was dead.") convinced him that America did not want
to know the truth of the War. So he wrote a series of other films:
Midnight Express, The Hand, Scarface, The Year of the Dragon
and *Salvador.*

Year of the Dragon, the story of a Vietnam veteran working
as a New York City detective in Chinatown, was part of a pack-
age to produce *Platoon.* Stone wrote the script for Michael Cimino on condition that Cimino would then produce *Platoon* and
Dino de Laurentiis would finance it. Ultimately both Cimino and
de Laurentiis dropped out of the production, replaced by Arnold
Kopelson and Helmdale Films (a British production company),
respectively. Filmed in the Philippines for only $6 million, *Pla-
toon* appeared on 19 December 1986 and was a huge success
(Corliss 57). It remains the most influential Vietnam War film.

The film's verisimilitude protected it from most critics. Although many disliked what Richard Blake calls "the gooey rendition of Samuel Barber's 'Adagio for Strings'" that provides a
counterpoint to the action, the melodramatic comments provided
by the hero's letters home to his grandmother, and the hero's final
act of murder, they refrained (for the most part—John Podhoretz
called it "one of the most repellent movies ever made in this country") from coming out against it. Pauline Kael, among the few
critics who give the film a generally unfavorable review, suggested why this was so.

> I know that "Platoon" is being acclaimed for its realism, and I
> expect to be chastened for being a woman finding fault with a
> war film. But I've probably seen as much combat as most of
> the men saying, "This is how war is" (95).

The veterans' assertion that "you had to be there" eliminated the
critic's authority to question a veteran's statement about the War.
This had been John Wayne's response to the cynical journalist in
The Green Berets; but while the 1968 critics treated it skepti-
cally, in the eighties it had become a valid defense.

Given the veterans' response to the film, experientially the War must have been very much the way Stone depicted it, at least for those soldiers who saw combat. Most of the events and characters come directly from Stone's personal experience.

> "I saw the enemy for the first time on my first night ambush" [Stone] recalls, "and I froze completely. Thank God the guy in the next position saw them and opened up. The ensuing firefight was very messy. I was wounded in the back of the neck—an inch to the right and I would have been dead—and the guy next to me had his arm blown off." He emptied his rifle clip at a man's feet, as Chris [Charlie Sheen] does in the movie. "He wouldn't stop smiling," says Stone, "and I just got pissed off and lost it. But I did save a girl who was being raped by two of the guys; I think they would've killed her. I went over and broke it up. Another kid—he's like Bunny [Kevin Dillon] in the movie—clubbed this old lady to death and then kind of boasted about it" (Corliss 60).

Chris Taylor, Stone's alter-ego, arrives in Vietnam in 1967, and his story describes life within this jungle hell. His guides are Staff Sergeant Barnes (Tom Berenger), the platoon's "Ahab" who makes things right through the force of his own violence, and the spiritual, almost effervescent Sergeant Elias (Willem Dafoe), Christ with an automatic weapon, who races swiftly and silently through the jungle killing Vietnamese as he moves.

Elias is a lyrical, asexual figure who loves the Vietnamese landscape. Throughout the film he is lithe and graceful as a deer; when Chris sees a stag in the blasted forest after the film's climactic air raid, it might be Elias reincarnated. Stone treats the landscape much the way he treats Elias. The camera work is mostly dolly and crane shots, the camera panning slowly across the faces and figures of the men in the landscape. The pace of the shooting is leisurely and elegant, moving with the lyrical, nostalgic strains of the "Adagio for Strings." The light filters gracefully through the thick jungle that hinders the men and makes their lives a misery.

Elias and the landscape both suffer devastation at the hands of Americans. After finding one of their men impaled on a stake, the platoon, including Chris, takes revenge on a nearby village.

Like the majority of the squad, Chris loses control. He "[empties] a rifle clip at a man's feet," then stands by as another soldier beats the man to death with his rifle. Barnes leads the men on their orgy of destruction, coldly shooting an old woman to force a confession from her husband. Chris describes Barnes as "our Ahab" through whom "we would set things right" and Stone has elaborated on this characterization: "I want him [Berenger] to play someone with evil in his heart, but play him with an understanding that will shed light on Melville's line, 'O this lovely light that shineth not on me ...'" (Stone 18).

The pressure the men feel from the heat, the miserable conditions in the Vietnamese jungle, and the cruelty of the Viet Cong combine to ignite the atrocities. The film makes no accusations about the purposelessness of the War or the incompetence of the military command; these are grunts and the film does not show them as having any political interest in the War. The question of purpose never seems to occur to them. (Many of the oral histories from the War call this assumption of an apolitical grunt into serious question.) This leaves only the conditions of Vietnam as explanation for the atrocities that occur; the horror arises from the land. The platoon reacts to the terrain of the war by splitting into two camps, the "heads" and the "juicers," each championed by one of the two sergeants.

> It was from these roots that the essential conflict between Elias and Barnes grew in my mind. Two gods. Two different views of the war. The angry Achilles versus the conscious-stricken Hector fighting for a lost cause on the dusty plains of Troy. It mirrored the very civil war that I'd witnessed in all the units I was in—on the one hand, the lifers, the juicers and the moron white element (part southern, part rural) against on the other, the hippie, dope-smoking, black, and progressive white element.... Right versus left (Stone 19).

Elias, the natural enemy of Barnes, is the leader of "the heads"—the pot-smoking group that contains all the film's sympathetic characters. The soldiers in the other half of the platoon give their allegiance to Barnes; they include the toadying Sergeant O'Neill (John C. McGinley), the psychotic Bunny (who beat the farmer and his mother to death in the village), a baby-faced.

incompetent Lieutenant (Mark Moses) and the cowardly Junior (Reggie Johnson). It is a neat division of good and evil that lends itself to cliché. It also implies (as *A Rumor of War* had) that certain men had a predisposition toward cruelty which Vietnam allowed them to indulge.

The film's most controversial moment comes when this division breaks down. Chris is a cross-over character who breaks under pressure in the village and joins the terror, then recovers his self-control and rescues two village women from rape. He is first attracted to Barnes strength, then repulsed by the naked cruelty of Barnes' methods. He learns to trust Elias instead, thereby making an enemy of Barnes. After the film's climactic bombing, he comes across the wounded Barnes and coldly shoots him. Since Rhah, who took over leadership of the heads on Elias' death, had earlier stated that "only Barnes can kill Barnes," it is easy to assume that Chris, too, has finally yielded to the evil force; he has adopted Barnes' tactics in Elias' cause, thereby betraying that cause.

The scene has bothered many critics. Pauline Kael describes it as the "violent fantasy" implicit behind Stone's explicit allegiance to Elias (96). Critic Richard A. Blake sees it as a final victory by Barnes.

> Chris, an image of the nation, clearly sides with Elias on a notional level, yet by his murder of a wounded man he becomes a reincarnation of Barnes. Despite Chris' pious posturings, Barnes has won. He and the country have lost their innocence, but have replaced it, not with wisdom, but with cynicism. The violent do indeed inherit the earth (159).

According to Stone, however:

> I also wanted to show that Chris came out of the war stained and soiled—all of us, every vet. I want vets to face up to it and be proud they came back. So what if there was some bad in us? That's the price you pay. Chris pays a big price. He becomes a murderer (Corliss 59).

Stone does not want to redeem his soldiers totally. One problem which veterans faced upon their return to America was that Americans refused to accept that their innocent young men had come home killers. In America, the traditional war story has the innocent youth become a killer for the duration of the war, then

return unsullied. Like the gunfighter who kills without culpability—since his killing is always justifiable —American soldiers are
expected to return from war wise but innocent. In Vietnam, there
seemed to be no cause to justify the soldiers' killing, and so they
returned covered in guilt and accused by society of war crimes. In
Platoon, Stone insists on the impossibility of this paradox; a veteran has a right to be guilty.

The crimes which American soldiers committed lie at the
root of the Vietnam combat film. One of the reasons it is so important and desirable to show "Viet Nam, the way it really was,
on film" (Corliss 54) is so that people will know what led to the
atrocities. Critics frequently describe the destruction of the village
as being similar to My Lai (although the scattered murders in the
film hardly approximate the brutality of the actual event in which
American GIs slaughtered over 300 men, women and children).
Platoon offers one explanation for what happened. Despite Chris'
sentiments about Barnes and Elias being in constant conflict for
his, and by extension America's, soul, it is not a simple explanation, because the hero kills but does not become another Barnes.
He "goes out of there a murderer," not just a cynical young man
but a man who has acted out his "violent fantasies," who has
yielded and knows it. He has not fulfilled some salvific paradox
that allows sin without stain. A former sergeant who participated
in the My Lai massacre clearly states an alternative attitude in a
1989 interview for Yorkshire Television's *Remember My Lai.*

> I feel that we carried out the orders in a moral fashion. The
> orders of destroying the village—of killing the people of the
> village, I feel that we carried out our orders and I feel that we
> did not—violate any moral standards.

Several films echo this defense, especially *The Siege of Firebase Gloria* and *Platoon Leader,* which justify orders like those
described by the My Lai sergeant. Chris, on the other hand, returns acknowledging his lost innocence and implies America
should not hide its complicity in the soldier's actions by insisting
that he be either as pure as when he left or else a homicidal maniac. "Innocence that changes," according to Stone, is "the key to
the movie" (McGilligan 60).

The Barnes/Elias split, however, allows *Platoon* to differentiate between two types of soldiers. Those who follow Barnes are
consistently weaker or morally corrupt. They lack the strength to
withstand the pressures of the War, and so they place their confi-
dence in Barnes' powerful anger. Elias, on the other hand, offers
his followers no power, merely guidance. His followers must be
strong enough to resist the urge to use force against the weaker
Vietnamese civilians. The men fight the true battle, Chris explains, within themselves, and the winners are those who have the
strength to resist Barnes' anger. The Nam is only the
battleground.

Platoon's success established the conventions of reality for
Vietnam. The grunts are working class, the jungle smothering, the
Viet Cong mere shapes in the darkness, and the Vietnamese people sullen or frightened peasants. The grunts show no interest in
the reasons for the War, just in surviving it. The good ones like
rock 'n roll. Racism scarcely exists, though blacks are usually
very hip and always band together. The soldier, though he does
not always realize it, is a tragic figure sacrificed to the moral and
political needs of others. The majority of combat films in the
eighties have relied on these conventions.

84 Charlie Mopic (1989) offers an alternative realism de-
void of romantic vision. The title refers to a Lessons Learned
Team, an army documentary crew accompanying a Long Range
Reconnaissance Patrol (LRRP) "to record procedures peculiar to
this situation." Mopic (*Mo*tion *Pic*ture) is the cameraman's nickname and the entire film is presented from his camera's point of
view, though not always while he operates it. The conceit of limit-
ing the film's perspective in this way limits the audience's perception of events to the experiential level, and no larger
picture—either physical or political—is shown. Even at the end,
when the camera lies forgotten in a rising helicopter, a soldier's
boot obscures its overview of Vietnam.

Instead, the camera records the details of the LRRP team's
life and work in Vietnam. Mopic records the details of a soldier
powdering his feet, cleaning and loading his weapon, taping his
dogtags, and boiling water. These are the rituals of the soldier's
life: the discipline or art of war. On one level, these actions are

mundane details of daily life in the bush. The attention the soldiers and camera pay to them, however, endow such details with a deeper significance. They become rites of safety: do them properly and you may survive. The grunts hold them sacred and do not hesitate to redress the Mopic lieutenant for disregarding them.

These details also provide meaning to the LRRP team's life in Vietnam. These grunts have no interest in the politics of the situation or the land they travel through. When they discover a ruined village and Mopic asks who destroyed it, "does it make a difference?" is the reply. When the Lieutenant comments on the beauty of Viet Nam, a member of the squad rejoins that they ought to destroy it. "Turn it into the big quartermaster in the sky, say hey motherfucker this place is beyond repair." If a meaning is to be found in the War, the soldiers will make it for themselves. "You're supposed to do your job the best you can whether you like it or not," explains another member of the team, and continues with a story about his father.

> Once I remember he was making this black oak china cabinet. Black oak. And, when the lady it was meant for said that he should paint it white, to match her floorboard trim, shit. He painted it white. And I mean it was beautiful black oak too. Grain like running water. And he painted it the smoothest, cleanest white you ever seen. Milk ain't that white. But you do your job.

This is not a world inhabited by the mythic heroes which Oliver Stone imagined. The metaphysical order comes from the lives of the soldiers; no outside imagination imposes it. This is part of the reason O.D., the leader of the LRRP team, resists having the camera crew along and refuses to be interviewed. The camera is an outsider that will attempt to impose another order on his life. He allows the crew along in the end because the army insists on it, but he won't reveal his personal reality. "That's my private life. Army got no business with my private life." He recognizes that the camera and the Mopic team belong to a separate order, but while they are in his territory he insists they obey his rules.

The ambitious Lieutenant tries to force his own order on the squad, an order based on rank and military discipline. Unlike the ritual base of the grunt's world, founded in utilitarian principles of staying alive, however, the officer's discipline provides little more than "advancement potential." O.D. breaks this discipline by thrusting the Lieutenant into the grunt's reality. When they must kill a wounded North Vietnamese soldier, he insists the Lieutenant does it.

> Knife makes it personal. It's time you drew blood LT. Your own, private KIA.... No, wait a second. You might want to know who you're killing. [takes papers from soldier and reads] His name's Trang, Nu Lin Trang. Age about nineteen. Got a family, looks like. Wife. Kid. Come on LT.

The Lieutenant thrusts the knife dramatically down into the body, as though he were driving a stake in a vampire's heart, but fails to kill the soldier. O.D. takes the knife and does it professionally, under the ribs with a twist. Like Mike Vronsky, O.D. insists that "this is this."

Mopic, too, tries to maintain his own reality. "Don't look at me, look at the camera," he tells the grunts he photographs, hoping to efface himself from the reality he films. Until the end of the mission, Mopic does nothing voluntarily except shoot film. He never fires a weapon or carries equipment. When the team members start dying, he does not carry a body. Only twice does this private discipline fail him—once when the team members steal his camera and interview him, and again at the end when he puts his camera down to help O.D. into the helicopter. This second time, he is shot and the helicopter leaves him behind, splitting him from his camera (and from the audience, which must stay with the recording apparatus).

84 Charlie Mopic offers one direct critique of the romantic visions of the War in *Platoon*. On the first night of the LRRP's mission, the grunts sit about the radio, listening to reports from a firebase that is under attack. When NVA soldiers overrun the base, a voice over the radio calls a bombing mission on his own perimeter. The voice is that of Dale Dye, who played the captain who called a bombing mission on his own perimeter in *Platoon*. In that film, the bombing was a Götterdämmerung of epic proportions; to the grunts listening on the radio, it is a sudden silence and the reality that a group of fellow soldiers have died. As the grunts say, "there it is."

Building the Land of Nam

Historically, the idea of an American outpost of civilization, a wild west fort, in Viet Nam may be absurd, but since John Wayne first defended Fort Dodge in *The Green Berets* Hollywood has been constructing a landscape and a storyline that make it possible, even inevitable. *Go Tell the Spartans* and *The Deer Hunter* established the iconography. The decontextualization that began in the seventies recreated Viet Nam as a romantic wilderness where the heroes travel in search of adventure, civilization, or themselves; in such a wilderness, firebases became outposts of American civilization. In the language of the grunts, this wilderness is "the Nam" and the land they came from is "the World."

The Nam is a land of inversions, where clean-faced American boys commit brutal atrocities; where meaningless clashes between isolated bands of soldiers are more common than actual battles and any battles are meaningless; where America's founding fathers, represented by their political totem (the Declaration of Independence) and their fighting methods (tenacity and guerrilla warfare) are the enemy and America represents the colonial imperialism those forefathers opposed. To correct these inversions, the soldier must find a haven like Firebase Gloria in which the traditional, masculine American role and character are maintained.

This creation of the Nam as a wilderness through which the American soldier must travel for twelve months, gradually gaining enough knowledge of the place to survive and become "short" (a short-timer was nearing the end of his tour), reflects the romantic tradition in American culture that stretches back to Cooper's Leatherstocking tales and the puritan captivity narratives. *The*

Deer Hunter is quite explicit about its origins; its title comes from Cooper's *The Deerslayer* and its central scene (the capture of the three friends by the Vietnamese) repeats the American captivity narratives. This deer hunter character recurs in various incarnations in the Vietnam combat films: Elias racing through the woods in *Platoon,* Hafner and his squad roaming the wilderness of Nam in *The Siege of Firebase Gloria,* a Viet Cong-fighter named Roach in *Platoon Leader* (1988) and O.D. in *84 Charlie Mopic.*

The films also resurrect the primitive warriors of the wilderness—the Indian of the American West—in the Viet Cong. These soldiers appear only briefly in the films, emerging mysteriously out of the grass, the forest, even the ground as though they are part of the landscape, like a snake hiding in the grass, waiting to strike. In one scene in *Platoon Leader,* the Viet Cong appear out of the forest like a herd of buffalo, trampling through the grass where the squad of amazed American grunts lie, disappear back into the forest; the horde is oblivious of the presence of the Americans though they are in danger of trampling on them. Such scenes transform the Viet Cong into a natural phenomenon rather than a politically or socially motivated group of men. The filmmakers, in response to criticism of this portrayal, argue that, to the soldier, the Vietnamese were an unseen enemy. The truth of that argument, coupled with the authority given the soldier's point of view by the American public and the lack of successful counter-portrayals, has succeeded in dehumanizing the Vietnamese in American cinema.

BAT-21 (1988) offers some antidote to this image of the enemy when a bombing intelligence expert, Colonel Iceal Hambleton (Gene Hackman), is shot down and calls a bombing strike from the ground. For the first time he must remain to see the aftermath of one of his strikes; as the camera traverses the wreckage of life and machinery, the airman turns away in distress. The film follows him as he witnesses the dirty face of war from the ground, traversing the countryside to reach a rendezvous point with the rescue planes. (The film is a dramatization of Hambleton's actual experience.)

He has several more encounters with the Vietnamese while struggling to reach the rendezvous. The bombing mission precedes an encounter with a farmer who finds Hambleton raiding his home and attacks him, by a young boy who offers his hat to Hambleton and exposes a trap the American is about to walk into, and a rescue attempt foiled by a brutal Viet Cong ambush. Hambleton enters all of these encounters from a position of weakness and ignorance. Apart from his bombing call, he has no way to dominate the situation. He is a hapless traveler in a world fraught with danger, and his rescue is the main storyline. It thus inverts the typical mise-en-scène in which the Americans have the power, giving it many of the overtones of the MIA/POW films even though Hambleton evades capture.

He discovers Viet Nam to be a pastoral land of farmers and kind-hearted people held in terror by the NVA. To foil an attempt to rescue Hambleton (as a colonel he would be an important prisoner), the NVA hold a village hostage. To attack the NVA the American rescue team would have to kill civilians, and after the enemy downs a helicopter and kills its pilot, the Americans refuse Hambleton's pleas and destroy the town. In contrast to the NVA's cold-blooded use of the civilians as hostages to American civility, the American bombing is clearly a reaction to the viciousness of the enemy, payback for the murder of a friend. That so many must die horrifies Hambleton, but he is helpless to stop the slaughter and continues forward to the next rendezvous.

Typically, however, the United States is represented not by helpless individuals struggling through a wilderness but by platoons or squads of fighting men. For their climactic conflicts, these combat films return to the western fort model. *Platoon*'s grunts defend a "defense perimeter" rather than a walled fort, but *The Siege of Firebase Gloria* makes the nature of the conflict implicit in its title. *Platoon Leader* moves the narrative one step further into the realm of the American West by associating a peaceful village with the American fort, so that the Americans become responsible for an actual community. The Viet Cong, rather than the Americans, massacre the peaceful villages, but the results are far closer to the My Lai model than the American efforts in *Platoon*. The Americans drive out the Vietnamese marauders, but not before the village has been set in flames and bodies of dead and wounded civilians litter the ground. *Siege* created a smaller community for the fort to defend by stationing nurses at the firebase. Both cases provide a just cause for the American presence and military methods—either to prevent a peaceful, neutral village from being destroyed or a nurse from being raped.

With this wilderness iconography established, the films can employ the narrative of the wilderness fort besieged by savages. The savages (Vietnamese) assault the fortress in suicidal waves that, after first breaking against the defenses, eventually override the resistance by force of numbers until the cavalry (America's military power in the form of aerial bombardment) drives them off. In *Platoon* that salvation signals a Götterdämmerung as the bombing counterpoints a satanic Barnes slamming a shovel blade down on the prostrate Chris; the bombing becomes a meeting of damnation and salvation, both expressed through devastation. In *Siege* and *Platoon Leader* (as years before in *The Green Berets*) the bombardment is less equivocal in its results: the air cavalry flies in and decimates the enemy. Afterward Vietnamese bodies litter the landscape and the American fighters can rest for a time.

Hamburger Hill differs from these versions of the War because the soldiers do not establish any outpost in the country. The grunts fight four long days to reach the peak of Hill 937, which dominates the Ashau Valley, but by the time the surviving members reach the top, the American and Vietnamese artillery has already destroyed it. Despite the high cost of the hill in American casualties, there is no suggestion that the soldiers will remain on the hill; there seems to be no reason why they would want to. Instead of an outpost, *Hamburger Hill* provides its soldiers with a safe haven, a peaceful riverside camp where the locals are friendly and the soldiers feel safe. Although there were famously "no fronts in Vietnam," the soldiers appear to be safely behind their own lines during the opening scenes of the film. The camera offers images of peace amidst pastoral beauty: a wooded landscape, a river gorge, local women bathing and washing their clothes in the river, children playing. Even an eventual artillery attack fails to mar its romantic beauty; it merely serves to remind the soldiers that this land is in danger from the forces in the Ashau Valley. *Platoon, Platoon Leader*, and *The Siege of Firebase Gloria*—films that use the narrative of the wilderness outpost—offer landscapes as pastoral as this river gorge, but in them the beauty hides poisonous snakes, ants, unfriendly villagers, and the Viet Cong. There is no haven in their Vietnam apart from the military outpost. The grunts in *Hamburger Hill*, on the other hand, have a safe landscape in which to play, whore, drink, and teach the fresh recruits without being overly concerned about possible attacks.

The actual twelve-month tour of duty that the soldiers underwent dictates the larger structure of these stories (as C.D.B. Bryan notes in his description of the generic Vietnam War novel, "Barely Suppressed Screams"). A soldier arrives in Vietnam and is labeled as an FNG (Fucking New Guy) or cherry. As Chris notes in *Platoon*, "Nobody cares about the new guys. They don't even want to know your name." Usually at least one cherry dies. Eventually a cherry who survives becomes accepted, grows disillusioned, and departs. As the short-timer Brownie (Erik King) describes it in *Casualties of War*:

> The Nam's a trip. The first thirty days you don't know shit, the last thirty days you don't give a shit.... [The cherry] is likely to end up wasted 'cause he don't know nothing, and you and me likely to end up in peril 'cause we don't care about nothing.

The events that mark passage through the Nam include the gain of knowledge (which allows a cherry to survive), acceptance into the ranks of the fellow soldiers, disillusion, and finally the passage of time (the most coveted rank for Vietnam soldiers in the films is "short-timer").

The rites of passage thus include the first firefight, the first atrocity, male-bonding, and the first time someone asks how much time you have left in the Nam. These are the moments referred to by veterans in postwar films like *In Country* and *Jacknife* and which provide the substance of the combat narratives like *A Rumor of War, Platoon, Hamburger Hill, Platoon Leader,* and *Casualties of War.* Not every soldier completes all the rites; those who fail are either unfortunate "good" soldiers who die or else among the ranks of the "bad" soldiers who fail to maintain their poise. Chris, whom the heads welcome, becomes a better soldier than any of those who side with Barnes. In the final battle he shares a foxhole with Junior, a black who refuses to join with the majority of blacks in the platoon; Chris manages to keep the panicking Junior alive before leaping from his position to run like a berserker among the attacking Vietnamese, racing through the night forest as Elias had earlier raced through the day. When the battle is over, Junior stabs his own leg and is medivacked out with Chris, the latter suffering from more honorable wounds.

Hamburger Hill illustrates this rite of passage through Vietnam. It is the story of the eleven day effort to take Dong Ap Bia, designated Hill 937 but named Hamburger Hill by the grunts because so many died fighting to reach its top. The FNGs fight first for status as veterans; after several days on the hill, two new FNGs arrive and the previous cherries laugh in relief. Afterward, when the lone surviving short-timer finally breaks down, the lone surviving former-FNG must bring him back to his senses so that together they can finally reach the hilltop. To the traditional list of individual differences which soldiers must overcome to form an effective fighting force—differences of race, personality, religion, and color—the Vietnam War film adds time in-country.

The first third of *Hamburger Hill* concentrates on the education of the FNGs, contrasting their growing cockiness against the hard-bitten cynicism of the short-timers. The FNGs are fresh faced and eager; they hardly need to shave yet when they arrive (in contrast to Sergeant Frantz [Dylan McDermott] who always seems to have last shaved three days before) and only develop stubble after experiencing combat. During the bucolic early scenes, when the platoon is encamped by a river gorge (framed in shots that resemble early American romance landscapes of the West) they learn the proper way to brush their teeth ("in a rapid vertical motion"), they fill out cards telling their loved ones how to contact them, they have water-fights by the river, and one dies when an artillery attack interrupts him flirting with young Vietnamese girls by the riverbank.

Meanwhile the experienced soldiers watch over them, tolerating their innocence or trying to dispel it with lessons about the Nam. Their general attitude is condescending. They do not mix with the new soldiers and refuse to allow them to participate in their conversation. When one short-timer says he looks forward to walking proudly down America's streets in his uniform and jump-boots, an FNG warns he had better not wear the uniform. Immediately the other old-timers berate the FNG for not understanding what the uniform means to a soldier. The misunderstanding is mutual, however, which marks another of the differences between the FNGs and the short-timers. The action in *Hamburger Hill* happens late in the War, after the antiwar movement has gained strength in the United States. The FNGs are aware of this but the old-timers are not. Because of this, the integration that occurs amongst this group of soldiers will have to include some accommodation to the FNGs.

In *Platoon,* Chris abandoned his attitudes from the World. He dropped out of college to come to Vietnam because he "didn't see why only the poor should be fighting this war"—a good, liberal viewpoint which another soldier quickly puts into the Nam's perspective: "You have to be rich in the first place to think like that." The antiwar movement in *Hamburger Hill* receives no more respect, but the grunts pay more attention to it; they treat it as though it were as dangerous to them as the Viet Cong enemy. Apart from the dispute about a veteran's right to wear his uniform with pride, the subject of the movement rises repeatedly in the second half of the film, which alternates between scenes of the soldiers' brutal assaults on the hill and the moments of calm in-between. During the calms, the soldiers talk about home, read letters from friends and sweethearts, or describe how they found themselves in Vietnam. One soldier plays a tape from his girlfriend in which she insists she does not believe the things her friends say about the soldiers. Another reads a letter from his girlfriend in which she explains that her "college-friends" have told her it would be immoral to write any more letters to an American soldier.

The message is clear and more demoralizing than the rigors of combat they undergo. The combined adversities bind the soldiers together against the "other"—represented less by the Vietnamese enemy than by the military forces requiring them to fight for the hill, the "long-hairs" and "college-types" back in the world, and any other groups that do not share in their hardship and enforced alienation. As Sergeant Frantz (a college student like

Chris in *Platoon* but without the latter's condescending attitude—the audience only learns he was a college student late in the
film) explains, people opposed to the War should at least come
over as medics or service personnel. "You don't have to like it,"
he states, "but you have to show up." When a reporter asks about
the assault on the hill, expressing doubts about the objective
(doubts which Frantz certainly shares) and questioning whether
they have any chance of success, the sergeant shuts him up. "You
have no right to be here. Do you understand that?" Like the journalist in *The Green Berets*, this reporter, dressed in clean, pressed
fatigues and asking suitably obnoxious questions, nods humbly to
the ragged sergeant.

The FNG's need to belong to the brotherhood of soldiers is
part of the larger theme of community that runs through the Vietnam War film. In the never-never Land of Nam, a soldier must be
part of a group because he cannot survive on his own. This highlights one of the crucial difficulties in the War, that of identifying
the allies and the enemy. Neil Sheehan describes the reaction of an
American advisor in the days before America had committed
troops, John Paul Vann (reputedly a model for Coppola's Colonel
Kurtz), to the idea of bringing American troops into what was essentially a civil war.

> The Viet Cong were so intermingled with the peasantry that
> the Saigon troops had difficulty distinguishing friend from
> foe. Think, Vann said, how much more difficult it would be
> for Americans. The American soldier would soon start to see
> the whole rural population as the enemy. The Army and the
> Marine Corps would create a bloody morass into which they
> and the Vietnamese peasantry would sink. "We'd end up
> shooting everything—men, women, kids, and the buffaloes,"
> Vann said. (Sheehan 383)

In such a chaos, any method that created order would be welcome, and the brotherhood of the soldiers at least let you know
who your friends were; you could then make general assumptions
about the enemy.

In *Full Metal Jacket* it is just after being reminded that he is
"fresh out of friends" that the main character shoots a wounded
female sniper; this is the act that finally instates him in the ranks

of the squad. Similarly all the squad members in *Casualties of War* had to join the rape of a Vietnamese girl and it was the hero's refusal to do so that alienated him. In *Platoon,* Chris is also ostracized when he stops a gang-rape during the rampage against the village; the rapists accuse him of being homosexual, tell him he does not belong in the Nam, and spit at him. "Social unanimity," according to Susan White, "involves violence against the other: in a capitalist-imperialist society that other is a Third World communist; under patriarchy it is a woman" (128). Gloria Emerson records one young grunt's agreement with the sentiment.

> The boy was in a mortar crew; he was saying that he thought lifers didn't really like women or want them around much. And then he said something startling and wise: "We are their women. They've got us" (7).

Thus when a split occurs in the social unanimity of the soldier-societies in these films, it often does so over the proper definition of the "other," the enemy; the need to differentiate amongst Asians, to discern between a good gook and a bad gook is often the cause of the dilemma. Barnes' violence in the village, the action that causes the final split between himself and Elias, is explicitly an attempt to force the village leader to confess to being a Communist by murdering his wife. Eventually the conflict resolves itself along gender lines; those who oppose indiscriminate violence against the Vietnamese share feminine traits and are ostracized in their turn by their fellow soldiers. The homo-erotic overtones of the scenes amongst the heads in *Platoon* are one example. Eriksson's helplessness at the moment of battle in *Casualties of War* is a second. Even in *The Siege of Firebase Gloria,* it is the female doctor and the FNG who complain against the brutal actions of DiNardo.

Siege takes the process one step further in the relation between DiNardo and Hafner. These two men have replaced women for one another. Hafner is mother, father, brother and (chaste) lover to DiNardo. A conflict arises between them because DiNardo had not come to his friend when his son died: "When the boy died you didn't come to me and let me put my arms around you and cry with you," Hafner complains. When the wounded DiNardo insists Hafner kill him, the latter caresses his friend and reminds him of their sexual adventures before providing the final bullet. No woman could provide this much love and nurturing. The woman in the film, a doctor, leaves the death scene because she cannot heal the fallen warrior and lacks the strength to kill him.

In *Casualties of War*, a young hero falls asleep on a subway and dreams of being in war-ravaged Nam. He wakes from the nightmare with a jolt, and is comforted by a young Vietnamese woman who reassures him that he has been dreaming. "It's over now, I think," she says to comfort him, and he gazes up into the clear California sky with a look on his face that the director, Brian DePalma, describes as "forgiven." In another film fifty years before, a young girl had also been told that she merely dreamed her marvelous adventures; but she wanted to return to Oz one day and so protested to her dog, Toto, "But it wasn't a dream. It was real!" The Vietnam soldier has no such desire in American films (though in truth the veterans have been among the first to visit the modern Viet Nam) and is happy to consign it to the realm of fantasy.

Living in the Land of Nam

Despite American cinema's almost slavish devotion to the soldier, even the most laudatory films had to admit that American GIs had committed actions that some people might describe as atrocities. Lt. Calley may have faded from the American consciousness along with My Lai, but the image of American violence associated with those names continues to haunt the American consciousness, as it continues to haunt Vietnam combat films. The question was, how could good American boys commit atrocities. *Platoon* provided one of the hardest answers when Chris became a little like Barnes and mercilessly shot his enemy. The Land of Nam was a place where men like Barnes flourished because all civilized restrictions were unknown. Innocents like Chris yielded their innocence or their lives.

The view that prevails in *The Siege of Firebase Gloria* is that, since no one could blame a soldier for being in such a place, no one could blame him for what that place did to him. Sergeant Hafner (Lee Ermey), who takes command of the besieged firebase, personifies a reality even more brutal than that of Barnes and justifies it by reference to the brutality he faces. The main characters, Hafner and his protégé DiNardo (Wings Hauser), are professional soldiers who will do whatever they must to win their personal part of the War. Their squad, made of men like DiNardo, "the kind of gung-ho soldier the marines are known for," has been operating without restraint on long-range reconnaissance. They visit a friendly village and find the Viet Cong have massacred everyone in it; nothing the Americans do subsequently can compare to the atrocities the camera shows there. When they arrive at Firebase Gloria on the eve of Tet, they find it manned by slovenly, undisciplined troops under the command of a doped-up lieutenant who receives his men stark-naked in the command bunker. DiNardo quickly frags the officer so Hafner can take control of the firebase just as the Viet Cong surround it.

The Viet Cong attack during the next several days in waves of men, and the defenders of the firebase repel each wave, leaving the ground covered with Vietnamese corpses. After one such assault, DiNardo sends men out to kill the wounded VC and brings one barely conscious enemy soldier to the base hospital to torture him. When the female surgeon, Captain Flanagan (Margi Gerard), orders him to stop, he refuses. She calls him an animal and he responds passionately.

> Lady, do you have any idea if Charlie got in here, what he would do? He would rape you and your nurses until you were dead. But you know what? He'd have to kill me first. Animal? I'm not an animal.

Justifying the torture of prisoners as a defense against rape is only one of the explanations the film offers for America's fighting tactics. From the first scene in the slaughtered village, the film makes it clear that the men in this war face a brutal, implacable enemy. Survival requires that the men become as savage as their foe. DiNardo orders the wounded shot to avoid "surprises." He frags the incompetent officer to save the lives of the men. When two Vietnamese women come too near the perimeter, he shoots them and they explode—they were sappers carrying dynamite. DiNardo expostulates to a stunned grunt:

> Even the girls have got balls. Instead of their mommies putting books in their hands and sending them to school, they wrap them up in dynamite and send them off to kill GIs. You got that. That's the enemy.

DiNardo's description of the enemy is an excuse to kill the women, and it sounds similar to what Bunny, a soldier in *Platoon*, yells at the mother of a man he has just beaten to death with his rifle:

> I betcha' the old bitch runs the whole fuckin' show. She prob'le cut Mannie's throat. She'd probably cut my balls off if

> I gave her the chance.... Let's do her. Let's do the whole
> fuckin' village.

Bunny is an extreme example; the filmmaker's lack of sympathy
for him makes the unfairness of his story clear. DiNardo, on the
other hand, has the filmmaker's sympathy and his enemy seems
undeniably evil—we saw the women explode! Chris had Stone's
sympathy as well, and when he decides to kill Barnes, although
the audience might not cheer, there is a sense of relief and of
justice.

Despite its more humanitarian temper, *Platoon*'s underlying
sympathy is with the more paranoid *Siege*. Stone's film ends with
hope as the youthful American rises above the madness of the
Nam; he has escaped not only Barnes' wrath but the greater menace of the Land itself. Barnes could only kill him; the Nam has
made him a killer. It seems to be the nature of the place. In
BAT-21, the American pilot shot down behind enemy lines wants
only to reach his own people again, but when a Vietnamese
farmer catches him stealing rice, he must kill the man to escape.
Afterward he looks up to see his victim's family watching helplessly, then stumbles hurriedly away like a common thief. Paradoxically the family's grief strengthens our sympathy for the
killer of their father. Hambleton is decent and good-natured; it is
unfair that he should have to carry the guilt for an old man's
murder.

All of these films admit that the Vietnamese and American
soldiers committed atrocities, but they repeatedly set the crimes of
the two in contrast as a way of forgiving the American side. In
BAT-21, for instance, shortly after Hambleton kills the farmer in
self-defense, a platoon of Viet Cong forces a downed pilot to step
on a mine while his friends watch. An even more heavy-handed
example comes in the more blood-thirsty *Platoon Leader*. A grunt
feels guilty about having accidentally shot-off the arm of a young
Vietnamese girl, so when he later finds her murdered by the Viet
Cong, he leads his squad in search of retribution. They find the
enemy bathing under a waterfall; a low-angle shot shows the
squad standing at the cliff edge like GI Jehovahs, glaring right-
eously down at their victims as they toss a dozen grenades from
the cliff above the water. Even in *Platoon*, the attack on the

village is a reaction to the mutilation of an American soldier; the men who ravage that village have lost control, but the men who strung-up the soldier acted coldly and deliberately.

Casualties of War tried to question this trend and as a consequence received heavy criticism from Vietnam veterans. It portrayed an American war crime that had actually occurred and insisted that the soldiers take responsibility for their actions. (Neither its director Brian DePalma nor its stars were veterans.) If we just try harder, the moral soldier Eriksson tells us, if we just hold to our principles, we will not succumb to the amorality that threatens in the Nam; we will return as innocent as when we left. The film's recreation of an American atrocity may come emotionally closer to My Lai than *Platoon* manages because, while *Platoon* terrorizes the village and then hardly refers to it again, preferring to concentrate on the lives of the soldiers for whom after all the burning of the village was only one of many horrors they experienced, in DePalma's film the atrocity defines the squad's entire stay in Vietnam.

The film, based on a 1969 *New Yorker* article by Daniel Lang, describes how a squad, worn down by their combat experience, kidnaps, rapes, and finally murders a young Vietnamese woman named Oahn. One member of the squad, Sven Eriksson, refuses to participate and brings the others to trial, where they receive stiff sentences. Lang makes it clear that none of them spent much time in jail, but the film only mentions (in a note at the end of the credits) that one member, the dim-witted Private Hatcher, eventually had his sentence reversed.

The opposing main characters are Sergeant Meserve (Sean Penn), a tough veteran nearing the end of his tour, and Private Eriksson (Michael J. Fox), an FNG who owes his life to Meserve. Meserve is a warrior-hero like Barnes, but he is not yet the same merciless killing machine; he still cares, and this is one of the reasons he breaks as completely as he does when a sniper kills his best friend. In contrast, Eriksson is a hapless newcomer who disregards the advice of the older squad members. He tries to make friends with the villagers and hands out candy bars, despite warnings that the villagers might very well be the enemy, and he only realizes the truth when a sniper from the village kills Brownie, the most popular member of the squad.

Until this point, the film has followed the general tour of duty storyline. The young innocent has arrived, survived his first brushes with death, and witnessed the cruelty of war. The difference, however, is that Brownie's death, while tragic, was not needlessly cruel; he was not the victim of a Viet Cong atrocity and no one mutilated his body. For cruelty and senseless violence, it can not compare to the squad's rape and murder of Oahn (Thuy Thu Le), which DePalma makes the cinematic centerpieces of the film.

Another equally important difference is in Eriksson's refusal to join in the American atrocity. He stands by himself during the abduction, even waiting behind a moment to apologize. He refuses to participate in the rape despite Meserve's threats and accusations of homosexuality. He departs for the jungle while the squad rapes the girl, and thus absolves himself from even the complicity of voyeurism (and absolves the audience which shares his point of view in this scene). Eriksson stands within the Nam as a moral voice that is all but overwhelmed by the squad's brutality, the army's indifference, and the essential horror of the Nam. He sets a moral standard by which to measure the other soldiers in the film, and by which measure all but a few come up short. He articulates this standard to his friend Rowan after watching as a soldier steps on a mine and the rest of the platoon just pass the body by or pause for a quick snapshot.

> This goddamn thing is turning us on our heads, Rowan. We're getting it backwards man. I mean just because each of us at any second can get blown away, everyone's acting like we can do anything, man. And it don't matter what we do. But I'm thinking maybe its the other way around, you know. Maybe the main thing is just the opposite. Because we might be dead in the next split second, maybe we gotta be extra careful what we do. Because maybe it matters more ... Jesus, maybe it matters more than we'll ever know.

The camera captures Eriksson's viewpoint and shows the pathetic, terrified young girl that the soldiers load with responsibility for their fears and miseries. DePalma films the murder with ballet-like precision in one of his extended signature sequences. Oahn, now more ghost than woman, rises from where the squad had left her for dead, struggles to walk upright along the railroad trestle—in too much agony to notice the firefight going on about her—stumbles past the crouching, horrified Meserve, and is brutally machine-gunned to death from both front and back before falling to the rocks below. No illusions remain about the monstrosity of the crime committed against her. A camera pan from her body across the wreckage of the firefight makes her as much a symbol for the film as for the squad.

DePalma insists on the acts of abduction, rape, and murder as bonding rituals. Meserve initiates the crime after a sniper shoots his buddy in a village they had identified as friendly. When Eriksson argues about the justice of the abduction, Meserve explains that she is a Viet Cong. He points to each member of the squad in turn, saying "he's not VC." Oahn, he explains, is definitely VC. Then he turns to Eriksson. "You I'm not so sure about." Another private who did not want to join in testifies at the trial that he committed the rape out of loyalty and fear of ostracism. Eriksson, on the other hand, has maintained his individuality through most of the film. He bonds with the rest of the squad only in the short period between Brownie's death and Meserve's announcement of the abduction plan. After hearing the plan, he grows increasingly distant from the others, and the camera stresses that distance, especially during the crime.

Eriksson's attempts to bring the squad to justice confirm that Meserve was right; the crime does bind together the Americans in the Nam. The army refuses to investigate and threatens Eriksson with retribution if he continues his efforts. He is, his captain explains, trying to bring the standards of civility that operate in the World into a place where they do not belong. The camera, however, continues on Eriksson's side and the diminutive Fox towers over Dale Dye's captain. An investigation eventually takes place and the squad members receive stiff sentences. DePalma films it simply, with the squad members testifying to the camera while an off-camera voice interrogates them. The voice is that of the watching, condemning world—the world that watched

Vietnam on television for over a decade and wondered who was to blame.

In *Full Metal Jacket* (1987), Stanley Kubrick argues against this exculpation and finds the reason for the soldier's failure closer to home. He does not allow for innocent consciences like Eriksson's. His soldiers are products created in the American bootcamp factory that builds an effective fighting unit from a group of individuals. The film begins with the camp barbers shaving the recruits ("as if they were being prepared for surgery on their brains" [Rafferty, 257]) to the tune of "Good-by my darling, hello Vietnam," and then introduces these bald young men to Sergeant Hartman (Lee Ermey again). Hartman is a drill instructor who destroys all the clichés of the character type. Lee Ermey was a professional soldier and drill instructor before becoming an actor, and Kubrick adapted Hartman's character from a three hundred page transcription of Ermey's improvisation. It is a virtuoso performance of verbal violence.

> If you ladies leave my island, if you survive recruit training, you will be a weapon. You will be a minister of death praying for war. But until that day you are pukes, you are the lowest form of life on Earth. You are not even human-fucking-beings. You are nothing but unorganized grabastic pieces of amphibian shit. Because I am hard you will not like me. But the more you hate me the more you will learn. I am hard but I am fair. There is no racial bigotry here. I do not look down on niggers, kikes, wops, or greasers. Here you are all equally worthless. And my job is to weed out all non-hackers who do not deserve to serve in my corps.

The process of weeding out non-hackers primarily means denying the recruits the status of "men" until they prove themselves worthy of the appellation through survival of Marine training. Until then they remain "ladies" and possible homosexuals. "Only steers and queers come from Texas," he informs a Texan, "and you don't look like a steer to me." Hartman stomps on individuality—he immediately beats the recruit whom he names Joker (Matthew Modine) when that recruit attempts to speak out of turn—but it is more important that the men be ashamed of their feminine tendencies and become hard. Until they become marines they will be "grabastic pieces of amphibian shit" and "ladies." He associates femininity with death and failure in battle.

> It is your killer instinct which must be harnessed if you are to survive in combat. Your rifle is only a tool. It is a hard heart that kills. If your killer instincts are not clean and strong, you will hesitate at the moment of truth. You will not kill. You will become dead marines. And then you will be in a world of shit. Because marines are not allowed to die without permission. Do you maggots understand?

Hartman's insistence that "it is a hard heart that kills," pushes the recruits into a crisis of identity as they struggle to be "reborn hard" as men.

Hartman makes Leonard Lawrence (Vincent D'Onofrio)—whom he re-names Gomer Pyle after the star of a sixties' sitcom set in a boot camp—for this crisis and struggle. Leonard is the least likely marine amongst the recruits. When Hartman abuses him during the opening monologue—calling him a "disgusting fatbody," exclaiming that he is so ugly he "ought to be a modern-art masterpiece," and associating his name with T.E. Lawrence, another effeminate soldier—Leonard can only smile like a child. Enraged, Hartman forces Pyle to choke himself on Hartman's outstretched hand. He refutes the paternalistic figure of the drill sergeant who only cares for the well-being of his men (the type played by John Wayne in *The Sands of Iwo Jima*, Jack Webb in *The DI*, Elias in *Platoon*, Louis Gossett Jr. in *An Officer and a Gentleman* and Ermey himself in *The Boys in Company C*, *The Siege of Firebase Gloria*, and *Purple Hearts*). Such paternalism suggests softness of heart, and that means death for a marine

Pyle's inability to be "reborn hard" eventually makes him the scapegoat for the entire platoon of "ladies" who need to be reborn. His insistent adolescent femininity and need for maternalistic care, which he can not receive amongst these ladies who want to be men, becomes the catalyst by which the ladies achieve their redemption within the corps. In a night barrack scene, the men ritually beat Private Pyle. In the blue-light of night in the barracks, they arise from their bunks, bind their victim by his bedclothes, and pass quietly by the writhing body to beat it with bars of soap wrapped in towels. The last to pass is Joker (Matthew Modine), who had treated Pyle with patience and kindness and now resists participation. The others insist, and finally Joker joins the ritual, pounding on the whimpering body six times before passing on. "It's only a dream," the last recruit warns Pyle before slipping away, and indeed the entire sequence has a dream-like quality to it with the menacing figures gliding silently through the darkness to where their victim lies sleeping. Afterward, Pyle's infantile behavior ceases; Hartman congratulates him on being "born again hard," and the platoon quickly moves to successful completion of their training and soon earn the right to be called men.

The platoon had suffered from a crisis of gender difference; Hartman had obscured their masculinity when he labeled them "ladies." Pyle is fat and weak (D'Onofrio gained over seventy pounds for the part), with a baby-face that responds positively to any sort of attention, including both Hartman's abuse and Joker's tender instruction, and this makes him a symbol of both the feminine side of the men and their infantile desire for maternal care. He exists outside the Marine Corps' defined group as an insistent reminder of the limits of their society and the fragility of its borders. "You have to do it," the Texan insists when Joker hesitates, and Joker yields to the implied threat that if he does not join the ritual he will have to join Pyle.

The result of the persecution is a general reconciliation amongst the platoon. The ritualized beating of Pyle has proved to them that the part of themselves he represents can be beaten. The men have acted out the myth propounded by Hartman and the Marine Corps, and by so doing have convinced themselves of its truth. They have finally achieved the discipline and unity of purpose needed to qualify them as men and Marines. The ritual beating of the feminine recruit has effectively purged them of their feminine natures and dependencies; they have achieved "the hard heart that kills."

Pyle's final act at Paris Island assures the community Hartman established: in the barracks head, again at night, Pyle shoots first Hartman, the recruits' last link to dependency, and then himself. By shooting Hartman, Pyle severs the last link between the newly made marines and their patriarch. His suicide, on the other hand, marks his elevation in their culture; he will later be re-incarnated in the brutal Animal Mother (Adam Baldwin) who resembles him physically—especially during the shooting of the Viet Cong sniper—and who wears the words "I am become death" on his helmet.

The shooting of the sniper in the film's final sequence is reminiscent of the earlier scapegoat scenes, although the place has changed from Paris Island to the Vietnamese city of Hue during the 1968 Tet offensive. Joker, now a reporter for *Stars and Stripes*, and a photographer named Rafterman (Kevyn Major-Howard) are traveling with a squad through the rubble of the city when a sniper pins them down. One soldier goes to scout the area and the sniper wounds him in the leg. As his buddies watch, the sniper continues to pick off pieces of the downed man and draws two more marines into the line of fire. Finally Animal Mother locates the source of fire and leads a raid on it. Joker and the photographer are the first to find their tormentor, who is unexpectedly revealed as a woman. Joker's gun jams at the moment of confrontation, but Rafterman manages to shoot her down; it is his first confirmed hit and leaves him jubilant.

He has failed to kill efficiently, however, and she lies dying on the floor, moaning or praying in Vietnamese. (Despite the training the recruits got at Paris Island, they remain poor soldiers rather than the killing machines Hartman had hoped to create.) The squad gathers around her in curiosity and awe. Joker's insistence that they can not leave her in agony elicits an angry response from Animal Mother. "You're fresh out of friends around here," he tells the Joker, and Joker's response is to kill the sniper with his handgun. He thus confirms his place in the squad and can join them as they march into the gathering dusk, singing an American anthem: "The Mickey Mouse Theme Song." Joker comments in voice-over:

> We have nailed our names in the pages of history enough for today. We hump down to the Perfume River to set in for the night. My thoughts drift back to erect-nipple wet dreams about Mary Jane Rottencrotch and the great homecoming fuck fantasy. I am so happy that I am alive, in one piece, and

short. I am in a world of shit. Yes. But I am alive. And I am not afraid.

Apart from Kubrick and DePalma, however filmmakers have been wary of casting aspersions on combat and soldiers. Most combat films offer the grunts' point of view and grant them honor and humanity. The cruelest soldiers are generally cast as villains. In *Eye of the Eagle* (1986), for instance, the enemy is a group of deserters who are ravaging the Nam for their own ends. If the hero is an officer, as in *Platoon Leader* and *The Iron Triangle* (1989), he fights alongside his men and earns their respect. Otherwise, officers are the enemy, as in *Eye of the Eagle II* (1988), in which a cowardly lieutenant leads his platoon to disaster, or *The Lost Idol* (1988) in which the officer massacres his squad to steal a priceless artifact. *The Iron Triangle*'s embrace of the grunt includes even the Viet Cong foot soldier as it adapts a captured Viet Cong diary to the screen. *BAT-21* took the convention so far as to have a pilot shot down and finally see the War from the ground—that is, from the grunt's perspective.

There was some question what the grunt's point of view was. The liberal-humanist view of *Platoon* provided one extreme; *The Siege of Firebase Gloria* provided another. While Stone's grunts are semi-mythical, apolitical warriors, their points of view limited to their immediate experience, the grunt in *Siege* is knowledgeable about the War and committed to the struggle for a free Viet Nam. Sergeant Hafner is surprisingly well informed about the course of the War and politics behind it. He predicts the Tet Offensive and in a voice-over narration explains that it is part of a North Vietnamese plot to destroy the Viet Cong and take over control of the War. Both narratives justify the deeds of the grunts, however. For Stone and the humanists, their brutality was a reaction to the brutality of their surroundings; for Hafner and the proponents of *realpolitik*, the grunts had to be hard and merciless to beat an enemy that put no limits on warfare.

Winning the War

Although they seldom managed to come to grips with the world of Viet Nam or the consequences of the War for either America or Southeast Asia, the Vietnam combat films did strive for a high level of experiential realism and accuracy regarding the subject of combat, and many veterans have attested to their success. There was one major exception to this, a group of films that were briefly successful in the middle of the eighties (one of them being amongst the most successful films of all time). These films insisted that the War was not over, that it could still be re-fought and won. They re-imagined Vietnam and combat as a personal proving ground for the great masculine America. Their action took place after the War had ended, and their heroes returned to the Land of Nam with a new, unmistakable goal: the rescue of American POWs. These MIA/POW films, which insist that American service men remain in Southeast Asia, show American warriors fighting a different Vietnam War, one freed of bureaucratic and political constraints, one in which the American warrior returns to his roots as a guerrilla fighter and delivers a symbolically crushing—if not decisive because struck in hindsight—blow. Instead of closing the book on the War, these films offer the hope of victory: the raid on the POW camp, the centerpiece of these films, is always successful and the hero can finally complete his mission.

The MIA soldiers, Americans listed as missing in action but believed to be held as prisoners of war, continue to be among the War's most enduring legacies. According to a 1991 Wall Street Journal/NBC News poll, 69% of Americans believe that the

Vietnamese still hold American soldiers prisoner (Franklin 45).
The evidence for their presence in Cambodia, Laos, and Viet Nam
is mostly circumstantial, but it has gathered the force of legend
for many people, so that it is politically inexpedient for any politician to unequivocally deny their existence. The producer of a
Sixty Minutes television article on the subject describes the evidence in her book, *Kiss the Boys Goodby: How the United States
Betrayed Its Own POWs in Vietnam.*

> Hundreds of refugees reported seeing American prisoners in
> all parts of Communist Southeast Asia in the early postwar
> years. Some of those refugees had spent time in prison with
> Americans. A few of them took their responsibility to report
> what they had seen seriously enough to testify under oath be-
> fore congressional committees. Analysts at the Pentagon's
> Defense Intelligence Agency (DIA), often took seriously one
> part of a witness' testimony only to debunk that part having
> to do with live men. For example, in the early eighties a for-
> mer Vietnamese colonel of Chinese descent testified in dis-
> guise before a congressional committee about a warehouse of
> remains of over four hundred Americans in the heart of Ha-
> noi. He explained the Vietnamese would cold-heartedly pull
> out some of those remains and return them to the United
> States when diplomatic concessions were required. The colo-
> nel, known as "The Mortician," passed lie-detector tests, and
> his story about the remains became part of DIA formal history
> (Jensen-Stevenson 9).

According to *Kiss the Boys Goodby,* Nixon had promised
4.5 billion dollars in aid to Viet Nam as part of the American
Peace Agreement pledge "to contribute to healing the wounds of
war and to post war reconstruction." Congress refused to honor
the promise, and Viet Nam kept the prisoners as "pearls" with
which to bargain in future negotiations. The story provides a neat
metaphor for both America's defeat in the War and the government's culpability and callous indifference to its lost or wounded
soldiers. It also ascribes a frightening amount of cruelty and de-
ceitfulness in the Vietnamese, a race that would hold up to 2,500
Americans hostage for twenty and more years merely as bargain-
ing chips. The racism becomes scarcely clear in anecdotes like the

one about the Mortician pulling corpses from a warehouse to meet an order.

The roots of the story lie in the brutalities suffered by American prisoners of war during the war years. The Hanoi government used America's failure to declare war on Viet Nam as an excuse to treat the prisoners as criminals rather than POWs protected by the Geneva Convention. Most accounts of the treatment the soldiers received describe it as cruel and brutal. (It was in part this brutality that persuaded Congress to withhold the reparations.) *The Hanoi Hilton* provides a cinematic treatment of life in one of the POW prisons, Hanoi's Hoa Lo Prison (the Hanoi Hilton of the title).

Pilot Patrick Williamson (Michael Moriarty) is shot down in 1964 and must endure nine years of solitary confinement, torture, betrayal by fellow Americans (including a famous actress, apparently modeled on Jane Fonda, who visits the prison and believes the lies which the Vietnamese tell her but not the facts told by the prisoners), and the antagonism of the prison's commandant, Cat (Aki Aleong), who insists on breaking the spirit of each of the prisoners. As in the World War II POW film, this need to break the Americans' spirit, and the Americans' stoic resistance, form the central conflict of the film. The torture sessions break all the Americans physically, but Cat never weakens their spirit. They maintain a loyal brotherhood throughout the long years, and in the end Williamson can look at Cat and say, "We won."

The question of why Cat should have felt it so imperative to break these men that he allows it to become a personal struggle between himself and Williamson never rises to the surface. The film treats it as a fact of nature, a narrative convention with its roots in World War II POW films and in traditional notions of oriental pride and "face." It is so vital, however, that Cuba sends a specialist to help in the task—as though a communist conspiracy lay behind the need to break these men down. If so, their proudly victorious departure from the prison at the film's end implies not just a victory over the Vietnamese, but a victory over the forces of communism in general.

Like the subjects of America's colonial captivity narratives, these POWs are captives in a wilderness under the control of a savage race and have no resources to rely upon beyond their own resolve and strength of will. These are the same resources that save the men at Firebase Gloria when the Viet Cong hordes surround it; they are the resources that save Mike, Nicky, and Steven when they are forced to play Russian roulette; even John Wayne's defense of Fort Dodge in *The Green Berets* depended finally on that strength of will. And that strength is rewarded every time. Eventually the Air Cav arrives, the bullet is not in the chamber—-or, in the case of *The Hanoi Hilton,* the War ends and the men are released.

This emphasis on strength of purpose suggests that it was a failure of nerve that lost the War for America. Since destiny rewards strength of will with victory, and the soldier maintained their will, someone must have betrayed the cause. Either destiny reneged on the bargain or some party to the American cause, not the soldier, failed in its resolve. This is the cry of John Rambo, the outcast veteran, at the end of *First Blood* (1983), "I do what I have to do to win, but somebody won't let us win," and it is the accusation behind his question at the opening of *Rambo: First Blood Part II* (1985), "Do we get to win this time?"

The Rambo series of films (which at present concludes with *Rambo III* (1988), though rumors have suggested a fourth installment in which Rambo fights an ecological battle) have been the most successful of all the Vietnam War films. Part two is amongst the most commercially successful of all American feature films. Released shortly after Viet Nam's tenth year victory celebration, *Rambo* earned the third highest first week gross of any film before it. The trilogy follows the career of a former Green Beret and Congressional Medal of Honor winner. He was the Vietnam soldier par excellence; "the best I ever trained," his mentor Colonel Trautman (Richard Crenna) says of him. In *First Blood,* he is the epitome of the wounded veteran: a drifter, alienated by a society that used him and now wishes to forget him, harboring a deep need to balance the scales of justice. His desperate cry at the film's end hints at the frustration that drives him to destroy a town when it thrusts him away instead of honoring him as he deserves.

At the film's conclusion, however, this town that fought Rambo is in flames and its leader lies wounded and at Rambo's mercy; yet the Vietnam veteran still loses. He stands alone in the police station, wounded but undeterred; outside, the state police and the National Guard wait to kill him. (The hero of *Billy Jack* faces a similar situation at the end of that film, and both situations resolve themselves the same way: a mothering figure [Billy's girlfriend, Rambo's mentor] enters the building to talk the fugitive into yielding peacefully.) Rambo kept his part of the bargain; he kept his will and resolve through the worst of torments. Yet victory remains elusive. Who is to blame, he wants to know; who is the "someone" that would not let him win in the War and who still obstinately prevents his victory?

John Rambo could not know it as he stood victorious but helpless, but the answer to that question, and his own path to final victory, had already been forged by a man named Bo Gritz. In November 1982, Former Lieutenant Colonel James (Bo) Gritz led a force of fifteen Laotions and three Americans on a mission to rescue American POWs believed to be held in Laos. The force was ambushed shortly after crossing the border, and one American was captured (he was reportedly held for $17,000 ransom). The raid was funded by millionaire (and future presidential candidate) H. Ross Perot and film stars William Shatner and Clint Eastwood (the latter two hoping for the movie rights). The U.S. State Department officially condemned the raid as harmful to government efforts to negotiate the return of any prisoners of war or their remains, though reportedly President Reagan supported the raid and sent Gritz a message in Thailand: "If you bring out one U.S. POW, I will start World War III to get the rest out" (Franklin 72).

The raid failed, Reagan did not start WW III, and neither Shatner nor Eastwood made the film, but the story did reach cinemas, albeit with considerable license (they get to win this time), in the form of *Uncommon Valor* (1983). This version begins in Vietnam with the desperate evacuation of a platoon under heavy fire. Several members of the squad are left behind, including Frank Rhodes, who will be the subject of the subsequent rescue mission. The scene is shot in soft-focus and slow motion. From within the helicopter the camera looks out at the young soldier, encumbered with a wounded buddy whom he carries on his back, reaching upward in desperation as the helicopter is forced to fly away. Steven Fore suggests that the primary motivation for all the film's subsequent action can be understood through the style of this first scene.

> Past and present questions of politics and morality are cloaked, deflected as the viewer is encouraged to engage the film's images on a purely personal, emotive level; it is implied here that the international social turmoil created by the war (and especially by America's role in it) is insignificant next to the personal turmoil caused by the loss of a friend (an American friend) (27).

This scene, and those immediately following it that show Frank's father searching for his son, define the motive for the coming raid as a personal one. Most of the men who go to rescue Frank were on the helicopter that left him, and it is Frank's father, Jason Rhodes (Gene Hackman), who recruits them. None of these vets has conquered the effects of the War; one is a beach bum, another an artist who sculpts warped figures of twisted metal; another is a mental patient who has been wandering the country with a live hand-grenade around his neck. All of them respond positively to Rhodes' request that they join him on a return to Southeast Asia. Rhodes realizes that each of them suffers from survivor's guilt combined with surpressed anger at having been unable to finish the job. Their journey back into the War will offer them a chance to resolve both needs. Rhodes expresses the stakes baldly in his pre-mission speech.

> You and I know that the books are still in the red. And the politicians know, too, the same politicians who never lost a single son in Vietnam, not one. Now they say we've been negotiating for ten years. Well, the other side's not buying, and while the politicians sit on their asses I'm gonna ask you to lay yours on the line—again—because, gentlemen, we are the only hope those POWs have. So we're going back there, and this time, this time nobody can dispute the rightness of what we're doing.

This time the issues will be simpler. It will be a soldier against his enemy; there will be no "somebody" to prevent their victory because Rhodes has identified who those somebodies are and eliminated them from the strategy. The vigilante nature of Rhodes' plan means he will act outside the sphere of the established authority: the government—the group that frowned on Bo Gritz's raid and reneged on the money for the MIAs. Like other vigilantes, this squad will accomplish by illegitimate means what the legitimate groups could not—not a military victory but a personal vindication of the soldier's valor and the rescue of their desperate MIA brethren.

Chuck Norris had adapted the POW rescue mission for his 1979 film *Good Guys Wear Black,* using the POW raid to ignite the main action. In his 1980s' saga of Colonel James Braddock, he made the mission the central action. Norris plays Colonel Braddock, a veteran who stands as living proof that MIAs are alive in captivity. He and a group of fellow POWs escaped from a Vietnamese prison camp seven years after the end of the War. Now he agitates in America for the release of the rest of the Americans in Southeast Asia. His story unfolds in two films, *Missing in Action* (1984) and *Missing in Action II: The Beginning* (1985). The third film in the series, *Braddock: Missing in Action III* (1988), abandons the original storyline; now Braddock is a free man in 1975, fleeing Saigon with his Vietnamese wife, and the MIAs are replaced with Amerasian children.

While *Uncommon Valor* might be classified as a combat film, including bootcamp scenes and a military raid, the *MIA* films are strictly within the realm of the vigilante story. Braddock works alone (apart from the incidental aid of a sidekick) to make right what the government cannot or will not repair. Unlike the band of alienated misfits Rhodes gathers, Braddock is a man with a firm sense of purpose and the drive to see that purpose achieved. These very masculine traits contrast with the distinctly feminine traits of Braddock's adversaries. A hapless negotiator who is willing to believe any lie the Vietnamese tell him leads an American government mission to investigate the possibility that MIAs remain alive in Viet Nam. The negotiator's female aide, Fitzgerald (Leonore Kasdorf) makes a few vain attempts to control Braddock, but he ignores her until he needs an alibi for a night's adventure, at which point he rips off her clothes, throws her on a bed, and forces her to lie to the investigating Vietnamese. Braddock invades the bedroom of the chief Vietnamese negotiator as boldly as he does Fitzgerald's, finds him sleeping in lace and pink satin bedclothes, and demands information with a knife to his throat. In effect, the veteran is the only masculine figure at the negotiations, and he is the only one who achieves what he is after.

The second film in the series (a prequel filmed at the same time and intended to be released first) is closer in conception to *The Hanoi Hilton* than *Uncommon Valor* as it details the hardships that Braddock and his fellow POWs underwent in their captivity. Again, it is the resolute will of the white American male that allows them to survive and eventually vanquish their less steadfast, non-white foe. The evil commandant, Colonel Yin (Soon-Teck Oh) is a more savage incarnation of *The Hanoi Hilton*'s Cat, and the contest of wills between the men and their captors erupts into physical violence and an escape.

Critics have frequently pointed out that these films obscure the issues of the War with the emotional tissue of guilt over America's treatment of its soldiers; but the films obscure even that treatment. They replace the problem (neglected veterans) with the metaphor (MIAs). Bringing the boys back home becomes the issue instead of how to treat them once they are here. *MIA III* provides a good example of this obfuscating tendency. The film concludes with a smiling Amerasian child leaving Viet Nam behind her forever while the soundtrack sings in praise of freedom; a note before the final credits announces the number of Amerasian children that remain "trapped in Vietnam." Of course, the problem is not that the children are trapped there, it is that their American fathers left them there and never returned for them. The film does not address where this smiling child will go once she crosses the bridge into Thailand.

An interesting variation on the MIA theme appears in *P.O.W.: The Escape* (1986). The action this time begins a few days before the end of the War. Colonel Cooper (David Carradine) is captured while on a mission to rescue POWs. (The U.S. military did stage such a raid on Son Tay Prison near the end of the War; it failed because the Vietnamese had cleared the camp shortly before.) The commandant of the prison camp, however, has a wife in Miami and a chest of valuables stolen from American soldiers and he agrees to lead the Americans to safety in return for passage to America! The adventures of the soldiers as they travel through North Viet Nam is reminiscent of nothing so much as a World War II escape film; they perform acts of sabotage, stop in local taverns, and come to the support of an outpost that is being overrun. The realities of the landscape and of history are randomly sacrificed to the movement of the story.

Rambo: First Blood Part II follows the lead of these films in its strategy to revitalize its wounded veteran. Rambo concluded *First Blood* in tears, wrapped in his mentor's overcoat to be turned over to the police. His efforts to resist ostracism and alienation had resulted in nothing more than the destruction of a town. In the sequel it becomes clear why any community he tried to enter would be destroyed. John Rambo is a hero of mythical proportions and potency; his attempt to reenter American society was like a male god attempting to copulate with a human only to have her burst into flame.

The film begins with an explosion that rocks a mountain; when the dust settles, Rambo stands revealed. Stallone honed his physique to such an extreme before the filming that he appears as solid as the rock he pounds in the federal work prison. The government sends him a messenger (his mentor Colonel Trautman again) and he exchanges this elemental landscape of rock and fire for the lush greenery of Vietnam. His helicopter circles around an immense Buddha; upon landing he is greeted as "the chosen one," and although the words are meant as a jest, it soon becomes obvious that the jester spoke more truth than he new. For as Rambo enters deeper into his domain ("What you choose to call Hell, he calls home," Trautman tells the congressman running the operation), he melds more completely into the landscape until it becomes impossible for the audience or his enemies to distinguish him from the mud, the water, or the trees.

Rambo's mistake in America had been that he tried to deny what he was—a great white masculine god. His attempts at passivity, even at passive resistance, were doomed to failure because they were denials. His return to Vietnam and to his mission (the rescue of his fellow soldiers) is an acceptance of his divinity. In America he cried out "somebody won't let me win." In Vietnam, no one can effect the outcome. Victory or defeat is, as Trautman says, indeed up to him.

Rambo is the masculine ego personified, and the Land of Nam becomes the land of the masculine unbound. Images of the hero's body dominate the film. The erotic subtext is manifest in the camera's frequent pans across the hard, sweaty muscles that bulge from his arms and chest. (Several pornographic remakes have been made, with titles like *Bimbo* and *Rambone*.) This is a man-ideal to be worshipped by women and by men, for Rambo is more than just a hunk of perfectly conditioned flesh. Rambo is a warrior who lives war. "I've always thought the mind was the best weapon," he explains, but by mind he means instinct. Rambo never thinks or plans. He acts swiftly and surely. He does not stop to measure success or progress—Murdoch, the effeminate bureaucrat, does that with his computers; Rambo just fights until the mission is completed.

He is the fulfillment of the figure Mike aspired to before experiencing the Nam. He is a descendent of Kurtz, the god of the Montagnards—only Kurtz went native and Rambo remains American. He balances the "conscious stricken Hector" of Elias and the "angry Achilles" of Barnes. He has the hard heart that kills but without the fear which that hardness hides in Joker, Pyle, and Hartman. He replaces the old deity, John Wayne; the "John Wayne thing" becomes "the Rambo thing." He achieves, finally, what these figures had attempted to do and failed; he reestablishes the old order, bringing the World to the Nam. The successful quest eliminates the need for questing by eliminating the romance landscape. The Americans are the freedom fighters again. He steals the American wilderness tactics back from the Vietnamese, revealing the duplicity of the enemy that tried to be American but in reality, Rambo shows us, was the Japanese of an earlier war.

Rambo III brings this warrior to the world arena. The specter of Vietnam had kept America from marching confidently into the World's troublespots. Now Rambo can confidently stride into the Afghanistan War and assume his role as protector of the little guy; at last he gets to fight with the rebels against the domineering world power. In a 1985 interview, Stallone summarized the myth/history Rambo offered.

> They just pushed ... until finally the giant said, "wait a minute. I'm big and strong, but I haven't done anything that's *that* atrocious.... There's nothing wrong with being fit and strong and powerful and, if necessary, to flex some muscle." We're back to geopolitics on an even keel. We're not coming in there quaking, "What do I do?" We're coming in as an equal. We're now in the proper weight class (Goldman 62).

This narrative puts America and its military in the role of the innocent victims who are finally, almost reluctantly, reclaiming their proper status as both giants and equals in the geopolitical world.

Other Lands of Nam

In the eighties, the grunt's view of the War had a privileged status in America. *Platoon* went furthest to establish what that view was, but numerous other combat films fleshed out the picture. This is not an uncommon feature of combat films; since the soldier is the one doing the fighting, he is the natural center of attention. What is uncommon in Vietnam combat films is the almost total isolation of the soldier from the rest of the military mission in the country—the nurses, doctors, officers, MPs, journalists, entertainers and bureaucrats without whom it is impossible to have a war, as well as the members of the other armed services—the sailors and pilots. Contact with these non-combatants has always been a vital part of the war film, providing character depth and variety of incident. The Vietnam War film, in contrast, usually kept the soldiers to themselves, as if they lived in a separate Nam.

Saigon, capital of South Viet Nam, appears in several films, almost invariably as a dingy urban landscape lit by broken neon lights, a seedy pleasure city for grunts seeking sex. A few films kept almost entirely to Saigon, most notably *Good Morning, Vietnam, Saigon Commandos* (1987), and *Off Limits* (1988). In *Good Morning, Vietnam,* Saigon appears at first to be a clean, well-lighted place full of beautiful women in immaculate white robes, but as Adrian Cronauer (Robin Williams) learns more about the War's effect on the city, he discovers darker streets filled with toothless old men and young Viet Cong saboteurs. *Saigon Commandos* and *Off Limits* are both cop films set in Vietnam. "Saigon Commandos" was a nickname for the military police in Saigon. Contrary to Hollywood tradition, however, these

MPs have more to do than arresting drunken GIs. In the Vietnam War, the MPs are waging a war of their own—not against the Viet Cong like everybody else, but against America's South Vietnamese allies who are using the War as an opportunity to expand the drug trade. *Off Limits* is another straightforward detective film, with the two detectives (Willem Dafoe and Gregory Hines) from the Criminal Investigations Detachment (CID) searching for a serial killer of prostitutes. Their immediate suspicions are that one of the many corrupt Vietnamese officials must be the killer, but they discover to their shock and dismay that it was their own commanding officer killing women who bore Amerasian children.

The press appear in many of the combat films, invariably to disadvantage. The first was probably John Wayne's foil Beckworth in *The Green Berets;* certainly his un-earned, liberal cynicism sets the standard. In *Hamburger Hill* the battle weary grunts tell the neatly pressed television reporter that he has no right to be in Vietnam, and he hangs his head in shame. In *The Siege of Firebase Gloria* the representative of the press is a drugged hippie who mocks the soldiers' efforts until the sergeant forces him to exchange his cameras for a gun and join the defense. Joker, the reporter for *Stars and Stripes* in *Full Metal Jacket,* hides behind sarcastic humor, but clearly wants the other grunts to accept him and is willing to sacrifice any convictions necessary. The honest, accurate, worthy journalist is extremely rare. Even Robin Williams as Adrian Cronauer, although well liked by the grunts, never manages to report the facts of the War. Apart from that film and an unsuccessful television pilot, *Shooter* (1988), the only film to take the journalists' side was the British *The Killing Fields*—and that was set in Cambodia, not Viet Nam.

The medical community generally did better than the journalists, despite being the subject of what might qualify as the most ridiculous Vietnam War film made to date. Regardless of its title, *Purple Hearts* (1984) has nothing to do with the medal a soldier receives when wounded (although the film is dedicated to the 347,309 purple heart winners in the War). The hearts in question are those of a young medic (Ken Wahl) and the nurse (Cheryl Ladd) whom he chases around such places as Saigon and Khe Sanh.

Wahl's gifted young doctor earns the respect of the soldiers because he seems to be willing to risk his life for them (they don't know about the nurse), and other doctors earn similar status by their willingness to serve the grunt. In contrast, the doctor in *The Siege of Firebase Gloria* earns the scorn of the soldiers because of her compassion for the enemy. Nurses usually earned the grunts' respect just by being in-country. *China Beach* (which first appeared in 1988 and was one of the most successful television series about the War) followed the daily life of the hospital and beach at the Viet Nam recreation center the grunts called China Beach. Many of the main characters in the series were women, and the stories relied on their relationships with the wounded and weary grunts who passed through their lives. For its final season, it intercut stories of life at China Beach with stories about the characters returning from the War, and followed one child search- ing for a mother who bore her in Viet Nam and then abandoned her.

The serial nature of a television program allowed a show like *China Beach* to treat many aspects of the War, if only a few of them in any depth, but the television format also enforces strict limitations on scriptwriters. *Tour of Duty* suffered especially from these limits. Inspired by *Platoon,* it began in 1987 by following a platoon's life in the bush. To expand the audience, however, the grunts had to have a home base from where they could meet women (nurses, reporters, officers), and so eventually they moved to a base camp and went on daily patrols. To justify the format the producers finally had to assign the platoon to the controversial Phoenix Project, turning the boys into assassins. That *Tour of Duty* only lasted a few years was due in part to the fact that the original tour of duty only lasted a year; after a season or two on the series, most of the popular characters had to die, go MIA, or end their tours and be sent home.

The cable network Home Box Office provided two of the more ambitious television shows on the War. One of these is a series called *Vietnam War Story,* which first appeared in 1987. It consists of half-hour stories about the War or the veterans. The other *Dear America: Letters Home from Vietnam* (1988), is one of the most effecting documentaries of the War. Scenes from

Vietnam accompany various popular actors reading letters that soldiers had sent home from the War. The effect is similar to that of seeing the personal tokens which family and friends have left by the Vietnam Veterans Memorial.

The nineties have seen two more areas of conflict open up to Hollywood. The first was the CIA's involvement and the secret war in Laos. *Air America* (1990) was based on Christopher Robbins' nonfiction book of the same name that described how the CIA flew arms to the fighters and returned to the airfield loaded with opium. In the film the CIA uses the opium money to finance its secret war, a claim Robbins never makes in his book. The film's accusations caused a minor flurry in the newspapers on its release, a flurry that died away as quickly as the film died at the box office. The other non-grunt combat film to arrive was *Flight of the Intruder* (1991), set aboard an aircraft carrier and following the adventures of some jet pilots who crash in the jungle and must find their way to safety. Essentially this is the same plot that was being used in the late fifties and early sixties; the main difference is that these downed pilots were making an unauthorized attack on Hanoi.

A popular topic among filmmakers was women and children, especially Amerasian children and their mothers left behind by American servicemen. *The Children of An Lac,* a 1980 television movie, told the story of Ina Balin and two other women who tried to evacuate a hundred Vietnamese orphans just before the fall of Saigon. *Don't Cry It's Only Thunder* (1982) gave a disreputable grunt a chance to redeem himself when a dying buddy forces him to promise to help the nuns at the local orphanage. Orphans and nuns also cropped up frequently in both the Vietnam television series. Colonel Braddock's final adventure in *Braddock: Missing in Action III* sends him back to Vietnam to rescue a son he did not know he had. Not content with just that feat, however, he also delivers a crowd of other Amerasian children from the clutches of the evil Communists. Braddock was not the only veteran to return and make amends to a deserted progeny. In *Green Eyes* (1976), Paul Winfield returned to Vietnam in search of *his* child, whom he could identify only by the unusual (for a Vietnamese child) color of his eyes. In 1985 *The Lady from Yesterday* reversed the

process and Tina Chen came to the States in search of the soldier
who had fathered *her* child.

Perhaps the most notably missing element in the American
Vietnam War film has been Viet Nam itself as a cultural entity.
Hollywood's emphasis on the soldier's story only partly explains
this omission, since that explanation assumes that the soldiers had
no interest in either the country where they were fighting and
dying or the history and reason for their fight. The material in oral
histories of the War shows that this was not altogether so, although many combat films presented it as a fact. Interestingly,
Apocalypse Now, in which Francis Coppola attempted to incorporate the whole of the War, originally contained a scene in a
French plantation, an important reference to the colonial history
of Viet Nam. Coppola filmed the scene (and the filming is included in *Hearts of Darkness,* the documentary about the film's
production) but did not include it in the finished product.

Several factors other than the grunts' presumed ignorance,
however, have obscured the issues behind the War—both during
the war years and later. One of these was the obsession with
Communism and the perceived threat to Southeast Asia, the famous Domino Theory that disregarded centuries of Vietnamese
history and conflict. Another factor, probably equally influential,
was the liberal establishment's conviction that the Communist
menace was an empty specter. Add to these contending factions
the press' attempt to make sense of the conflict, the antiwar
movement's general condemnation of American efforts, as well as
the government's failed attempts to wage the War cheaply and
quietly, and the result is a war without a generally accepted past
and a country that Americans knew only as the site of a war. After that war, America refused to recognize Viet Nam as victorious
or as a legitimate nation, and the government and people tried to
put the entire miserable experience behind them. The veterans
maintained enough popular sentiment to inspire films about themselves, but Viet Nam had few people on its side.

Still, a few films did try to provide some historical and cultural background. One of these was *The Iron Triangle.* It claims
to be based on a captured Viet Cong diary, and it tells the story of
an American officer and a Viet Cong guerrilla who learn that as

soldiers they have more in common then either realized. The dedi-
cated guerrilla (Liem Whatley) captures an American captain
(Beau Bridges) who speaks Vietnamese, and then must defend his
prize from an ambitious, corrupt Hanoi party member. Like the
Viet Cong regiment in *The Siege of Firebase Gloria*, the Viet
Cong force described here resembles nothing so much as an
American fighting group. Apart from cosmetic differences involv-
ing recreation and accent, the main difference is that the Viet
Cong lack the American firepower and must operate in hiding.
Even the film's subplot—the conflict between the party official
and the guerrilla—mirrors the common conflict in Vietnam War
films between the grunts and their officers.

Whatley portrays the young Viet Cong soldier Ho as a sensi-
tive, dedicated soldier driven to be a guerrilla when the South
Vietnamese government murders his father. During the film, however, he discovers that his chosen side is no more humane than his
chosen enemy. He constantly conflicts with the "ambitious and
stupid" party official over captured weapons, prisoners, and
glory. It is the party official, linked with Hanoi more than to the
guerrillas, who mistreats or orders the mistreatment of prisoners,
who kills a fellow soldier to further his own ambition, and who
relishes his chances to torture and kill the helpless. He employs
the propaganda narratives of the Hanoi government to justify his
own brutality, repeatedly threatening his rival with retribution
from the party. Ho, on the other hand, balks at killing a propagan-
dizing South Vietnamese woman, falls in love, and remains behind at the final attack to heroically guard the retreat. *The Iron
Triangle*'s description of this guerrilla and his motives does little
more than assume that all soldiers are alike and apolitical. Ho's
motives are personal and his commitment to Hanoi weaker than
his commitment to friends and fellow soldiers. The anti-American
propaganda and the need for revenge were not enough to keep him
committed even before he met his American captive. The filmmaker's good-natured desire to see the enemy as being just like us
strongly colored his portrait.

Good Morning, Vietnam also addresses these limits to
America's perceptions of the effect and character of the War and
Viet Nam. Robin Williams plays Adrian Cronauer, a popular

disk-jockey on Armed Forces Radio during the War who enters into the social life of Saigon and befriends a Vietnamese brother and sister. The highlights of the film are Cronauer's radio shows. Williams, originally an improvisational comic, improvised much of the dialogue in these scenes in which he makes fun of everything from Nixon ("We'd all like to hear your Mister Ed imitation.") to Ho Chi Minh ("Ho Chi Minh and Colonel Sanders really the same person? You be the judge.") to the self-immolations of the Buddhist priests ("It's so hot I saw one of those little guys with the orange robes burst into flame!"). Among the most common referents in this monologue is *The Wizard of Oz* ("It's the Wicked Witch of the West—it's Hanoi Hannah!"). In his final broadcast, played as his plane departs, he quips "The ruby slippers. Put them on and say 'there's no place like home.'"

The references begin as part of his satire of the War and life in Vietnam. He also compares the country to *The Twilight Zone* ("You have entered—The Demilitarized Zone"). His activity in the country, however, belies this romantic, a-temporal, a-cultural other-world. He insists on conversing with the local people, trying their food, visiting them in their villages, and courting a young Vietnamese woman (Chintaro Sukapatana) through Vietnamese customs (on their one date ten members of her family accompany them). His best friend in the country is a Vietnamese youth, Tuan (Tung Thanh Tran), who introduces him to the culture.

Cronauer lacks American ambition and arrogance, and he treats the local population without condescension. He talks with them rather than to them; a sign that he thinks of them as equals is his willingness to exchanges insults with them. The filmmakers go out of their way to portray this humanitarian, egalitarian vision of Cronauer: in one scene he attempts to break the racial barrier in a GI bar, and in another he visits Tuan's village, allowing himself to be guided into the non-American Viet Nam. In the latter scene, the muted soundtrack shifts the emphasis from the very vocal Cronauer to the pastoral culture of which he is a guest.

His humanitarian vision ultimately reveals itself as utopian, however. Despite his liberal attitude, he is an outsider like Dorothy in Oz, and though he enters the country with egalitarian assumptions, he also carries with him his preconceptions. He insists on believing that he can separate himself from the military force of which he is a part. He expects personal friendship to transcend the social and political situation in the country, and he feels betrayed when it does not. Tuan, he learns, is a Viet Cong terrorist. The news upsets his romantic vision of the country and he races away to confront his friend in a section of Saigon he had not entered before. Previously the city had appeared as a clean, well-lighted place where beautiful young women in white ao-dais walk along verdant riverbanks. Now Tuan's sister leads him down a squalid alley where dirty figures peer out curiously through the smoke and shadows. He sees Tuan conferring with a group of Viet Cong at the end of the alley and chases him down another blind lane to accuse him of betrayal.

> You were my friend. I trusted you—I fought to get you into
> that bar and then you blow the place up! Listen. I gave you
> my friendship and my trust. Now they tell me that my best
> friend is the god damned enemy.

The complaint is that of the well-intentioned liberal who fails to see the insignificance of his personal effort when it is his own people who cause the problem. His birth has forced him into the enemy camp. Cronauer's accusation that Tuan killed two men rouses anger from the Viet Cong soldier.

> Big Fucking deal. My mother is dead. And my brother, who
> be twenty-nine years old, he dead. Shot by Americans. My
> neighbor—dead. His wife—dead. Why? Because we're not
> human to them. We're all enemies!

Tuan disappears and his words are ignored. "We're here to help these people," Cronauer sighs, resorting at last to the American cliché without noticing that he is suddenly speaking in the plural. "This will not look good on a resume," he shouts as he walks helplessly away to play baseball with his English class. For the film's conclusion, the other side of this foreign land is again forgotten. The liberal message that we can all get along if we just ignore our differences is illustrated by a ball game in which even the MPs join while the soundtrack plays the Rivieras singing:

> We're out there having fun
> Underneath the warm California sun.

Even Tuan's sister comes by to wish the warm-hearted Cronauer good-bye and express regret that their cultures must keep them apart.

In his final reference to Oz ("The ruby slippers!") Cronauer recognizes the he has been in a mysterious land and, like Eriksson at the end of *Casualties of War*, is now safely away. Viet Nam refused to fit his vision of it, and he must leave because of this failure on his part. The country was not the exotic utopia he (and many Americans in the antiwar movement) wanted it to be. When confronted with that fact, he ignored it and insisted on a reaffirmation of the visionary version of the country as an oddly configured America. In the same way many of the antiwar protesters, when confronted with the brutality of the North Vietnamese and Viet Cong, managed to ignore the facts and continue to support them.

The Killing Fields, director Roland Joffé's first feature film, is set not in Viet Nam but in Cambodia, and it is a British, not American, film. It is difficult to exclude it from any study of Vietnam War films, however, as it provides one of the fullest treatments of what the War meant for Southeast Asia. A brief, pre-credit sequence narrated by Waterston as Sydney Schanberg explains the situation. It opens with images of a peaceful Cambodia—a child sitting on a water buffalo while storm-clouds approach, peasants bathing at a riverbank; then, as Schanberg speaks, these pastoral images change to signs of war—helicopters litter the sky and patrol boats head toward the camera:

> Cambodia. To many westerners it seemed a paradise, another world, a secret world. But the war in neighboring Vietnam burst its borders. And the fighting soon spread to neutral Cambodia.

As this opening makes clear, *The Killing Fields* abandons the ahistorical, decontextualized vision of "the Nam," replacing it with a context of cause and effect—the War is the cause and the destruction of Cambodia is the effect. As the story opens, the War has already begun in Cambodia. The streets of Phnom Pen suffer from terrorist bombings while the streets of other Cambodian cities suffer from American bombings. Schanberg and Pran (Haing S. Ngor) are investigating the accidental American bombing of the Cambodian city of Neak Luong. The camera shows Schanberg's distress at the destruction he sees around him. Slow pans reveal children sitting on rubble, individual men and women stumbling aimlessly across the wreckage of their city, and families mourning or trying to recover from the cataclysm that has rocked their home. Meanwhile government forces execute Khmer Rouge prisoners while sipping cokes or listening to Paul McCartney's "Band on the Run" on a radio.

This and the other sequences during the first two-thirds of the film graphically depict the devastation of the land and the people. Schanberg tells the story, though, not Pran or some other Cambodian, and his story reflects an American's character and interests rather than Cambodia's history or unique problems. At an awards banquet in 1976, Schanberg explains that his goal as a journalist was to make the administration's abstract notion of Cambodia into a concrete reality; the film achieves this goal by stressing the experiential reality of the holocaust the country experienced, but it limits the reality to the experience of foreign journalists. Schanberg, and the film while Schanberg remains its central character, never delves into the history of this nation, never investigates the political or social origins of the Khmer Rouge (beyond the effect America's bombing had on their rise). It shows them as young and fanatic but fails to explain that fanaticism.

The camera work in this first section of the film is jagged and hectic. A multitude of objects and actions fill each frame, making it difficult to concentrate on any one in particular; close-ups are frequently shot over a shoulder; the music is harsh and intrusive. The opening shot of Schanberg, shown in the pre-credit sequence, suggests that this hectic perspective is his. The shot is an out-take from the sequence at the bombed city. In it Schanberg expresses distress mixed with curiosity; his eyes move from one point to another, not concentrating on details but seeing the big picture.

The character of Dith Pran suffers from this perspective. Sydney treats him with the same condescension with which he treats the rest of the country. As one critic notes, Pran is "one step removed from Gunga Din" (Hoberman). He acts as

Schanberg's translator, gofer, and occasional savior, and in return
Schanberg treats him like a copy boy. The American fails to con-
sider, or perhaps to see, the risks Pran takes on numerous occa-
sions and especially on the occasion of his choosing to stay in
Cambodia after his family escapes. This choice causes a crisis for
Schanberg when it leaves Pran stranded in the killing fields of
Kampuchea. Other journalists accuse Schanberg of having used
Pran, and though he can assert that Pran chose to stay of his own
accord, he knows that Pran stayed for him. Ultimately the film
uses this situation as another critique of America's misuse of the
country. Schanberg comes to represent America, "a needy super-
power that brought a tiny country into a war and then abandoned
it," as David Denby notes in his review of the film:

> They load onto Schanberg's shoulders the burden of Ameri-
> ca's guilt. But this is both unfair and peculiarly sentimen-
> tal—a displacement of rage and disgust from what should be
> their true objects (Nixon and Kissinger) onto a single crying
> man. And it lets America off the hook too easily. The ambi-
> tious but generally conscientious Sydney Schanberg can easily
> be forgiven; the United States cannot (125).

The Killing Fields is, however, two stories told in distinct
ways. The first tells of the ambitious Sydney Schanberg, the
equally ambitious United States, and their two servants, Dith Pran
and Cambodia. The second, told during the last third of the film,
describes what happens to the abandoned servants. It is a slower,
more measured tale that generally abandons suspense for sorrow.
The camera proceeds slowly, filling the frame with landscapes
and still objects. Fewer cuts interrupt its movement. The music,
too, which had been very intrusive in the first sections, all but disappears, replaced by the slow, quiet voice of Dith Pran's thoughts
(addressed to Schanberg), the drone of radio propaganda, or the
sounds of footsteps, murmuring voices, and birdsongs. "Here only
silence survives," Pran notes, and the silence highlights the enormity of the catastrophe from which Cambodia—now
Kampuchea—suffers.

   This film style reflects the film's first image of Pran the way
the earlier style reflected Schanberg's. Pran's image appears in
the same opening sequence and is an out-take of the same scene in

the bombed city. While Schanberg's face and eyes moved constantly, noting and reacting to the scene around him, Pran's eyes move slowly from left to right of the frame and then freeze. His reaction to the chaos hides behind an expressionless face. Once Schanberg leaves, the film presents Pran's story of Cambodia in contrast to Schanberg's, thus giving each side a spokesman and elevating Pran from the status of a Gunga Din.

Through Pran's character, the camera reveals a dimension of Cambodia that Schanberg missed or ignored. In the first two-thirds, Pran occasionally displays a perspective that differs from Schanberg's and the other reporters', but these foreign observers usually ignore the native's reaction. When the Khmer Rouge arrive in Phnom Pen, Pran joins the other Cambodians in the street acclaiming peace: "No more fighting! No more war!" The foreign journalists, however, react suspiciously and desire to investigate further. The two reactions reflect the two experiences of the War: the Cambodians have watched their homeland destroyed around them while the journalists have watched another small nation destroyed. For the Cambodians, peace means the hope of life—for the journalists it means the end of a job.

In the last third, the point of view moves from hotels and embassies to labor camps and killing fields. Instead of Schanberg's detail-filled, fast-paced, foreign perspective, the film presents Pran's slow, thoughtful gaze quietly watching. The enormity of what happens must be slowly assimilated. Through Pran the film reveals the Khmer Rouge as a savage group of ideologues—an image perceived by Schanberg and accepted as the whole truth—but also as a variety of groups struggling for control of their revolution and their destiny. Pran's second Khmer captor is a caring father and humanitarian who attempts to stop the killing. Pran's escape to Thailand takes him through a landscape that ranges from fields filled with skeletons to ancient temples crumbling in the mountains.

At its conclusion, however, the film returns to Schanberg's story. When Pran finally sees the Red Cross camps on the Thailand border, the camera cuts immediately to Schanberg racing triumphantly down a hallway at the *New York Times*. He travels immediately to Thailand to greet his friend, and they reunite to the sound of John Lennon's "Imagine," a sentimental song that might be the least suitable music the filmmakers could provide. "The song is worse than mindless in this context," wrote J. Hoberman in *The Village Voice*, "since Cambodia Year Zero was, in fact, a horrific version of Lennon's no-money, no-religion, no-possessions utopia." It reflects again Schanberg's perceptions of this conflict. In an earlier scene, Schanberg listens to Puccini's Asian romance *Turandot* while he edits a documentary on Cambodia; the opera reaches a crescendo as Schanberg fast-forwards through images of destruction; Schanberg seems unable to escape the urge to give his war a romance soundtrack.

Two French films have recently attempted to penetrate the culture in Viet Nam but have fallen prey to the same self-reflective tendency as most American efforts. Both *The Lover* (1992) and *Indo-Chine* (1993) begin before America's large-scale involvement in the War. The events in *The Lover* unfold in the 1920s, in a colonial Viet Nam where warfare was not yet an issue. The story describes a culture that once existed in the country, although not a Vietnamese culture but a colonial one. The daughter of an impoverished French colonist indulges in a passionate affair with a wealthy Chinese man in Saigon's Cholon district. The Vietnamese themselves are all around, but they have no more personality or dignity than in Stone's *Platoon*. The film treats the culture and the people living in Indochina as exotic background to the more significant lives of the French and Chinese colonialists, much the way American films have used them as a menacing background to the soldiers' lives. Similarly, it is a tale of a French colonialist and a French officer that concerns *Indo-Chine*. The action in both of these films occurs in a romantic past between the Wars, when France still maintained its colonial empire. *The Lover* goes so far as to have the voice of Jeanne Moreau narrative the tale and provide a romantic coda at the conclusion, making the nubile young Jane March and her erotic lover Tony Leung as much a fantasy of youth as a memory of it. Despite the detailed recreation of 1920s Saigon, it is the glossy, soft-focus photography by David Hamilton that defines this colonial past.

The first French combat film to feature the French Vietnamese War is *Diên Biên Phû*, directed by Pierre Schoendoerffer in

1991. Like Oliver Stone, Schoendoerffer adapts his own experiences to a film he both wrote and produced. The French director of 1967's documentary *The Anderson Platoon* was a military cameraman at the climactic battle of the French colonial war; he was one of the 10,000 prisoners captured by the armies of General Giap and one of the 3,000 to survive the imprisonment. Because Schoendoerffer based it on a specific incident, the film is almost more true to personal experience than Stone's was. Schoendoerffer himself is one of the characters and is played by his own son Ludovic.

Like *The Lover* and *Indo-Chine, Diên Biên Phû* was filmed in Viet Nam with the cooperation of the current Vietnamese government, and it was budgeted at $25 million (among the highest budgets for any French film). What makes this especially noteworthy is that, although there was no shortage of French cinematic responses to the conflict during the war years, French filmmakers have failed to produce any substantial body of work about the War. This makes them unique amongst the three countries most involved in the conflict. Despite the almost constant state of warfare that Viet Nam has suffered under during this century, a Vietnamese film industry has been active since the first half of the century. The Communist government founded the documentary section of the official Vietnamese Cinema Department in 1953 and was on hand to film the victory at Dien Bien Phu. It employed over forty cameramen and managed to produce several short films every year during the American War. The Cinema Department meanwhile produced three-to-six feature films yearly and, since 1975, has produced eighteen-to-twenty features each ear. It is currently producing a ten-hour film history of Vietnamese history and culture, *Vietnam—Building and Defending Our Country*. The 1989 American tour of Vietnamese films, The Vietnam Film Project, was a revelation to American critics and moviemakers, many of whom expected to find only rough-hewn, ideological propaganda pieces. Instead they discovered a body of well-crafted, humane tales in which the French and American wars provided the backdrop as often as they did the subject. In 1993 the cinema world acknowledged the Vietnamese film industry by nominating one of its films, *The Scent of Green Papaya*, for an Oscar.

In 1993 Oliver Stone made what he described as the conclusion to his Vietnam trilogy, *Heaven and Earth*. The first two-thirds had told the soldier's and the veteran's story. In the last he identified another victim of the War, the Vietnamese people. Like Joffé in *The Killing Fields*, Stone describes a peaceful, pastoral Indo-Chinese country ravaged by war. Stone, however, does not provide an American intermediary through whom to view this country. Instead, he provides a native interpreter, a peasant girl from a small village near Da Nang who aided the Viet Cong as a child, was tortured by the South Vietnamese, raped by the North Vietnamese, eventually prostituted herself to the Americans, and finally married an American sergeant and came to America.

Le Ly Hayslip, the Vietnamese woman at the center of Stone's film, wrote two memoirs of the War and her eventual success in America. The first she titled *When Heaven and Earth Changed Places* and in it she "tried to show how we peasants survived—and still survive today—as both makers and victims of our war." The second, *Child of War, Woman of Peace*, tells of her successful efforts to survive in the United States and how she founded the East Meets West charitable foundation. Stone is generally faithful to the facts from the books, though he concludes before Le Ly manages to succeed in America. The major exception to his fidelity is the character of Steve (Tommy Lee Jones), whom Stone creates from Ed Munro, an older sergeant who Le Ly marries to escape Viet Nam, and Dennis Hayslip a dangerously paranoid veteran whom Le Ly marries after Ed's death. For Stone, these two men are a single character, the Vietnam Veteran torn (like Chris and Ron Kovic) between conscience and anger. It is also a character that takes over the narrative center when he arrives half-way through. This is partly an effect of casting. The young, inexperienced Hiep Thi Le (who plays Le Ly) can barely stand her own against the forceful Jones. The force of the character is also an effect of Stone's consciousness, however. Steve is the character that has repeatedly fascinated Stone in his films. Le Ly is of interest to him because of her similarity to the character, and because she offers a different view of him—a Vietnamese view.

In some ways her roles in the story are the same as Oahn's in *Casualties of War*. She is both the innocent victim of the War and the forgiving angel for its soldiers. Stone describes her life, and the life of her village, as being tragically destroyed by the fighting. Stone and his cameraman Robert Richardson photograph the opening scenes beautifully. We see the people going about their daily affairs of family, farming, and religion. A pair of monks in brilliant orange robes pass through the verdant green rice paddies where the peasants work in the sunshine. "Then one day, in the summer of 1953, the French came," Le Ly tells us in a voice-over. The French arrive and destroy the village, then they leave, the village is rebuilt, everything is back to the pastoral idyll, and the credit sequence has not yet ended. The camera zooms up and away as Le Ly skips childishly through the paddies. When she once again warns that "the peasant countryside changed forever," she marks out the narrative structure of the film. The events of the French war are to be reenacted by the Americans and the end will be the same—the village will be destroyed but the people will rise again from the ashes and nothing will have changed.

Amongst other details, this narrative contradicts Le Ly's statement that everything changed in Viet Nam after 1963, including the government. Stone films the arrival of the modern South Vietnamese and American armies in one of the film's most lyrical sequences. While Le Ly works in the paddies, a wind arises from nowhere to startle the water buffalo and the birds, and to toss her hat from her and blow it across the waving grass. The wind whips-up the water against her, and she sees the settling helicopter through a wash of wind and water. This is the War entering the village life, and the villages must stand against it as they might stand against the monsoons. They are victims of the North Vietnamese, who come in the night to seduce them with speeches then return to kill the disloyal, and they are victims of the South Vietnamese who suspect all of them (often with good reason) and torture them to learn for certain. Later they are the victims of the Americans, who turn their daughters into prostitutes, their sons into cripples, and their village into a wasteland. Meanwhile they ask only to be left alone to work their fields and worship their ancestors.

Le Ly Hayslip's portrait of her village and its inhabitants differs from Stone's only in subtle shades (she was a consultant on the film and applauded Stone's rendition of her life). In one scene, the Viet Cong come to the village and kill two peasants they claim are disloyal. The night visitors terrify Le Ly—the VC are terrible in their dark vengeance—and she huddles close to her father. In the book, Le Ly describes the scene's context.

> "The other was a village busybody—a veteran of the Viet Minh who, after a long imprisonment, had become a government informer. He came to our house often and asked my mother about my brother Bon, making her—and all the other mothers who had sons in the North—worry for their lives. Now the informer himself had been informed against and I felt, deep in my young girl's heart, that he, like Manh, had gotten what he deserved. It was my first taste of vengeance and I found that revenge, like the blood that once ran from my nose during our war games on the playground, tasted sweeter than I expected. It made even a puny little farm girl feel like someone important." (Hayslip 38)

Le Ly and her fellow villagers were not innocent bystanders to the War. She and most of the other villagers actively supported the North. The film makes this clear in several scenes, but the first half is a litany of suffering in which the historical and personal contexts are lost. Stone wants Le Ly to be a victim, and so he allows her no culpability in her own tragic tale. Among the greatest strengths of *Platoon* was its insistence that the soldier be allowed to be guilty, to admit that he did terrible things in the Nam. Ron Kovic's emotional survival eventually depends on his ability to admit that he killed women, children, and another soldier in the Nam. For the grunt, Stone can postulate an "innocence that changes," but he denies the Vietnamese that right.

The reason becomes clear in the second half of the film. This is, again, a soldier's story. A Vietnamese peasant woman may be the main character, but America and the American soldier dominate that life. Once she meets her future husband, her role in the film is finally established. Steve is a guilt-racked soldier who

spends his tour in Viet Nam running "black ops"—assassinations
and other covert activities. He first appears gentle and kind, but in
the States he descends into brutish behavior. Eventually he threatens Le Ly with a shotgun (sparking a flashback to her attack by
the Viet Cong) and kidnaps their son before finally ending his own
life with a shotgun. The emotions behind his marriage become
clear in a family Thanksgiving dinner, when his sister makes a
crass remark about Le Ly being ungrateful for America's bounty.
He retorts angrily that Le Ly's people have suffered enough and
describes how the peasants, when the soldiers arrived in a village,
would beg them "please sir, don't kill me." Le Ly looks up grate-
fully at her defender, but Steve has not been speaking for her
benefit. He was the one who brought the conversation around to
the subject and he was the one to draw the insult out of his sister.
He defends her at the cost of insisting on her primary role as victim, as does the film.

In return he gets an angel to forgive him. By saving her and
defending her, he hopes to earn forgiveness for his sins—murder,
rape, war crimes, "you name it." Le Ly's Buddhist convictions
provide her with the sympathy to see Steve as a fellow victim of
karma. "Different skin," she tells him, "same suffering," and she
goes on to explain about "soul guilt," the accumulation of faults a
soul gathers over a myriad of lifetimes. "I too was a soldier in
past lives," she explains. Steve, however, is too emotionally
scarred to accept her forgiveness when she offers it and finally
kills himself.

America's "soul debt" manifested itself in the Vietnam Syndrome of the seventies, and the country recovered from its debilitating effects with the revisionism of the Reagan Revolution.
Heaven and Earth follows that model and concludes with Le Ly's
visit to her ancestral home and a family reunion. The country has
again grown healthy and back to normal—just as it had after the
French war during the credit sequence. The paddies are green and
lush and the people left in peace. Bitter feeling and recriminations
remain, but they are subdued around the family dining table. Le
Ly's brother Bon, who fought for the North, accuses her of deserting her land during its time of hardship, and explains that life
had continued to be hard after the liberation. The long fight for

freedom did not immediately bring peace, but more wars with the
Chinese and Cambodians. Le Ly's mother, however, chastens her
son for his bitterness. She tells Le Ly she did right going to America to save her sons. In the end, she admits, the War and its hardships made the Vietnamese better people.

Despite the conciliatory ending's resemblance to *Casualties
of War*'s fairy-tale conclusion, Stone has rooted his tale deeply in
the reality of Viet Nam. The characters of her father (Haing S.
Ngor) and mother (Joan Chen) are more fully figured than Stone
allows Le Ly to become, and they provide the strongest evidence
of what the War meant for the Vietnamese. While Le Ly endures
her sequence of personal tragedies, her parents continue to struggle for survival in the village. They endure their own tragedies
and tortures, but being already mature adults the War effects
them less intimately. Le Ly is a product of the War, but her parents are forged by their history and heritage; the War wears them
down rather than shapes them. The mother supports the North
and sends her sons to fight; her father believes in neither party. He
trusts only the traditions and land of his ancestors. After her
brothers go to join the Viet Cong, he takes Le Ly aside to tell her
about the history of Viet Nam, of its heritage of women warriors
and independence. He tries to lay on her the burden of loving and
respecting that land and independence. But he does not want his
family to fight and chastises his wife for sending her boys to war.
He is like the ruined stone temple that sits in the midst of the
paddy fields, old and beaten by the times, but enduring without
conflict. Haing Ngor's weathered face comes to symbolize the en-
durance of the Buddhist farmer.

Her mother, on the other hand, is a fighter. At first she is
eager for her boys to fight for their independence, then as life
deteriorates she fights desperately just to protect her family.
Deeply loyal to her family and culture, its customs bind her to a
stoic denial of her self. She seldom shows love or affection, even
when saving her daughter from prison or destitution. Stony faced
with a mouth discolored from chewing betel nuts, she is the Vietnamese peasant that infuriated Stone's soldiers in *Platoon* because she would not react as they expected.

These two characters owe very little to Stone's Land of Nam. They exist independently of the American experience, and in their creation Stone retained more fidelity and depth than he allowed for their daughter. Le Ly provides a bridge between the two cultures. Through her we see the American effort and the American grunt, and Stone chose and refined his source to provide a suitable vision. Hayslip dedicates her books to peace and the need for the two cultures to reengage each other on a new field. She provides ready material for Stone's preconceptions, but Stone never gives her the narrative authority that Haing Ngor's Dith Pran managed in *The Killing Fields*. When Schanberg left Pran in Cambodia, the Cambodian took control of the story. Stone's film style is too aggressive to allow any of his characters to take control. He does, however, manage to admit that they exist apart from their lives in the Land of Nam.

The romance of the Land of Nam, like the romance of the American West or Arthurian Britain, depends on the assumption that the Land, or the West, or the countryside surrounding Camelot, is an uncivilized wilderness that can only benefit from the civilizing tendencies of the warrior nations. Once it was admitted that the Indians had a successful culture in their own right, the American Western had to move on to a post-romantic ethos. Now that American films are beginning to provide a voice for the Vietnamese and the American government is opening up relations with Viet Nam, the Vietnamese are gaining a voice of their own. The Land of Nam may at last have to make way for Viet Nam.

Appendixes

Chronology of American Vietnam War Films

1948
Rogue's Regiment
Saigon

1952
A Yank in Indo-China

1955
Jump into Hell

1957
China Gate

1958
The Quiet American

1959
Five Gates to Hell

1962
Brushfire

1963
The Ugly American

1964
A Yank in Viet-Nam

1965
Motor Psycho

Operation CIA
To the Shores of Hell

1966
The Lost Command
Some May Live (TVM)

1967
The Born Losers
Live for Life

1968
Angels from Hell
The Angry Breed
Blue Movie
The Edge
The Green Berets
Greetings
The Initiation
The Night of the Living Dead
Targets
Tiger by the Tail
Windflowers: The Story of a Draft
  Dodger

1969
The Activist
Alice's Restaurant

The Ballad of Andy Crocker (TVM)
The Big Bounce
Easy Rider
Explosion
The Gay Deceivers
Hail, Hero!
I Feel It Coming
Medium Cool
The Model Shop
Satan's Sadists

1970
Captain Milkshake
Cowards
Getting Straight
Hi, Mom
Homer
Ice
Joe
Little Big Man
The Losers
Norwood
RPM (Revolutions Per Minute)
The Ravager
The Revolutionary
Soldier Blue
The Strawberry Statement
Zabriskie Point

1971
Billy Jack
The Bus Is Coming
Chrome and Hot Leather
Clay Pigeon
Glory Boy
The Hard Ride
Jud
Prism
Summertree
Taking Off
Welcome Home, Johnny Bristol

1972
AWOL
Black Gunn
The Blood of Ghastly Horror
Deathdream
Drive, He Said
Georgia, Georgia
Journey through Rosebud
Limbo
Outside In
Parades
Slaughter
Slaughterhouse-Five
Stanley
To Kill a Clown
Trial of the Catonsville 9
Ulzana's Raid
Vanishing Point
The Visitors

1973
American Graffitti
Electra Glide in Blue
Gordon's War
Magnum Force
The P.O.W.
Slaughter's Big Rip-Off
The Stone Killer
Trained to Kill
Two People

1974
The Bears and I
The Black Six
Blackenstein
The Crazy World of Julius Vrooder
The Trial of Billy Jack
Two
Welcome Home, Soldier Boys

1975
The Desperate Miles (TVM)
Katherine (TVM)

Milestones
Tracks

1976
Black Sunday
The Enforcer
Green Eyes (TVM)
Mean Johnny Barrows
Poor White Trash II

1977
Billy Jack Goes to Washington
Fighting Mad
Heroes
Just a Little Inconvenience (TVM)
Rolling Thunder
Special Delivery
Taxi Driver
Twilight's Last Gleaming

1978
The Big Fix
Big Wednesday
The Boys in Company C
Coming Home
The Deer Hunter
Go Tell the Spartans
Hair
Our Winning Season
Who'll Stop the Rain

1979
Apocalypse Now
Friendly Fire (TVM)
Good Guys Wear Black
More American Graffiti
Night Flowers
Saint Jack
When Hell Was in Season (TVM)
When You Comin' Back Red Ryder?

1980
The Children of An Lac (TVM)
Don't Answer the Phone

The Exterminator
Fighting Back (TVM)
Kent State (TVM)
Magnum, P.I. (TVM)
The Ninth Configuration
Operation Nam
The Promise of Love (TVM)
Return of the Secaucus Seven
A Rumor of War (TVM)
The Six O'Clock Follies (TVM)
A Small Circle of Friends
The Stunt Man

1981
Cutter's Way
The Exterminator II
Eyewitness
Fly Away Home (TVM)
Four Friends
Modern Problems
Search and Destroy
Southern Comfort

1982
Ashes and Embers
Don't Cry It's Only Thunder
Fighting Back
Firefox
First Blood
Invasion of the Flesh Hunters
Some Kind of Hero

1983
The A-Team (TVM)
Americana
The Big Chill
Blue Thunder
The Long Journey Home (TVM)
Memorial Day (TVM)
No Dead Heroes
Streamers
Twilight Zone: The Movie
Uncommon Valor

1984

Airwolf (TVM)
American Commandos
Birdy
Final Mission
Fleshburn
G. I. Executioner
Heated Vengence
The Killing Fields
The Last Hunter
Limosine
Missing in Action
Purple Hearts
Secret Honor
Soldier's Revenge

1985

Alamo Bay
The Annihilators
Bimbo
Cease Fire
Fandango
Fatal Vision (TVM)
The Lady from Yesterday (TVM)
Latino
Missing in Action 2: The Beginning
The Park Is Mine (TVM)
Rambo: First Blood, Part Two
Volunteers
White Nights
Year of the Dragon

1986

Back to School
Eye of the Eagle
Eye of the Tiger
Heartbreak Ridge
House
P.O.W. The Escape
Platoon
Resting Place (TVM)
The Return of Mickey Spillane's
   Mike Hammer (TVM)

Whatever It Takes

1987

Backfire
Full Metal Jacket
Gardens of Stone
Good Morning, Vietnam
Hamburger Hill
The Hanoi Hilton
In Love and War (TVM)
Lethal Weapon
Proud Men (TVM)
Saigon Commandos
Steele Justice
Suspect
Tour of Duty (TVM)
Vietnam (TVM)

1988

Above the Law
BAT-21
Betrayed
Braddock: Missing in Action III
China Beach (TVM)
Dear America: Letters Home from
   Vietnam (TVM)
Distant Thunder
Eye of the Eagle II
Fear
Gleaming the Cube
The Lost Idol
My Father, My Son (TVM)
1969
Off Limits
Platoon Leader
The Presidio
Rambo III
Running on Empty
Siege of Firebase Gloria
'68
Shooter (TVM)
To Heal a Nation (TVM)
Trained to Kill

Vietnam War Story (TVM)

1989
Born on the Fourth of July
Casualties of War
84 Charlie Mopic
In Country
The Iron Triangle
Jacknife
Lethal Weapon 2
The Long Road Home (TVM)
The Lost Platoon
Physical Evidence
Welcome Home

1990
Air America
Graveyard Shift
Jacob's Ladder
The Last Flight Out (TVM)
The Last Platoon
Leathernecks
The Lost Idol
Quantum Leap (TVM)
Vietnam, Texas

1991
Flight of the Intruder
JFK
Lethal Weapon 3

1992
For the Boys
Scent of a Woman
Universal Soldier

1993
Heaven and Earth
The Last Hit

Filmography, 1948–1993

Included in this filmography are all the American and some select foreign films I could discover that used the Vietnam War as subject matter, theme or context. Occasionally in video rental shops I still come across ones I had never heard about, but on the whole I believe this is a comprehensive list. It includes made for television movies (TVM) and a representative smattering of foreign films. I have elected not to include a list of documentaries about the War; such a list would be valuable and interesting, but is beyond the scope of this book. Those interested in documentaries might look at the filmography provided by Dittmar and Michaud in *From Hanoi to Hollywood: The Vietnam War in American Film*. The titles and details here have been culled from a variety of sources, including the films themselves, videotapes, original press releases, *Halliwell's Film Guide*, *Sight and Sound*, and John Willis' *Screen World*.

A-Team, The. TVM Rod Holcomb. With George Peppard, Dwight Schultz, Tim Dunigan, Mr. T. PROD: John Ashley, Patrick Hasburgh (Universal TV, Stephen J. Cannell). NBC-TV, 1983.
A squad of green berets is ordered to rob the Bank of Hanoi four days after the war ends. Afterwards, the army denies responsibility and wants to prosecute, so the squad goes underground in America and hires itself out to people in need.

AWOL (U.S./Sweden). Herb Freed. With Russ Thacker, Isabella Kaliff. PROD: (BFB). W: Richard Z. Chesnoff, Herb Freed. BFB, 1972.
This Swedish film recounts the adventures of a U.S. deserter.

Above the Law. Andrew Davis. With Steve Seagal, Pam Grier, Henry Silva. PROD: Stephen Seagal, Davis. W: Steven Pressfield, Ronald Shusett, Davis from story by Davis & Seagal. PH: Robert Steadman. M: David M. Frank. Warner, 1988.

A cop who once fought in Vietnam now combats drug dealers and corrupt officials. Also known as Nico.

Activist, The. Art Napoleon. With Michael Smith, Leslie Bilburn. PROD: Art Napoleon. Jana, 1969.
Two students fall in love while protesting the war, but the boy's dedication to the cause eventually splits them apart.

Air America. Roger Spottiswoode. With Mel Gibson, Robert Downey Jr. PROD: Daniel Melnick (Carolco/Indie). W: John Eskow, Richard Rush from the book by Christopher Robbins. PH: Roger Deakins. M: Charles Gross. Guild, 1990.
A traffic copter pilot is enlisted to work for Air America, a CIA airline running contraband into Laos. While there he discovers that they are also flying opium out of the country for the local drug lords.

Airwolf. TVM Donald P. Bellisario. With Jan-Michael Vincent. PROD: (Belisarius). W: Donald P. Bellisario. Universal TV, 1984.
A former Vietnam chopper pilot agrees to help the government retrieve its super-helicopter if they promise to find for certain whether MIA's are still alive in Southeast Asia. He keeps the helicopter as collateral.

Alamo Bay. Louis Malle. With Ed Harris, Amy Madigan, Ho Nguyen. PROD: Louis and Vincent Malle (Delphi III). W: Alice Arlen from a true story. PH: Curtis Clarke. M: Ry Cooder. Tri-Star, 1985.
A Vietnam veteran joins the K.K.K. when Vietnam refugees seem to be destroying his shrimp fishing business. From an actual incident.

Alice's Restaurant. Arthur Penn. With Arlo Guthrie, Pat Quinn, James Broderick. PROD: Hillard Elkins, Joe Manduke (Florin). W: Venable Herndon, Penn from Guthrie's song 'Alice's Restaurant Massacre'. PH: Michael Nebbia. M: Arlo Guthrie. United Artists, 1969.
Arlo Guthrie avoids the draft and seeks friendship amongst the counter-cultural society that gathers around Alice's home and restaurant. From a song by Guthrie.

American Commandos. Bobby A. Suarez. With Christopher Mitchum, John Phillip Law. PROD: Just Betzer. W: Ken Metcalf and Bobby A. Suarez. Panorama, 1984.
The government sends a group of Vietnam veterans to the Golden Triangle as a special narcotics team. Also known as Hitman.

American Graffiti. George Lucas. With Richard Dreyfuss, Ronny Howard, Paul Le Mat. PROD: Francis Coppola, Gary Kurtz

(Lucasfilm/Coppola). **W:** Lucas, Gloria Katz, Willard Huyck. **Pʜ:** Ron Eveslage, Jan D'Alquen. Universal, 1973.
This elegiac look at the end of '50s America concludes by mentioning that some of the characters will go to Vietnam and that one of the more sympathetic characters will die there.

Americana. David Carradine. With David Carradine, Barbara Hershey. **Pʀod:** Carradine. **W:** Richard Carr from Henry Morton Robinson's story 'The Perfect Round'. **Pʜ:** Michael Stringer. **M:** Craig Hundley. Crown International, 1983.
A veteran travelling across the American West pauses in a rural Kansas town to rebuild an abandoned carousel, provoking first friendship then animosity from the townspeople. Filmed in 1973.

Angels from Hell. Bruce Kessler. With Tom Stern, Arlene Martel, Ted Markland. **Pʀod:** Kurt Neuman (Fanfare Film). **W:** Jerome Wish. **Pʜ:** Herman Knox. American International, 1968.
A returning veteran uses his military training to organize a biker gang into a fighting unit that clashes with the police.

Angry Breed, The. David Commons. With Jan Sterling, James MacArthur, William Windom, Murray McLeod. **Pʀod:** David Commons (David Commons Assoc. and Harold Goldman Assoc.). **W:** David Commons. CUE, 1968.
When an aspiring actor saves a scriptwriter's life in Vietnam, he earns a chance to star in a new film. Unfortunately problems develop and he clashes with the director over his daughter and with a motorcycle gang leader who also wants the role.

Annihilators, The. Charles E. Sellier, Jr. With Christopher Stone, Andy Wood. **Pʀod:** *Allan C. Pederson, Tom Chapman.* **W:** Brian Russell. **Pʜ:** Henning Schellerup. **M:** Bob Summers. New World, 1985.
A group of Vietnam veterans joins together to help the innocent in a small California town, à la The A-Team.

Apocalypse Now. Francis Ford Coppola. With Martin Sheen, Robert Duvall, Marlon Brando. **Pʀod:** Coppola (Omni-Zoetrope). **W:** John Milius, Coppola, Michael Herr. **Pʜ:** Vittorio Storaro. **M:** Carmine Coppola, Francis Coppola. United Artists, 1979.
An American military assassin travels up-river into Cambodia on a mission to kill an American colonel who has gone beyond the limits of the military's code of warfare. Based on Conrad's Heart of Darkness *and Homer's* Odyssey.

Ashes and Embers. Hale Gerima. With John Anderson, Evelyn Blackwell, Norman Blalock. Prod: *Gerima*. W: Gerima. Mypheduh, 1982.
Eight years after the war, a black veteran continues to work out his personal demons within Black American society.

BAT-21. Peter Markle. With Gene Hackman, Danny Glover. W: William C. Anderson, George Gordon from *BAT-21* by William C. Anderson. M: Christopher Young. Tri-Star, 1988.
A military strategist is shot down in Vietnam and sees the country firsthand while avoiding the NVA and trying to rendezvous with a rescue team.

Back to School. Alan Metter. With Rodney Dangerfield, Sally Kellerman, Burt Young. Prod: Chuck Russell (Paper Clip). W: Steven Kampmann, Harold Ramis, Will Porter, Peter Topokvei. Ph: Thomas E. Ackerman. M: Danny Elfman. Orion, 1986.
A history professor who fought in Vietnam rants about conspiracies and combat when the subject turns to recent American military history in a comedy about college life.

Backfire. Gilbert Cates. With Karen Allen, Keith Carradine, Jeff Fahey. Prod: Danton Rissner (ITC). W: Larry Brand, Rebecca Reynolds. Ph: Tak Fujimoto. M: David Shire. Virgin, 1987.
The life of a wealthy but unstable veteran and his working class wife is disrupted by the arrival of a stranger.

Ballad of Andy Crocker, The. tvm George McCowan. With Lee Majors, Joey Heatherton, Jimmy Dean, Agnes Moorehead. Prod: (Thomas-Spelling). W: Stuart Margolin, 1969.
A veteran returns to his home town and finds that his sweetheart has married and his former business partner is now a crook.

Bears and I, The. Bernard McEveety. With Patrick Wayne, Chief Dan George, Andrew Duggan. Prod: Winston Hibler (Walt Disney). W: John Whedon from the novel by Robert Franklin Leslie. Ph: Ted D. Landon. M: Buddy Baker. Buena Vista, 1974.
A veteran goes to live in the woods, adopts three bear cubs, becomes a park ranger, and settles disputes between Indians and local bigots.

Betrayed. Henri Costa-Gravas. With Debra Winger, Tom Berenger, John Heard. Prod: Joe Eszterhas (Irwin Winkler). W: Eszterhas. Ph: Patrick Blossier. M: Bill Conti. MGM/UA, 1988.
The leaders of a band of white supremacists and Neo-Nazis in the American Midwest attract a high number of Vietnam veterans, many of whom provide the leadership.

Big Bounce, The. Alex March. With Ryan O'Neal, Leigh Taylor-Young, Van Heflin. **PROD:** William Dozier (Greenway). **W:** William Dozier from the novel by Elmore Leonard. **PH:** Howard R. Schwartz. **M:** Michael Curb. Warner, 1969.
A veteran drifts through a series of sordid encounters rather than return home to his family. A beautiful woman tries to lead him into a life of crime, but he prefers the life of a migrant worker.

Big Chill, The. Lawrence Kasdan. With William Hurt, Glenn Close, Kevin Kline. **PROD:** Michael Shamberg (Carson). **W:** Kasdan, Barbara Benedek. **PH:** John Bailey. Columbia, 1983.
A group of college friends from the sixties reunites in the eighties after the suicide of the most idealistic of them.

Big Fix, The. Jeremy Paul Kagan. With Richard Dreyfuss, Susan Anspach, John Lithgow, Bonnie Bedelia. **PROD:** Carl Borack, Dreyfuss. **W:** Roger L. Simon from his novel. **PH:** Frank Stanley. **M:** Bill Conti. Universal, 1978.
An activist from the sixties becomes a private eye in the seventies. His investigation of another former radical leads him to question the protest movement and his own former commitments.

Big Wednesday. John Milius. With Jan-Michael Vincent, William Katt, Gary Busey. **PROD:** Buzz Feitshans (surfing sequences), Greg MacGillivray (A-Team). **W:** Milius, Dennis Aaberg. **PH:** Bruce Surtees (surfing sequences), Greg MacGillivray. **M:** Basil Poledouris. Warner, 1978.
Three surfers encounter the pitfalls of reaching adulthood—one of which is responsibility for fighting or avoiding the Vietnam War—while waiting for the big wave (Big Wednesday) to come. Also known as Summer of Innocence.

Billy Jack. T.C. Frank (Tom Laughlin). With Tom Laughlin, Delores Taylor. **PROD:** Mary Rose Solti (National Student Film Corporation). **W:** T.C. Frank, Teresa Christina (Delores Taylor). **PH:** Fred Koenekamp, John Stephens. **M:** Mundell Lowe. Warner, 1971.
A half-breed Indian uses his Green Beret training to protect an innovative school in the Arizona desert.

Billy Jack Goes to Washington. T.C. Frank (Tom Laughlin). With Tom Laughlin, Delores Taylor, E.G. Marshall. **PROD:** Frank Capra, Jr. **W:** T.C. Frank, Teresa Cristina (Delores Taylor) from the screenplay *Mr. Smith Goes to Washington* by Sydney Buchman. **PH:** Jack Merta. **M:** Elmer Bernstein. Taylor-Laughlin, 1977.

Final episode in the Billy Jack series has the veteran half-breed take his causes to the capital.

Bimbo. Red Light Video, 1985.
Pornographic story of a woman who goes to Vietnam to rescue her POW husband.

Birdy. Alan Parker. With Matthew Modine, Nicolas Cage. Prod: Alan Marshall (A&M Films). W: Sandy Kroopf, Jack Behr from the novel by William Wharton. Ph: Michael Seresin. M: Peter Gabriel. Tri-Star-Delphi III, 1984.
A veteran, whose face has been scarred by flames in Vietnam, attempts to help his childhood friend recover from a trauma caused by combat. From a novel about World War II.

Black Gunn. Robert Hartford-Davis. With Jim Brown. Prod: John Heyman, Norman Priggen (Champion). W: Franklin Coen, Robert Shearer. Ph: Richard H. Kline. M: Tony Osborne. Columbia, 1972.
A black veteran leads an attack against the drug dealers when his brother is killed.

Black Six, The. Matt Cimber (Matteo Ottaviano). With Gene Washington, Carl Eller, Lem Barney. W: George Theakos. Cinemation, 1974.
After a biker gang kills a black man for dating a white woman, the man's brother leads five other black veterans on an assault against them.

Black Sunday. John Frankenheimer. With Robert Shaw, Bruce Dern, Marthe Keller. Prod: Robert Evans. W: Ernest Lehman, Ivan Moffat, Kenneth Ross from the novel by Thomas Harris. Ph: John A. Alonzo. M: John Williams. Paramount, 1977.
A veteran agrees to fly the Goodyear Blimp for Middle-East terrorists who plan to blow-up the Super Bowl.

Blackenstein. William A. Levey. With John Hart, Joe DiSue. 1974.
Dr. Frankenstein offers to replace the limbs lost by a black soldier in the Vietnam War.

Blood of Ghastly Horror, The. Al Adamson. With John Carradine, Kent Taylor, Tommy Kirk, Regina Carrol. Ph: Vilmos Zsigmond. 1972.
A veteran is the subject of a mad-scientist's brain transplant experiment. Also known as The Fiend with the Electronic Brain, Psycho-a-Go-Go!, The Love Maniac, *and* The Man with the Synthetic Brain.

Blue Movie. Andy Warhol. 1968.

Andy Warhol's film of two people in bed making love and talking about various issues includes discussion of the Vietnam War.

Blue Thunder. John Badham. With Roy Scheider, Malcolm McDowell, Candy Clark, Warrren Oates. PROD: Gordon Carroll (Rastar). W: Dan O'Bannon, Don Jakoby. PH: John A. Alonzo, Frank Holgate (aerial sequences) M: Arthur B. Rubinstein. Columbia, 1983.
A Vietnam veteran working for LAPD Aerial Surveillance is assigned to test an antiterrorist helicopter designed by another veteran. He discovers the chopper is meant for use against civilians and destroys both it and its designer.

Born Losers, The. T.C. Frank (Tom Laughlin). With Tom Laughlin, Elizabeth James. PROD: Donald Henderson. W: E. James Lloyd. PH: Gregory Sandor. M: Mike Curb. American International, 1967.
A biker gang terrorizes a Southern California town until Vietnam veteran Billy Jack stands against them. This is the first in a series of four Billy Jack films.

Born on the Fourth of July. Oliver Stone. With Tom Cruise, Willem Dafoe, Caroline Kava, Raymond J. Barry. PROD: A. Kitman Ho and Oliver Stone (Ixtlan). W: Oliver Stone and Ron Kovik from the memoir by Ron Kovik. PH: Robert Richardson. M: John Williams. Universal,1989.
A Vietnam veteran returns home from war and must cope with paraplegia, guilt, the antiwar movement, and his sense of personal failure in Vietnam.

Boys in Company C, The (U.S./Hong Kong). Sidney J. Furie. With Stan Shaw, Andrew Stevens, Craig Wasson, Lee Ermey. PROD: Andrew Morgan (Golden Harvest/Good Times Films). W: Rick Natkin, Furie. PH: Godfrey Godar. M: Jaime Mendoza-Nava. Columbia, 1978.
A group of draftees survive boot camp together and go to Vietnam. There they encounter an insane situation that drives them to work together for their own survival.

Braddock: Missing in Action III. Aaron Norris. With Chuck Norris, Aki Aleong, Yehudi Efroni. PROD: Menahim Golan, Yoram Globus (Golan-Globus). W: James Bruner and Chuck Norris. PH: Joao Fernandes. M: Jay Chattaway. Cannon, 1988.
Braddock returns to Vietnam when he learns that his Vietnamese wife and son are alive. Although his wife is soon killed by the communists, he is able to lead a band of orphans to safety. The story contradicts the storyline of the earlier films in the series.

Brushfire!. Jack Warner Jr. With John Ireland, Jo Morrow, Everett Sloane. PROD: Jack Warner, Jr. (Obelisk). W: Irwin R. Blacker. PH: Ed Fitzgerald. M: Irving Gertz. Paramount, 1962.
Americans are captured while aiding anti-Communists in South-East Asia.

Bus Is Coming, The. Wendell James Franklin. With Mike Simms. PROD: Horace Jackson. William Thompson International, 1971.
A black veteran returns home to investigate the murder of his brother.

Captain Milkshake. Richard Crawford. With Geoff Gage, Andrea Cagan. Richmark Productions, 1970.
A marine befriends drug-smuggling hippies while on leave. Despite their encouragement to desert, he returns to the army and is killed in Vietnam.

Casualties of War. Brian De Palma. With Michael J. Fox, Sean Penn. PROD: Art Linson. W: David Rabe from a *New Yorker* article by Daniel Lang. PH: Stephen H. Burum. M: Ennio Morricone. Columbia/Tri-Star, 1989.
A soldier watches helplessly as his squad kidnaps and rapes a Vietnamese girl, but later he manages to bring the squad to justice.

Cease Fire. David Nutter. With Don Johnson, Lisa Blount. PROD: William Grefe (Double-Helix Films/ELF). W: George Fernandez from his play *Vietnam Trilogy*. PH: Henning Schellerup. M: Gary Fry. Cineworld, 1985.
A veteran is still haunted by his war experience fifteen years later, but he refuses to admit he has a problem until another veteran commits suicide.

Children of An Lac, The.TVM John Llewellyn Moxey. With Shirley Jones, Ina Balin, Beulah Quo. PROD: Jay Benson (Charles Fryes). W: Blanche Hanalis. CBS-TV, 1980.
Three women try to evacuate hundreds of orphans just before the fall of Saigon. Ina Balin plays herself in this docudrama.

China Beach.TVM Rod Holcomb. With Dana Delany, Jeff Kober, Michael Boatman, Marg Helgenberger. PROD: John Sacret Young (Sacret, Warner-TV). W: John Sacret Young. PH: Charles Minsky. M: John Rubenstein. ABC-TV, 1988.
The pilot for a successful television series about an army recreation center and hospital at China Beach focuses on the women involved in the war.

China Gate. Samuel Fuller. With Gene Barry, Angie Dickinson, Nat King Cole, Lee Van Cleef. PROD: Fuller (Globe Enterprises). W: Fuller. PH: Joseph Biroc. M: Victor Young, Max Steiner. 20th Century-Fox, 1957.

A Eurasian saloon owner leads a gang of mercenaries on a raid to destroy a communist munitions dump.

Chrome and Hot Leather. Lee Frost. With William Smith, Tony Young, Marvin Gaye. PROD: Wes Bishop. W: Michael Haynes, David Neibel, Don Tait. PH: Lee Frost. M: Porter Jordon. American International, 1971.
After a biker gang kills a soldier's girlfriend, four Green Berets form their own biker gang and use military training and equipment to destroy the killers.

Clay Pigeon. Tom Stern, Lane Slate. With Telly Savalas, Tom Stern, Robert Vaughn. PROD: Tom Stern (Tracom). W: Ronald Buck, Buddy Ruskin, Jack Gross Jr. from a story by Ruskin-Gross. PH: Alan Stensvold. M: Gavin Murrell. MGM, 1971.
A soldier leaps on a grenade and, in the moment before he dies, imagines that he survives and returns to the United States to fight the drug dealers. Also known as Trip to Kill.

Coming Home. Hal Ashby. With Jane Fonda, Jon Voight, Bruce Dern. PROD: Jerome Hellman (Jerome Hellman Enterprises/Jayne). W: Waldo Salt, Robert C. Jones from story by Nancy Dowd. PH: Haskell Wexler. United Artists, 1978.
While her Marine captain husband is in Vietnam, a woman volunteers at a V.A. hospital and becomes emotionally and sexually involved with one of the patients. Her husband returns, disillusioned by the war, and tries to confront his wife's unfaithfulness.

Cowards. Simon Nuchtern. With John Ross, Susan Sparling. PROD: Simon Nuchtern (Lewis Mishkin-Simon Nuchtern). W: Nuchtern. PH: Robert T. Megginson. Jaylo International, 1970.
A youth must decide whether to accept being drafted, to evade the draft in Canada, or to fight against the draft. His father's accusations of cowardice make him chose to join a raid against a draft board office.

Crazy World of Julius Vrooder, The. Arthur Hiller. With Timothy Bottoms, Barbara Seagull, Lawrence Presman, Albert Salmi. PROD: Edward Rissien, Arthur Hiller (Playboy). W: Daryl Henry. PH: David Walsh. 20th Century-Fox, 1974.
A veteran escapes from his bed in a mental hospital and hides out in the city.

Cutter's Way. Ivan Passer. With Jeff Bridges, John Heard, Lisa Eichorn. PROD: Paul R. Gurian (Gurian Entertainment). W: Jeffrey Alan Fiskin from Newton Thornburg's novel *Cutter and Bone*. PH: Jordan Cronenweth. M: Jack Nitzsche. United Artists, 1981.

A veteran who lost a leg and an eye in the war encourages his friend, who had been deferred, to investigate the murder of a stranger. Also known as Cutter and Bone.

Deathdream (Canada). Bob Clark. With John Marley, Richard Backus, Lynn Carlin. PROD: (Quadrant Films, Impact Films). Europix International, 1972.
A veteran returns to his family after being reported killed in action, but he soon shows a craving for blood. Also known as Dead of Night *and* Night Walk.

Deer Hunter, The. Michael Cimino. With Robert De Niro, John Cazale, John Savage, Christopher Walken, Meryl Streep. PROD: Barry Spikings, Michael Deeley, Cimino, John Peverall (EMI). W: Deric Washburn from a story by Cimino, Louis Garfinkle, Quinn K. Redeker, and Washburn. PH: Vilmos Zsigmond. M: Stanley Myers. Universal, 1978.
A trio of patriotic steel workers goes to Vietnam and finds that the experience alters their sense of self and community.

Desperate Miles, The.TVM Daniel Haller. With Tony Musante, Joanna Petter, Jeanette Nolan. PROD: Joel Rogosin. Universal, 1975.
A disabled veteran travels 130 miles in his wheelchair to prove his independence. From a true story.

Diên Biên Phû. Pierre Schoendoerffer. With Jean Rochefort, Patrick Catalifo, Ludovic Schoendoerffer, Donald Pleasance. PROD: Jacques Kirsner. W: Schoendoerffer. PH: Raoul Coutard. Seko Film, 1991.
The story of the French defeat at Dien Bien Phu as seen by an American journalist. Filmed in Vietnam with the assistance of the French and Vietnamese armies.

Distant Thunder. Rick Rosenthal. With John Lithgow, Ralph Macchio, Kerrie Keane. W: Robert Stitzel. Paramount, 1988.
A Vietnam veteran who has been hiding with other vets in the mountains comes out of the woods when a friend commits suicide. He tries to reenter society by taking a job and contacting the son he never knew.

Don't Answer the Phone! Robert Hammer. With James Westmoreland, Flo Gerrish, Ben Frank. PROD: Hammer (Scorpion). W: Hammer. PH: James Carter. M: Byron Allred. Crown International, 1980.
A psychotic veteran kills a doctor's patients and girls who live alone. Also known as The Hollywood Strangler.

Don't Cry It's Only Thunder. Peter Werner. With Dennis Christopher, Susan St. James, Lisa Lu, James Whitmore Jr. PROD: Walt deFarla. W: Paul Hensler. PH: Don McAlpine. M: Maurce Jarre. Sanrio Communications, 1982.
A soldier promises his dying friend that he will protect an orphanage in Vietnam.

Dragon Lady. Joel M. Reed. With Tom Kenna, Victoria Racimo, Angelique Pettyjohn. Troma Team, 1984.
A veteran operating a bar in Singapore becomes a mercenary killer known as the G.I. Executioner tracking down a Red Chinese scientist. Also known as GI Executioner *and* Wit's End.

Drive, He Said. Jack Nicholson. With Michael Margotta, William Tepper, Karen Black, Bruce Dern. PROD: Steve Blauner (Drive/BBS). W: Jeremy Larner, Nicholson from novel by Larner. PH: Bill Butler. M: David B. Shire. Columbia, 1972.
A college basketball star attempts to fail his physical by staying awake for several days before his induction physical.

Easy Rider. Dennis Hopper. With Peter Fonda, Dennis Hopper, Jack Nicholson. PROD: Peter Fonda (Pando/Raybert). W: Fonda, Hopper, Terry Southern. PH: Laszlo Kovacs. Columbia, 1969.
Two men use a drug sale to finance a motorcycle trip across the United States to New Orleans.

Edge, The. Robert Kramer. With Jack Rader, Tom Griffin. PROD: Robert Kramer, Robert Machover (Blue Van, Alpha 60). W: Robert Kramer. PH: Robert Machover. Blue Van, Alpha 60, 1968.
A veteran attempts to assassinate the president in retaliation for Vietnam. Won the Prix Georges Sadoul.

84 Charlie Mopic. Patrick Duncan. With Richard Brooks, Nicholas Cascone, Jonathon Emerson, Jason Tomlins. PROD: Michael Nolin (The Charlie Mopic Company). W: Duncan. PH: Alan Casco. M: Donavon. RCA/Columbia, 1989.
An army documentary Motion Picture (MOPIC) crew accompanies a crack squad on Long Range Reconnaissance Patrol to document their activities and methods. The film maintains the point of view of the MOPIC cameraman's camera throughout.

Electra Glide in Blue. James William Guercio. With Robert Blake, Mitchell Ryan. PROD: Guercio, Robert Hitzig. W: Robert Boris. PH: Conrad Hall. M: Guercio. United Artists, 1973.
A small-town motorcycle cop becomes disillusioned.

Enforcer, The. James Fargo. With Clint Eastwood, Tyne Daly, Harry Guardino. **Prod**: Robert Daley (Malpaso). **W**: Stirling Silliphant, Dean Riesner from a story by Gail Morgan Hickman & S.W. Schurr. **Ph**: Charles W. Short. **M**: Jerry Fielding. Warner, 1976.
Dirty Harry and a female partner defeat an underground terrorist group in San Francisco.

Explosion (Canada). Jules Bricken. With Gordon Thomson, Don Stroud. **Prod**: (Swank Motion Pictures). **W**: Alene and Jules Bricken. American International, 1969.
When a young man's brother dies in Vietnam, he leaves for Canada to avoid the draft and enters a life of crime.

Exterminator, The. James Glickenhaus. With Christopher George, Robert Ginty, Samantha Eggar. **Prod**: Mark Buntzman (Interstar). **W**: Glickenhaus. **Ph**: Robert M. Baldwin. **M**: Joe Renzetti. Avco Embassy, 1980.
A Vietnam veteran goes on a brutal rampage to avenge the murder of a fellow veteran.

Exterminator 2, The. Mark Buntzman. With Robert Ginty, Deborah Geffner, Mario Van Peebles. **Prod**: Buntzman, William Sachs. **W**: Buntzman, William Sachs. **Ph**: Bob Baldwin, Joseph Mangine. **M**: David Spear. Cannon, 1984.
The vigilante veteran continues to fight crime in the streets, now with a flame thrower.

Eye of the Eagle. Cirio H. Santiago. With Brett Clark, Robert Patrick, William Steis. **W**: Joseph Zucchero. Concorde, 1986.
A soldier must fight a group of deserters in Vietnam who have formed a terrorist squad for criminal gains.

Eye of the Eagle II. Carl Franklin. With William Field, Andy Wood, Ken Jacobson. 1988.
A squad is decimated because of its cowardly commander. The only survivor is saved by a beautiful refugee, whom he must then save when the commander kidnaps her for prostitution purposes. Also known as Inside the Enemy *and* KIA.

Eye of the Tiger. Richard C. Sarafian. With Gary Busey, Yaphet Kotto. **Prod**: Tony Scotti. **Ph**: Peter Collister. **W**: Michael Montgomery. Scotti Brothers, 1986.
A veteran seeks revenge against a gang of bikers who ravaged his home town.

Eyewitness. Peter Yates. With William Hurt, Sigourney Weaver, Christopher Plummer, James Woods. Prod: Yates. W: Steven Tesich. Ph: Matthew F. Leonetti. M: Stanley Silverman. 20th Century-Fox, 1981.
A veteran pretends to be a witness to the murder of an Oriental businessman in order to meet the television journalist covering the story. His best friend, another veteran, becomes the prime suspect. Also known as The Janitor.

Fandango. Kevin Reynolds. With Kevin Costner, Judd Nelson, Sam Robards. Prod: Tim Zinnemann (Amblin Entertainment). W: Reynolds from Reynold's student film *Proof.* Ph: Thomas Del Ruth. M: Alan Silvestri. Warner, 1985.
Five students graduate from college and, faced with the draft, go on a road trip to recover a bottle of wine they had buried on the Mexican border.

Fatal Vision. TVM David Greene. With Karl Malden, Eva Marie Saint, Gary Coal. Prod: Richard L. O'Connor. W: John Gay from the book by Joe McGinnis. Ph: Steven Larner. NBC-TV, 1985.
A former Green Beret faces trial for the murder of his wife and daughters. From an actual incident.

Fear. Robert A. Ferretti. With Cliff DeYoung, Kay Lenz. 1988.
A veteran leads ex-cons in a terrorist rampage against a family camping in the wilderness.

Fighting Back.TVM Robert Lieberman. With Robert Urich, Art Carney, Bonnie Bedelia. Prod: Jerry McNeely (MTM). W: McNeely from a true story. Ph: Stevan Larner. M: Fred Karlin. ABC, 1980.
Rocky Bleier returns to the Pittsburgh Steelers after being wounded in Vietnam. From a true story.

Fighting Back. Lewis Teague. With Tom Skerritt, Michael Sarrazin, Patti LuPone, Yaphet Kotto. Prod: D. Constantine Conte (Dino de Laurentiis). W: Tom Hedley, David Zelag Goodman. Ph: Franco DiGiacomo. M: Piero Piccioni. Paramount, 1982.
When a veteran's wife and mother are killed, he forms a community vigilante group that grows increasingly out of control. Also known as Death Vengeance.

Fighting Mad (U.S./Philippines). Cirio H. Santiago. With James M. Iglehart, Jayne Kennedy, Leon Isaac. 1977.
When a soldier is left to die in Vietnam, he is captured by Japanese who do not know that World War II has ended.

Final Mission (Philippines). Cirio H. Santiago. With Robert Young, John Dresden, Kaz Gavas. **Prod:** Anthony Maharaj (Santiago/Maharaj). **W:** Anthony Maharaj. **M:** George Carvarente. Cannon, 1984.
When an LA SWAT member witnesses the murder of his family, he traces the killers back to Laos, where he discovers an American deserter with an old grudge against him.

Firefox. Clint Eastwood. With Clint Eastwood, Freddie Jones, David Huffman. **Prod:** Clint Eastwood (Malpaso). **W:** Alex Lasker, Wendell Willman from novel by Craig Thomas. **Ph:** Bruce Surtees. **M:** Maurice Jarre. Warner, 1982.
A Vietnam veteran pilot is sent on a mission to steal the Soviet Union's latest fighter aircraft despite suffering from Post-Traumatic Stress flashbacks.

First Blood. Ted Kotcheff. With Sylvester Stallone, Richard Crenna, Brian Dennehy. **Prod:** Buzz Feitshans (Carolco). **W:** Michael Kozoll, William Sackheim & Stallone from the novel by David Morrell. **Ph:** Andrew Laszlo. **M:** Jerry Goldsmith. Anabasis/Orion, 1982.
A small-town sheriff hassles a drifter without realizing that it is a Green Beret who has been pushed around by everyone since his return from the War. The veteran, John Rambo, decides to fight back this time and destroys the sheriff's town.

Five Gates to Hell. James Clavell. With Dolores Michaels, Neville Brand, Kevin Scott, Benson Fong. **Prod:** James Clavell. **W:** James Clavell. **Ph:** Sam Leavitt. **M:** Paul Dunlap. 20th Century-Fox, 1959.
A U.S. medical team is captured by a warband and forced to treat its leader. When they fail, the warband kills all of them except a few of the nurses who escape through "sheer use of their sexual powers" (Variety).

Fleshburn. George Gage. With Steve Kanaly, Karen Carlson, Macon McCalman. **Prod:** Beth Gage (Amritraj). **W:** George Gage, Beth Gage from Brian Garfield's novel *Fear in a Handful of Dust*. **Ph:** Bill Pecchi. **M:** Arthur Kempel. Crown International, 1984.
A deranged Native American veteran escapes from a mental hospital where he has been incarcerated for murder. He seeks vengeance against the psychiatrists he blames for putting him there by stranding them in the middle of the desert.

Flight of the Intruder. John Milius. With Danny Glover, Willem Dafoe, Brad Johnson, Rosanna Arquette. **Prod:** Mace Neufeld, Robert Rehme. **W:** Robert Dillon, David Shaber from novel by Stephen

Coonts. **PH:** Fred J. Koenekamp. **M:** Basil Pouledouris. Paramount, 1991.

Bomber pilots from an aircraft carrier off the coast of Vietnam decide to bomb Hanoi but are shot down.

Fly Away Home.TVM Paul Krasny. With Bruce Boxleitner, Tiana Alexandra, Brian Dennehy. **PROD:** Stirling Silliphant (An Lac, Warner TV). **W:** Stirling Silliphant. ABC-TV, 1981.

The pilot film for an ensemble drama set in South Vietnam features American, North Vietnamese, and South Vietnamese characters in various storylines.

For the Boys. Mark Rydell. With Bette Midler, James Caan. **PROD:** Bette Midler, Bonnie Bruckheimer, Margaret South (All Girls). **W:** Marshall Brickman, Neal Jimenez, Lindy Laub. **PH:** Stephen Goldblatt. **M:** David Grusin. 20th Century-Fox, 1992.

A pair of entertainers tours the fronts in World War II, the Korean War, and finally Vietnam where their son dies.

Four Friends. Arthur Penn. With Craig Wasson, Jodi Thelen, Jim Metzler, Michael Huddleston. **PROD:** Penn, Gene Lasko (Cinema 77/Geria, Florin). **W:** Steven Tesich. **PH:** Ghislain Cloquet. **M:** Elizabeth Swados. Filmways, 1981.

An idealistic, young Yugoslavian immigrant experiences the sixties. Also known as George's Friends.

Friendly Fire.TVM Harry May. With Carol Burnett, Ned Beatty, Sam Waterston. **PROD:** Philip Barry, Fay Kanin (Marble Arch). **W:** Fay Kanin from the book by C.D.B. Bryan. ABC-TV Films, 1979.

An Iowan farm couple investigates the death of their son who was killed by friendly fire in Vietnam.

Full Metal Jacket. Stanley Kubrick. With Matthew Modine, Lee Ermy, Adam Baldwin, Vincent D'Onofrio. **PROD:** Kubrick, Philip Hobbs (Natant). **W:** Kubrick, Michael Herr, Gustav Hasford from Hasford's novel *The Short-Timers.* **PH:** Douglas Milsome. **M:** Abigail Mead. Warner, 1987.

A group of recruits struggle through the de-humanizing instruction of a brutal sergeant in basic training. Later, in Vietnam, these recruits come to depend on being inhuman to survive the battle of Hue.

Gardens of Stone. Francis Coppola. With James Caan, Anjelica Huston, D.B. Sweeney, James Earl Jones. **PROD:** Michael I. Levy and Francis Coppola (Tri-Star/ML Delphi Premier). **W:** Ronald Bass from the novel by Nicolas Proffitt. **P**ʜ: Jordan Cronenweth. **M**: Carmine Coppola. Tri-Star, 1987.

A young soldier who wants to fight in Vietnam is assigned to the burial brigade at Arlington National Cemetery, where he meets an experienced sergeant who wants a chance to train young soldiers for Vietnam so fewer of them will die.

Gay Deceivers, The. Bruce Kessler. With Kevin Coughlin, Brooke Bundy, Larry Casey. **P**ʀᴏᴅ: Joe Solomon (Fanfare Film). **W**: Jerome Wish from story by Abe Polsky, Gil Lasky. Fanfare Film, 1969.

When two draftees pretend to be gay to avoid induction, the draft board hounds them until they confess and face the draft board as straights, only to find the new board is gay.

Georgia, Georgia. Stig Bjorkman. With Diana Sands, Dirk Benedict, Minnie Gentry. **W**: Maya Angelou. Cinerama Releasing Corp., 1972.

A black singer involves herself with a white singer and American defectors.

Getting Straight. Richard Rush. With Elliott Gould, Candice Bergen. **P**ʀᴏᴅ: Richard Rush (The Organization). **W**: Robert Kaufman from the novel by Ken Kolb. **P**ʜ: Laszlo Kovacs. **M**: Ronald Stein. Columbia, 1970.

A Vietnam veteran and former radical enters graduate school and must confront his past convictions when they conflict with his current desire to settle down and find a job.

Gleaming the Cube. Graeme Clifford. With Christian Slater, Steven Bauer, Richard Herd. **P**ʀᴏᴅ: Lawrence Turman (Rank/Gladden Entertainment). **W**: Michael Tolkin. **P**ʜ: Reed Smoot. **M**: Jay Ferguson. 20th Century-Fox, 1988.

A skateboard fanatic investigates the murder of his adopted Vietnamese brother.

Glory Boy. Edwin Sherin. With Arthur Kennedy, Michael Moriarty, William Devane. **P**ʀᴏᴅ: Philip Waxman (Waxman-Minskoff). **W**: Stanford Whitmore from John Sanford's novel *The Old Man's Place*. **P**ʜ: Richard C. Glouner. **M**: Charles Gross. Cinerama Releasing, 1971.

When a veteran returns home with two military buddies, tensions rise amongst his father, the vets, and a girlfriend; the result is rape and murder. Also known as The Old Man's Place.

Go Tell the Spartans. Ted Post. With Burt Lancaster, Craig Wasson. **P**ʀᴏᴅ: Allan F. Bodoh, Mitchell Cannold (Spartan Company/Mar Vista). **W**: Wendell Mayes from Daniel Ford's novel *Incident at Muc*

Wa. **Pн:** Harry Stradling, Jr. **M:** Dick Halligan. Avco Embassy Films, 1978.
A group of professional, disheartened soldiers lead a rabble of Vietnamese soldiery to the defense of a useless, abandoned village that the French had once tried and failed to defend.

Good Guys Wear Black. Ted Post. With Chuck Norris, Anne Archer. **Prod:** Allan F. Bodoh (Action One Film). **W:** Bruce Cohn, Mark Medoff from story by Joseph Fraley. **Pн:** Bob Steadman. **M:** Craig Safan. Mar Vista, 1979.
At the end of the war, the chief American negotiator betrays an American commando squad into a Vietnamese ambush to facilitate the peace negotiations. Years later when he is about to become Secretary of State, he sends a Vietnamese hitman to kill the survivors.

Good Morning, Vietnam. Barry Levinson. With Robin Williams, Forest Whitaker, Tung Thanh Tran, Chintara Sukapatana. **Prod:** Mark Johnson, Larry Brezner (Buena Vista). **W:** Larry Brezner, Mitch Markowitz. **Pн:** Peter Sova. **M:** Alex North. Touchstone, 1987.
A Radio Armed Forces disk jockey is popular with the troops and the Vietnamese but antagonizes his superiors. Based on the life of Adrian Cronauer.

Gordon's War. Ossie Davis. With Paul Winfield, Carl Lee, David Downing. **Prod:** Robert L. Schaffel (Palomar). **W:** Howard Friedlander, Ed Spielman. **Pн:** Victor J. Kemper. **M:** Andy Bodale, Al Ellis. 20th Century-Fox, 1973.
When a Black veteran comes home to find his wife has overdosed on drugs, he bands his veteran friends together to destroy the pushers.

Graveyard Shift. Ralph S. Singleton. With David Andrews, Kelly Wolf, Brad Dourif. **Prod:** William J. Dunn, Ralph S. Singleton (Graveyard). **W:** John Esposito, from a Stephen King short story. **Pн:** Peter Stein. **M:** Anthony Marinelli, Brian Banks. Columbia Tri-Star, 1990.
A veteran working as an exterminator encounters a giant, man-eating rat.

Green Berets, The. John Wayne, Ray Kellogg. With John Wayne, David Janssen, Aldo Ray, Craig Jue, Irene Tsu. **Prod:** Michael Wayne (Batjac). **W:** James Lee Barrett from the novel by Robin Moore. **Pн:** Winton C. Hoch. **M:** Miklos Rozsa. Warner, 1968.
A Green Beret command defends a military outpost and kidnaps a Viet Cong official.

Green Eyes.TVM John Erman. With Paul Winfield, Rita Tushingham. **PROD:** David Seltzer (Lorimar). **W:** David Seltzer. **M:** Fred Karlin. ABC-TV Films, 1976.
A veteran returns to Vietnam to search for the son he had with a Vietnamese prostitute.

Greetings. Brian De Palma. With Jonathon Warden, Robert De Niro, Gerrit Graham. **PROD:** Charles Hirsch (Sigma). **W:** Charles Hirsch, DePalma. **PH:** Robert Fiori. **M:** The Children of Paradise. West End Films, 1968.
Three companions work on ways to avoid the draft while also pursuing their daily pursuits: voyeurism, the Kennedy assassination, and dating agencies.

Hail, Hero!. David Miller. With Michael Douglas, Arthur Kennedy. **PROD:** Harold D. Cohen (Halcyon). **W:** David Mamber from the novel by John Weston. **PH:** Robert Hauser. **M:** Jerome Moross. National General, 1969.
A wealthy youth who opposes the war enlists to please his family, to make amends for crippling his older brother, and to learn why men fight.

Hair. Milos Forman. With John Savage, Treat Williams. **PROD:** Lester Persky, Michael Butler (CIP). **W:** Michael Weller from musical play by Galt MacDermot, Gerome Ragni/James Rado. **PH:** Miroslav Ondricek, Richard Kratina, Jean Talvin. **M:** Galt MacDermot. United Artists, 1978.
A tribe of hippies waylays a draftee in Central Park for a last twenty-four hours of adventure and fun.

Hamburger Hill. John Irvin. With Anthony Barrile, Don James, Dylan McDermott, Courtney Vance. **PROD:** Marcia Nasatir and Jim Carabatsos (RKO). **W:** Jim Carabatsos. **PH:** Peter MacDonald. **M:** Philip Glass. Paramount, 1987.
Raw recruits and hardened veterans must work together to reach the top of a strategic hill. From an actual battle.

Hanoi Hilton, The. Lionel Chetwynd. With Michael Moriarty, Aki Aleong, Paul Le Mat. **PROD:** Menahem Golan and Yoram Globus (Golan-Globus). **W:** Lionel Chetwynd. **PH:** Mark Irwin. **M:** Jimmy Webb. Cannon Films, 1987.
POWs survive for years in Hanoi's infamous prison.

Hard Ride, The. Burt Topper. With Robert Fuller, Sherry Bain, Tony Russell. **PROD:** Charles Hanawalt (AIP/Burwalt). **W:** Burt Topper. **PH:** Robert Sparks. **M:** Harley Hatcher. Anglo-EMI, 1971.

A soldier accompanies the body of a black friend home and encounters his white sweetheart and the Indian leader of his motorcycle gang.

Heartbreak Ridge. Clint Eastwood. With Clint Eastwood, Marsha Mason, Mario Van Peebles. **PROD:** Eastwood (Malpaso/Jay Weston). **W:** James Carabatsos. **PH:** Jack N. Green. **M:** Lennie Niehaus. Warner, 1986.
A veteran of Korea and Vietnam is now a drill instructor who finally gets to lead his men to victory at Grenada.

Heated Vengeance. Edward Murphy. With Richard Hatch. **PROD:** Edward Murphy. **W:** Edward Murphy. **M:** Jim Price. 1984.
When a veteran returns to Vietnam to find the woman he deserted there, he discovers a group of American deserters who band together to kill him.

Heaven and Earth. Oliver Stone. With Tommy Lee Jones, Joan Chen, Haing S. Ngor, Hiep Thi Le. **PROD:** Stone, Arnon Milchan, Robert Kline, A. Kitman Ho (Regency/Le Studio Canal+/Alcor). **W:** Stone from the memoirs *When Heaven and Earth Changed Places,* by Le Ly Hayslip and Jay Wurts, and *Child of War, Woman of Peace,* by Le Ly and James Hayslip. **PH:** Robert Richardson. **M:** Kitaro. Warner, 1993
Le Ly is a Vietnamese girl who suffers at the hands of the South Vietnamese, North Vietnamese, and Americans during the war. Eventually she marries an American soldier and comes to America but learns that there is no paradise here either.

Heroes. Jeremy Paul Kagan. With Henry Winkler, Sally Field, Harrison Ford. **PROD:** David Foster, Lawrence Turman (Turman-Foster Company). **W:** James Carabatsos (David Freeman, uncredited). **PH:** Frank Stanley. **M:** Jack Nitzsche, Richard Hazard. Universal, 1977.
A comically deranged veteran travels to Eureka, California to start a worm farm with a buddy he has forgotten died in Vietnam.

Hi, Mom!. Brian De Palma. With Robert De Niro, Jennifer Salt, Lara Parker, Gerrit Graham. **PROD:** Charles Hirsch (Sigma III). **W:** De Palma from story by De Palma, Charles Hirsch. **PH:** Robert Elfstrom. **M:** Eric Kaz. West End Films, 1970.
A returning veteran becomes involved in the radical movements of New York City. Comic sequel to Greetings. *Also known as* Confessions of a Peeping John *and* Blue Manhattan.

Homer. John Trent. With Don Scardino, Tisa Farrow, Alex Nicol. **PROD:** Terence Nene, Steven North (Palomar). **W:** Claude Harz from a story by Harz, Matt Clark. **PH:** Lazlo George. **M:** Scardino. National General, 1970.

A young man hides his opposition to the war from his parents until his best friend is killed in action.

House. Steve Miner. With William Katt, George Wendt, Richard Moll, Kay Lenz. PROD: Sean Cunningham. W: Ethan Wiley. PH: Mac Ahlberg. M: Harry Manfredini. New World, 1986.
A veteran's son is kidnapped by the ghost of a Vietnam buddy who disappeared in the War.

I Feel It Coming. Sidney Knight. With Sammy Cole, Dandy Thomas. PROD: Jean Jacques Robeau. Sam Lake Enterprises, 1969.

Ice. Robert Kramer. PROD: David C. Stone (Monument Film/AFI). W: Robert Kramer. PH: Robert Machover. 1970.
In the near future, America is fighting an imperialist war against Mexico and a band of American guerrillas tries to overthrow the government.

In Country. Norman Jewison. With Emily Lloyd, Bruce Willis, John Terry, Joan Allen. PROD: Norman Jewison, Richard Roth. W: Frank Pierson, Cynthia Cidre from Bobbie Ann Mason's novel. PH: Russell Boyd. M: James Horner. Warner, 1989.
A girl struggles to learn about her father who died in Vietnam before she was born and about the war that killed him.

In Love and War.TVM Paul Aaron. With Jane Alexander, James Woods, Concetta Tomei. PROD: Carol Schreder (Carol Schreder, Tisch/Avnet). W: Carol Schreder from the book by Jim & Sybil Stockdale. PH: Gayne Rescher. M: Charles Gross. NBC-TV, 1987.
True story of Jim Stockdale, who was shot down over Vietnam, and his wife Sybil whose campaign against the U.S. government's seeming inaction over the POW's plight eventually gains her husband's release. In 1992, Stockdale would be Ross Perot's presidential running mate.

Indo-Chine. (FR/VN) Régis Wargnier. With Catherine Deneuve, Vincent Perez, Jean Yanne. PROD: (Paradis Films/Générale d'images W: Régis Wargnier, Louis Gardel, Erik Orsenna, Catherine Cohen. PH: Françios Catonné. 1992.
In 1930s Indo-China, a woman governs her rubber plantation but loses her French lover, a naval officer, to her adopted Indochinese daughter.

Initiation, The. William Welburn. With Denise Lynn, Rich Stausser, Sean Ohlen. PROD: Tom Parker. Original Films, 1968.

Invasion of the Flesh Hunters. 1982.
Vietnam veterans become cannibals.

Iron Triangle, The. Eric Weston. With Beau Bridges, Haing S. Ngor,
Liem Whatley. Prod: Angela P. Schapiro, Tony Scotti (Eurobrothers).
W: Eric Weston, John Bushelman, Larry Hilbrand from a diary found
on a dead NVA soldier. Ph: Irv Goodnoff. M: Michael LLoyd, John
D'Anrea, Nick Strimple. Medusa/International Video, 1989.
*An American officer is captured by a young NVA soldier, but when a Hanoi
party official tries to claim the prisoner, the NVA soldier and the American
must learn to work together to survive.*

JFK. Oliver Stone. With Kevin Costner, Gary Oldman, Tommy Lee
Jones. Prod: A. Kitman Ho, Stone (Warner with Le Studio
Canal+/Regency Enterprises/Alcor Films). W: Stone, Zachary Sklar
from *On the Trail of the Assassins* by Jim Garrison and *Crossfire: The
Plot that Killed Kennedy* by Jim Marrs. Ph: Robert Richardson. M:
John Williams. Warner, 1991.
*Using a mixture of original footage, re-enactments, and fictional drama, Ol-
iver Stone argues that Kennedy's assassination was engineered by the
military/industrial bureaucracy to prevent his lessening the U.S. commitment
to Vietnam.*

Jacknife. David Jones. With Robert De Niro, Ed Harris, Kathy Baker.
Prod: Robert Schaffel, Carol Baum (King's Road). W: Stephen Met-
calfe from his play *Strange Snow*. Ph: Brian West. Vestron, 1989.
*A truck driver reunites with a war buddy who suffers from survivor's guilt
and helps him to put the war behind him.*

Jacob's Ladder. Adrian Lyne. With Tim Robbins, Elizabeth Pena,
Danny Aiello. Prod: Alan Marshall (Carolco). W: Bruce Joel Rubin.
Ph: Jeffrey L. Kimball. M: Maurice Jarre. Guild, 1990.
*A veteran discovers that he was the victim of military experiments while in
Vietnam and that he may actually be dead.*

Joe. John G. Avildsen. With Peter Boyle, Susan Sarandon, Dennis
Patrick. Prod: David Gil. W: Norman Wexler. Ph: Avildsen. M:
Bobby Scott. Cannon Films, 1970.
*When a wealthy man accidentally kills his daughter's drug-dealing lover, a
hard-hat bigot encourages him to follow-up with the slaughter of a counter-
culture group in which, he learns too late, his daughter is a member.*

Journey through Rosebud. Tom Gries. With Robert Foster, Kistoffer
Tabori. Prod: David Gil. GSF, 1972.
*An Indian veteran who had allowed his fellow white soldiers to commit atroci-
ties in Vietnam is now an alcoholic. He provides sanctuary on the reservation
to a draft dodger, is betrayed by the dodger, and kills himself.*

Jud. Gunther Collins. With Joseph Kaufmann, Robert Demon. **Prod:** Igo Kantor (Duque Films). **W:** Gunther Collins. **Ph:** Isidore Mankofsky. **M:** Stu Phillips. Maron Films 1971.
A veteran returns to the states and finds that people expect help from him that he is unable to give.

Jump into Hell. David Butler. With Jaques Sernas, Kurt Kasznar, Arnold Moss, Peter Van Eyck, Pat Blake. **Prod:** David Weisbart. **W:** Irving Wallace. **Ph:** J. Peverell Marley. **M:** David Buttolph. Warner, 1955.
Four French paratroopers jump to the aid of the French defenders at Dien Bien Phu.

Just a Little Inconvenience.tvm Theodore J. Flicker. With Lee Majors, James Stacey, Barbara Hershey. **Prod:** Allan Balter (Fawcett-Majors/Universal TV). **W:** Theodore J. Flicker, Allan Balter. **Ph:** Duke Callaghan. **M:** Jimmie Haskell. 1977.
A paraplegic veteran blames his wounds on his best friend, until that friend designs a ski-system that allows the vet to participate in his favorite sport once again.

Katherine.tvm Jeremy Paul Kagan. With Art Carney, Sissy Spacek. **Prod:** Gerald I. Isenberg (Jozak). **W:** Jeremy Kagan. **Ph:** Frank Stanley. ABC-TV, 1975.
A wealthy young woman is drawn into the radical movement and eventually dies when a bomb she is carrying explodes before she can place it.

Kent State.tvm James Goldstone. With Jane Fleiss, Charlie Lang, Talia Balsam. **Prod:** (Interplanetary). **W:** Gerald Green, Richard Kramer. **Ph:** Steve Larner. **M:** Ken Lauber. NBC-TV, 1980.
The events that led to the Kent State Massacre are dramatized.

Killing Fields, The (GB). Roland Joffé. With Sam Waterston, Haing S. Ngor, John Malkovich. **Prod:** David Puttnam (Goldcrest/Enigma). **W:** Bruce Robinson from the article "The Death and Life of Dith Pran" by Sydney Schanberg. **Ph:** Chris Menges. **M:** Mike Oldfield. Warner, 1984.
An American journalist remains in Cambodia after the American withdrawal, putting his native interpreter in danger. After the journalist leaves, the interpreter must survive Pol Pot's oppression and flee the country.

Lady from Yesterday, The (USA).tvm Robert Day. With Wayne Rogers, Bonnie Bedelia, Tina Chen. 1985.
A Vietnamese woman confronts the married American executive who fathered her son ten years before in Vietnam.

Last Flight Out.tvm Larry Elikann. With Richard Crenna, James Earl Jones, Haing S. Ngor. **Prod:** William Cohen. **W:** Walter Halsey Davis. 1990.
The story of the last American jetliner to leave Saigon in April 1975 is told with an all-star cast.

Last Hit, The. Jan Egleson. With Bryan Brown, Brooke Adams, Harris Yulin. **Prod:** Rob Christianson, Rob Rosenberg. **W:** Walter Klenhard, Alan Sharp. 1993.
The government offers a deserter immunity if he will become an assassin.

Last Hunter, The (IT). Anthony M. Dawson (Antonio Margheriti). With David Warbeck, Tisa Farrow. **Prod:** Gianfranco Couyoumdjian (Flora Films/Gico Cinematografica). **W:** Dardano Sacchetti. **Ph:** Riccardo Pallottini. **M:** Franco Micalizzi. World Northal, 1984.
Gilbert Adair describes this as a "spaghetti Vietnam War film." Also known as Caccatori II *and* Hunter of the Apocalypse.

Last Platoon. Paul D. Robinson. With Richard Hatch, Max Laurel, Anthony Sawyer. American Imperial, 1990.
A cynical sergeant is ordered to lead a squad of new recruits and criminals on a special mission with a band of Vietnamese guerrillas. His Vietnamese girlfriend is one of the guerrillas, and he must rescue her when she is captured.

Latino. Haskell Wexler. With Robert Beltran, Annette Cardona, Tony Plana. **Prod:** Benjamin Berg (LucasFilm). **W:** Wexler. **Ph:** Tom Sigel. Cinecom International, 1985.
A Chicano Green Beret veteran encounters a personal conflict when he is sent to advise the Contras in Nicaragua.

Leathernecks. Paul D. Robinson. With Richard Hatch, James Mitchum. American Imperial, 1990.
A crack squad is ordered to capture two deserters, one of whom is a war hero and friend of the squad's leader.

Lethal Weapon. Richard Donner. With Mel Gibson, Danny Glover, Gary Busey. **Prod:** Richard Donner, Joel Silver. **W:** Shane Black. **Ph:** Stephen Goldblatt. **M:** Michael Kamen, Eric Clapton. Warner, 1987.
A high-strung vet, suicidal after his wife's murder, is teamed up with a vet who is now a socially secure, family-man on the LAPD. Together they fight a drug ring composed of Vietnam veterans who exploit connections in SE Asia to smuggle heroin.

Lethal Weapon 2. Richard Donner. With Mel Gibson, Danny Glover, Joe Pesci. Prod: Richard Donner, Joel Silvers (Silver) W: Jeffrey Boam from a story by Shane Black and Warren Murphy. Ph: Stephen Goldblatt. M: Michael Kamen, Eric Clapton, David Sanborn. Warner, 1989.
The Vietnam veteran cop remains addicted to risk as he and his partner attack a drug-kingpin protected by diplomatic immunity.

Lethal Weapon 3. Richard Donner. With Mel Gibson, Danny Glover, Joe Pesci, Rene Russo. Prod: Richard Donner and Joel Silver W: Jeffrey Boam, Robert Mark Kaman. Ph: Jan De Bont. M: Michael Kamen, Eric Clapton, David Sanborn. Warner, 1991.
The Vietnam veteran cop remains addicted to risk as he and his partner ....

Little Big Man. Arthur Penn. With Dustin Hoffman, Martin Balsam, Faye Dunaway, Chief Dan George. Prod: Stuart Miller (Stockbridge/Hiller/Cinema Center). W: Calder Willingham from the novel by Thomas Berger. Ph: Harry Stradling. M: John Hammond. 1970.
The only white man to survive Custer's last stand recounts his life among both the Indians and the white men to a reporter. The film is frequently described as a allegory of the Vietnam War.

Limbo. Mark Robson. With Kate Jackson, Kathleen Nolan, Katherine Justice. Prod: Linda Gottlieb (The Filmmaker's Group, Omaha/Orange Films). W: Joan Silver, James Bridges from Silver's novel. Ph: Charles Wheeler. M: Anita Kerr. Universal, 1972.
The wives of soldiers who are missing in action face uncertain futures. One supports the war, one opposes it, and one is uncommitted about it. Also known as Women in Limb *and* Chained to Yesterday.

Limousine. Augustin B. Ramos. Prod: Augustin B. Ramos (A.B. Ramos). 1984.
Short film about a Vietnam veteran .

Live for Life (France/Italy). Claude Lelouch. With Yves Montand, Annie Girardot, Candice Bergen. Prod: (Ariane/Vides) W: Pierre Uytterhoeven, LeLouch. Ph: Lelouch. M: Francis Lai. UA, 1967.
A French documentary producer falls in love with an American model. Also known as Vivre pour Vivre.

Long Journey Home, The.tvm Rod Holcomb. With Meredith Baxter Birney, David Birney. Prod: Ervin Zavada (Andrea Baynes, Grail,

Lorimar-TV). **W:** Karen Clark. **Pʜ:** Ed Koons. **M:** J.A.C. Redford. CBS-TV, 1983.
A veteran listed as MIA but actually working undercover returns home in secret to try and steal his wife's money. It begins with a meeting of the Wives of MIAs.

Long Road Home, The. With Denis Forest. 1989.
After receiving his draft notice, a young man takes a job at a Canadian summer camp and considers what to do.

Losers, The. Jack Starrett. With William Smith, Bernie Hamilton, Adam Roarke. **Pʀod:** Joe Solomon (Fanfare Film). **W:** Alan Caillou. **Pʜ:** Nonong Rasca. **M:** Stu Phillips. MGM-EMI, 1970.
The government sends a motorcycle gang to rescue an American diplomat who has been captured by the Communist Chinese in Cambodia.

Lost Command, The. Mark Robson. With Anthony Quinn, Alain Delon, George Segal. **Pʀod:** Mark Robson (Red Lion). **W:** Nelson Gidding from *The Centurians* by Jean Larteguy. **Pʜ:** Robert Surtees. **M:** Franz Waxman. Columbia, 1966.
French soldiers lose valiantly at Dien Bien Phu and go on to fight for a losing cause in Algeria.

Lost Idol, The. P. Chalong. With Erik Estrada, James Phillips, Myra Chason. **Pʀod:** P. Chalong. **W:** James Phillips, Tony S. Suwat. **Pʜ:** Visidh Stone. **M:** Anuwat Suebsuwan. 1988.
When an army officer discovers a priceless golden statue in Cambodia, he massacres his unit, hides the statue, and returns for it years later, only to find a survivor of the unit waiting for him.

Lost Platoon. David A. Prior. With David Parry, William Knight, Michael Wayne. **Pʜ:** James Rosenthal. Action International, 1989.
A platoon of vampires has fought in World Wars I and II, Korea, and Vietnam, and they are now fighting in Central America.

Lover, The (FR/GB). Jean-Jacques Annaud. With Jane March, Tony Leung. **Pʀod:** Claude Berri, Timothy Burrill (Renn Films A2/Burrill with Biai Phong Film) **W:** Gérard Brach, Annaud from the novel by Marguerite Duras. **Pʜ:** Robert Fraisse. **M:** Gabriel Yared. Guild, 1992.
A young French girl becomes the lover of a wealthy Chinese man in 1920s Saigon, but their love is constricted and finally forbidden by the social systems of the period. Filmed in Vietnam.

Magnum Force. Ted Post. With Clint Eastwood, Hal Holbrook, Mitchell Ryan. PROD: Robert Daley (Malpaso). W: John Milius, Michael Cimino. PH: Frank Stanley. M: Lalo Schifrin. Warner, 1973.
Dirty Harry combats a group of veterans enlisted as motorcycle cops by a corrupt police captain who uses them as a vigilante force.

Magnum, P. I. TVM Roger Young. With Tom Selleck, John Hillerman, Roger E. Mosley, Larry Manetti. PROD: J. Rickley Dumm (Belisarius, Glen A. Larson, Universal TV). CBS-TV, 1980.
A veteran turned private eye tries to clear one army buddy and encounters another. Pilot for the series.

Mean Johnny Barrows. Fred Williamson. With Fred Williamson, Roddy McDowall, Jenny Sherman. PROD: (Ramana). Atlas Films, 1976.
A veteran becomes involved with the Mafia.

Medium Cool. Haskell Wexler. With Robert Forster, Verna Bloom, Peter Bonerz. PROD: Tully Friedman, Wexler (H&J). W: Wexler. PH: Wexler. M: Mike Bloomfield. Paramount, 1969.
A news cameraman who prides himself on professional detachment finds himself caught in the war protests he attempts to shoot.

Memorial Day.TVM Joseph Sargent. With Mike Farrell, Shelley Fabares, Keith Mitchell. W: Michael Bortman. 1983.
A veteran encounters some war-buddies on memorial day and relives the memories.

Milestones. Robert Kramer and John Douglas. With Helen Grace Paley, Mary Chapelle, David C. Stone. PROD: Barbara Stone, David C. Stone. W: Kramer & Douglas. PH: Kramer & Douglas. NY Cinema, 1975.
A group of men and woman review their past in the counterculture. The film was banned in South Africa.

Missing in Action. Joseph Zito. With Chuck Norris, M. Emmett Walsh, Leonore Kasdorf, James Hong. PROD: Menahem Golan and Yoram Globus (Golan-Globus). W: James Bruner from story by John Crowther, Lance Ho. PH: Joao Fernandes. M: Jay Chattaway. Cannon Films, 1984.
An ex-POW returns to Vietnam to prove POWs still exist by freeing some of them.

Missing in Action 2: The Beginning. Lance Hool. With Chuck Norris, Soon Teck-Oh. PROD: Menahem Golan and Yoram Globus (Golan-

Globus). **W:** Arthur Silver, Larry Levinson and Steve Bing. **Ph:** Jorge
Stahl Jr. **M:** Brian May. Cannon Films, 1985.
*POWs kept in captivity years after the war must fight their Vietnamese cap-
tors and their fellow prisoners to survive and escape. A prequel to the first
film.*

Model Shop, The. Jacques Demy. With Anouk Aimée, Gary Lock-
wood. **Prod:** Jacques Demy. **W:** Jacques Demy. **Ph:** Michael Hugo. **M:**
Spirit. Columbia, 1969.
*An architect tries to enjoy his last twenty-four hours before induction in Los
Angeles.*

Modern Problems. Ken Shapiro. With Chevy Chase, Patti D'Arbon-
ville. **Prod:** Alan Greisman, Michael Shamberg. **W:** Shapiro, Tom
Sherohman, Arthur Sellers. **Ph:** Edmund Koons. **M:** Dominic Fron-
tiere. 1981.
A disabled Vietnam veteran works as an air traffic controller.

More American Graffiti. B.W.L. Norton. With Ron Howard, Charlie
Martin Smith. **Prod:** Howard Kazanjian (LucasFilm). **W:** B.W.L. Norton. **Ph:** Caleb Deschanel. Universal, 1979.
*Terry "the Toad" goes to Vietnam and attempts to desert, while Steve Hol-
lander gets involved in campus activism.*

Motor Psycho. Russ Meyer. With Jaji, Alex Rocco. **Prod:** Russ
Meyer. Eve, 1965.
A Vietnam veteran is a member of a motorcycle gang.

My Father, My Son.tvm Jeff Bleckner. With Keith Carradine, Karl
Malden. **Prod:** Fred Weintraub (Fred Weintraub, John J. McMahon).
W: Jacqueline Feather, David Seidler from the book by Elmo Zumwalt
Jr. & Elmo Zumwalt III. **Ph:** Cliff Ralke. **M:** Laurence Rosenthal.
CBS-TV, 1988.
*Story of Admiral Elmo Zumwalt who ordered the use of Agent Orange, and of
his son Elmo Zumwalt III who died of cancer after swimming through water
covered with Agent Orange in Vietnam.*

National Lampoon's Animal House. John Landis. With Thomas
Hulce, John Belushi, Stephen Furst. **Prod:** Matty Simons, Ivan Reit-
man. **W:** Harold Ramis, Douglas Kenney, Chris Miller. **Ph:** Charles
Correll. **M:** Elmer Bernstein. Universal, 1978.
*Although it is set in the early sixties, the college president's cruelest attempt
to squash the unruly fraternity boys is to expel them and inform their draft
boards that they are eligible. A coda explains that the ROTC fanatic dies in
Vietnam at the hands of his own men.*

Night Flowers. Luis San Andres. With Jose Perez, Gabriel Walsh. **W:** Gabriel Walsh. Leonard Franklin Associates, 1979.

Night of the Living Dead. George A. Romero. With Judith O'Dea, Duane Jones, Karl Hardman. **PROD:** (Image Ten). **W:** John A. Russo. 1968.
The dead rise and attack the living in what some have described as a critique of the Vietnam War.

1969. Ernest Thompson. With Robert Downey, Jr., Bruce Dern, Kiefer Sutherland. **PROD:** Daniel Grodnik, Bill Badalato (Atlantic). **W:** Thompson. **PH:** Jules Brenner. **M:** Michael Small. Entertainment, 1988.
Two students experience the sixties. When one of them drops out of college because of drug problems, they travel in a van to see the country, steal their draft cards, and consider escaping to Canada.

Ninth Configuration, The. William Peter Blatty. With Stacey Keach, Scott Wilson, Jason Miller. **PROD:** Blatty (ITC/Lorimar). **W:** Blatty. **PH:** Gerry Fisher. **M:** Barry DeVorzon. Warner, 1980.
A veteran thinks he has been assigned as chief of a special asylum for deranged veterans, but he is actually its chief patient and suffering from survivor guilt and a Christ complex. Also known as Twinkle, Twinkle Killer Kane.

No Dead Heroes. J.C. Miller. With John Dresden, Max Thayer, Dave Anderson, Nick Nicholson. **PROD:** J.C. Miller (Maharaj-Miller). **W:** Miller, Arthur Gelfield. **M:** Marita Welman. Cineventures, 1983.

Norwood. Jack Haley Jr. With Glen Campbell, Kim Darby, Joe Namath. **PROD:** Hal B. Wallis. **W:** Marguerite Roberts from the novel by Charles Portis. **PH:** Robert B. Hauser. **M:** Al DeLory. Paramount, 1970.
A veteran trying to break into the country singing world travels from Texas to New York to collect $70 that another veteran owes him.

Off Limits. Christopher Crowe. With Willem Dafoe, Gregory Hines, Amanda Pays. **PROD:** Alan Barnette (American Entertainment Partners). **W:** Crowe, Jack Thibeau. **PH:** David Gribble. **M:** James Newton Howard. 20th Century-Fox, 1988.
Two detectives from the Criminal Investigations Detachment track down the murderer of Vietnamese prostitutes in 1968 Saigon. Also known as Saigon.

Open Season. (U.S./Spain/Switzerland). Peter Collinson. With Peter Fonda, John Philip Law, William Holden. **PROD:** Jose S. Vicuna,

George H. Brown (Impala-Arpa). **W:** David Osborn, Liz Charles-Williams. **PH:** Fernando Arribas. **M:** Ruggero Cini. Columbia, 1974.
Three Vietnam veterans hunt humans. Also known as Los Cazadores.

Operation CIA. Christian Nyby. With Burt Reynolds, Danielle Aubry. **PROD:** Peer J. Oppenheimer (Hei Ra Matt). **W:** Bill Ballinger, Oppenheimer. **PH:** Richard Moore. **M:** Paul Dunlap. Allied Artists, 1965.
A CIA agent struggles to avert the assassination of the American ambassador in Saigon, and nearly fails when his French lover is revealed as a Viet Cong double-agent.

Operation Nam. Larry Ludman. With Oliver Tobias, Ethan Wayne, Donald Pleasance. **PROD:** (Falvia Internation Film). Fabriano de Angeles, 1980.
Action drama set in the jungles of Vietnam.

Our Winning Season. Joseph Ruben. With Scott Jacoby, Deborah Benson, Joe Penny. **PROD:** Joe Roth. **W:** Nick Niciphor. **PH:** Stephen Katz. **M:** Charles Fox. American International, 1978.
A group of young men survive High School in the sixties but face Vietnam in their futures.

Outside In. Allan Baron. With Darrel Larson, Heather Menzies. **PROD:** George Edwards (George Edwards-Sal Grasso-Media Trend). **W:** Robert Hutchinson from a story by Hutchinson, Baron. **PH:** Mario Tosi. **M:** Randy Edelman. Harold Robbins International, 1972.
A draft dodger secretly returns from Canada to attend his father's funeral.

P.O.W., The. Phillip Dossick. With Howard Jahre. **PROD:** David Moltak, Jane Dossick. 1973.
A paraplegic veteran in a wheelchair struggles to reenter society while two filmmakers prepare documentaries about him.

P.O.W.: The Escape. Gideon Amir. With David Carradine, Charles R. Floyd, Mako. **PROD:** Menahem Golan and Yoram Globus (Golan-Globus). **W:** Jeremy Lipp, James Bruner, Malcolm Barbour and John Langley from a story by Avi Kleinberger and Gideon Amir. **PH:** Yechiel Ne'eman. **M:** Michael Linn. Cannon, 1986.
An American colonel is captured trying to rescue POWs at the end of the war, but he still manages to lead an escape from the camp where he is held.

Parades. Robert J. Siegel. With Russ Thacker, Brad Sullivan. **PROD:** Robert J. Siegel (Confron). **W:** George Tabori. **PH:** Sol Negrin. **M:** Garry Sherman. 1972.

A frail youth claiming to have an artificial heart is drafted, goes AWOL, and suffers from the brutality of the stockades.

Park is Mine, The (TVM). Steven Hilliard Stern. With Tommy Lee Jones, Helen Shaver, Yaphet Kotto. PROD: Denis Heroux, John Kemeny. **W:** Lyle Gorch from book by Stephen Peters. **PH:** Laszlo George. **M:** Tangerine Dream. 20th Century-Fox, 1985.

A veteran suffering from Agent Orange-induced cancer commits suicide after wiring Central Park with explosives, but another unemployed veteran carries on the dream of taking the park "hostage" to make a statement about veterans' rights.

Physical Evidence. Michael Crichton. With Burt Reynolds, Theresa Russell, Ned Beaty. PROD: Martin Ransohoff (Columbia). **W:** Bill Phillips from a strory by Steve Ransohoff, Phillips. **PH:** John A. Alonzo. **M:** Henry Mancini. Rank, 1988.

When an ex-cop is arrested for murder, the trial judge refuses to allow mention of his service in the Phoenix assassination project in the case against him.

Platoon. Oliver Stone. With Tom Berenger, Willem Dafoe, Charlie Sheen. PROD: Arnold Kopelson (Helmdale Film). **W:** Stone. **PH:** Robert Richardson. **M:** Georges Delerue. Orion, 1986.

A young soldier in Vietnam must choose between two sergeants, one violent and angry, the other conscience stricken.

Platoon Leader. Aaron Norris. With Michael Dudikoff. PROD: Menahim Golan and Yoram Globus (Golan-Globus), from the memoir by James R. McDonough. Cannon Films, 1988.

An inexperienced lieutenant must gain the trust of his battle-hardened platoon.

Poor White Trash II. S.F. Browning. With Gene Ross, Ann Stafford, Norma Moore. PROD: Browning. **W:** Mary Davis, Gene Ross. **M:** Robert Farrar. Dimension, 1983.

A veteran becomes an axe-murderer who assaults a couple on their summer holiday. Also known as Poor White Trash *and* Scum of the Earth.

Predator. John McTiernan. With Arnold Schwarzenegger, Carl Weathers, Elpidia Carrillo. PROD: Lawrence Gordan, Joel Silver, John Davis. **W:** Jim Thomas, John Thomas. **PH:** Donald McAlpine. **M:** Alan Silvestri. 20th Century-Fox, 1987.

A squad of American commandos go to Central America on what they believe is a rescue mission. In fact, the government has sent them on a covert operation against communist revolutionaries. They defeat the communists easily, but face a deadlier foe in an alien who has come to Earth on a hunting trip.

Presidio, The. Peter Hyams. With Sean Connery, Mark Harmon, Meg Ryan, Jack Warden. **Prod:** D. Constantine Conte. **W:** Larry Ferguson. **Ph:** Hyams. **M:** Bruce Broughton. Paramount/UIP, 1988.
A group of Vietnam veterans run a smuggling operation out of a military base in San Francisco.

Prism. Anitra Pivnick. With Paul Greier, Dale Soules, Nancy Volkman, Ozzi Tortora. **Prod:** Bob Silverstein, Jay Freund, Anitra Pivnick (Corn King Films). **W:** Anitra Pivnick. **Ph:** Jay Freund. **M:** Tom Manoff. 1971.
A lawyer defends draft dodgers and resisters.

Prologue. Robin Spry. 1968.

Promise of Love, The.TVM Don Taylor. With Valerie Bertinelli, Shelly Long, Jameson Parker. **Prod:** Jay Benson (Pierre Cassette). **W:** Harry & Renee Longstreet, Carol Saraceno. **Ph:** Don Birnkrant. **M:** Paul Chihara. CBS-TV, 1980.
A young bride must rebuild her life after her husband dies in Vietnam.

Proud Men.TVM William A. Graham. With Charlton Heston, Peter Strauss, Nan Martin. **Prod:** Robert M. Sertner, Fraser C. Heston (Cowboy, Agememnon Films, von Zernack-Samuels). **W:** Jeff Andrus. **Ph:** Denis Lewiston. **M:** Laurence Rosenthal. ABC-TV, 1987.
A deserter, now living in Paris, comes home to Wyoming when he receives word that his father is dying.

Purple Hearts. Sidney J. Furie. With Cheryl Ladd, Ken Wahl. **Prod:** Furie (Ladd). **W:** Rick Natkin and Furie. **Ph:** Jan Kiesser. **M:** Robert Folk. Warner, 1984.
A navy medic pursues a nurse across Vietnam.

Quantum Leap.TVM With Scott Bakula, Harry Dean Stanton. **Prod:** (Bellisarius). NBC-TV, 1990.
The series hero is reincarnated as a Vietnam soldier whose squad goes on a mission to rescue POWs but is betrayed by a Vietnamese interpreter.

Quiet American, The. Joseph L. Mankiewicz. With Michael Redgrave, Audie Murphy, Claude Dauphin, Georgia Moll. **Prod:** Mankiewicz (Figaro). **W:** Mankiewicz from the novel by Graham

Greene. **Ph:** Robert L. Krasker. **M:** Mario Nascimbene. United Artists, 1958.

An idealistic young American tries to establish a plastics industry in Vietnam, but is betrayed to the communists by a jealous English journalist who convinces himself that the American is plotting terrorism.

RPM (Revolutions Per Minute). Stanley Kramer. With Anthony Quinn, Ann-Margret, Gary Lockwood, Paul Winfield. **Prod:** Kramer. **W:** Erich Segal. **Ph:** Michel Hugo, Perry Botkin, Jr. **M:** Barry de Vorzon. Columbia, 1970.

When students take over the administration offices in a small college, a radical professor is appointed to negotiate with them. Unfortunately he finds himself caught between sympathy for their youthful idealism and his new responsibilities.

Rambo: First Blood, Part Two. George P. Cosmatos. With Sylvester Stallone, Richard Crenna, Julia Nickson. **Prod:** Buzz Feitshans (Anabasis Investments NV). **W:** Stallone, James Cameron from characters created by David Morrell. **Ph:** Jack Cardiff. **M:** Jerry Goldsmith. Tri-Star, 1985.

A Vietnam veteran is released from prison for a secret mission to prove that no POWs exist in Vietnam. When he finds some, however, he disobeys orders and rescues them.

Rambo III. Peter MacDonald. With Sylvester Stallone, Richard Crenna. Tri-Star, 1988.

Rambo leaves the peace he has found in Thailand to rescue Colonel Trautman from the Russians in Afghanistan.

Ravager, The. Charles Nizet. With Pierre Gaston. **Prod:** Dave Ackerman. **Prod:** (Green Dolphin). 1970.

A veteran, deranged from witnessing a Viet Cong rape and murder, returns to the States, steals a load of dynamite, and bombs lovers in their cars.

Resting Place.tvm John Korty. With John Lithgow, Morgan Freeman, M. Emmett Walsh. **Prod:** Robert Huddleston. **W:** Walter Halsey Davis. **Ph:** William Wages. **M:** Paul Chihara. 1986.

A war-hero's funeral causes a small-town controversy and a military scandal. He is black and may have been the victim of racism in Vietnam. He is certainly its victim at home.

Return of Mickey Spillane's Mike Hammer, The.tvm Ray Danton. With Stacey Keach, Lindsay Bloom, Don Stroud. 1986.

Mike Hammer investigates a group of Viet vets who steal and sell children in Hollywood. Pilot for a new series of Mike Hammer mysteries.

Return of the Secaucus Seven, The. John Sayles. With Mark Arnott, Gordon Clapp, Maggie Cousineau. Prod: William Aydelott, Jeffrey Nelson (Salsipuedes). W: John Sayles. Ph: Austin de Besche. M: K. Mason Daring. Libra Films, 1980.
A group of college friends from the sixties reunites for a weekend and examines how their lives have changed over the years.

Revolutionary, The. Paul Williams. With Jon Voight, Jennifer Salt, Robert Duvall. Prod: Edward R. Pressman (Pressman-Williams). W: Hans Kõningsberger based on his novel. Ph: Brian Probyn. M: Mike Small. United Artists, 1970.
An allegorical tale describes the development of a young radical revolutionary in a nonspecific country.

Rogues' Regiment. Robert Florey. With Dick Powell, Marta Toren, Vincent Price. Prod: Robert Buckner. W: Buckner. Ph: Maury Gertsman. M: Danielle Amfitheatrof. Universal-International, 1948.
An American joins the French Foreign Legion in Vietnam to track down an escaped Nazi war criminal. The enemy are Vietnam nationalists supplied by USSR through German (Nazi) smugglers.

Rolling Thunder. John Flynn. With William Devane, Tommy Lee Jones, Linda Haynes. Prod: Norman T. Herman (AIP). W: Paul Schrader, Heywood Gould from story by Schrader. Ph: Jordan Cronenweth. M: Barry DeVorzon. American International, 1977.
A POW returns home to find a welcoming community, but soon learns his wife wants to leave him. When thieves murder his wife and son, he sets out for vengeance.

Rumor of War, A.tvm Richard T. Heffron. With Brad Davis, Keith Carradine, Brian Dennehy, Stacy Keach. Prod: David Manson (Stonehenge, Charles Fries). W: John Sacret Young from Philup Caputo's memoir. Ph: Jorge Stahl, Jr. and Stevan Larner. M: Charles Gross. CBS-TV, 1980.
A wild young man joins the marines to do something with his life. In Vietnam he loses his ideals, and, finally worn down by all the death, participates in the murder of two Vietnamese civilians.

Running on Empty. Sidney Lumet. With Judd Hirsch, Christine Lahti, River Phoenix. Prod: Amy Robinson, Griffin Dunne (Lorimar/Double Play). W: Naomi Foner. Ph: Gerry Fisher. M: Tony Mottola. Warner, 1988.
A radical couple, still on the run twenty years after accidentally killing a man during a war protest, try to raise their family and live normal lives.

Saigon. Leslie Fenton. With Veronica Lake, Alan Ladd, Douglas Dick. PROD: Wolfson. W: P. J. Wolfson and Arthur Sheekman from a story by Julian Zimet. PH: John F. Seitz. M: Robert Emmett Dolan. Paramount, 1948.
When a pilot takes a dying friend on a last fling to Saigon, they become involved in intrigue and murder.

Saigon Commandos. With PJ Soles, Richard Young. Concorde, 1987.
American MPs stationed in Saigon fight the corrupt Vietnamese politicians who run the heroin trade.

Saint Jack. Peter Bogdanovich. With Ben Gazzara, Denholm Elliott. PROD: Roger Corman (Shoals Creek/Playboy/Copa deOro). W: Bogdanovich, Howard Sackler, Paul Theroux from Theroux's novel. PH: Robby Muller. New World, 1979.
An American runs a brothel for American servicemen in Vietnam.

Satan's Sadists. Al Adamson. With Russ Tamblyn, Scott Brady. PROD: Al Adamson (Kennis-Frazer Films). W: Dennis Wayne. PH: Gary Graver. M: Harley Hatcher. Independent International, 1969.
A veteran must battle with a motorcycle gang.

Scent of a Woman. Martin Brest. With Al Pacino, Chris O'Donnell. PROD: Martin Brest (UIP/Universal/City Lights). W: Bo Goldman from *Profumo di Donna* (dir. Dino Risi) and novel *Il Buio e il Miele* by Giovanni Arpino. PH: Donald E. Thorin. M: Thomas Newman. Universal 1992.
A blind Vietnam veteran plans to commit suicide after a last fling in New York City.

Search and Destroy. William Fruet. With Perry King, Don Stroud, Tisa Farrow, Park Jong Soo. PROD: James Margellis. W: Don Enright. Film Ventures, 1981.
A former South Vietnamese official living in the United States seeks revenge against American soldiers.

Secret Honor. Robert Altman. With Philip Baker Hall. PROD: Altman. W: Donald Freed, Arnold M. Stone from their play. PH: Pierre Mignot. M: George Burt. Sandcastle 5, 1984.
In this one-man show, Nixon rambles into a tape recorder about his political career, including Vietnam and Watergate, and reveals himself as the true hero of the War.

Shooter. TVM Gary Nelson. With Jeffrey Nordling, Alan Ruck, Rosalind Chau, Helen Hunt. PROD: Barry Berg (UBU and Paramount

Network TV). **W:** David Hume Kennerly, Stephen Kline. **PH:** Gayne Rescher. **M:** Paul Chihara. 1988.
An attempted series pilot features photographers and journalists in Vietnam.

Siege of Firebase Gloria, The (U.S./Australia). Brian Trenchard-Smith. With R. Lee Ermey, Wings Hauser. **PROD:** (Eastern Film Management). 1988.
A squad of hardened soldiers takes control of the defense of a firebase during the 1968 Tet offensive. From a true incident.

Six O'Clock Follies, The.TVM Robert Sweeney. With A.C. Weary, Larry Fishburne, Philip Charles MacKenzie. **PROD:** Norman Steinberg, Marvin Kupfer (Warner TV). **W:** Norman Steinberg, Marvin Kupfer. 1980.
The Vietnam War serves as a backdrop for a comedy-drama about an Army television station.

'68. Steven Kovacs. With Eric Larson, Robert Locke, Neil Young. **PROD:** Dale Djerassi, Isabel Maxwell, Kovacs (New World). **W:** Kovacs. **PH:** Daniel Lacambre. Entertainment, 1988.
The son of a Hungarian immigrant volunteers for the army to prove his patriotism and his manhood, but changes his mind and reveals his homosexuality during the induction procedures.

Slaughter. Jack Starrett. With Jim Brown, Rip Torn. **PROD:** Monroe Sachson (Slaughter United). **W:** Mark Hanna, Don Williams. **PH:** Rosalio Sonanio. **M:** Luchi DeJesús. American International, 1972.
A black Green Beret wages war on the syndicate after it kills his parents.

Slaughter's Big Rip-Off. Gordon Douglas. With Jim Brown, Ed McMahon. **PROD:** Monroe Sachson. **W:** Charles Johnson. **PH:** Charles Wheeler. **M:** James Brown, Fred Wesley. American International, 1973.
Slaughter continues to fight the drug syndicates.

Slaughterhouse-Five. George Roy Hill. With Michael Sacks, Ron Leibman, Eugène Roche. **PROD:** Paul Monash (Vanodas). **W:** Stephen Geller from the novel by Kurt Vonnegut Jr. **PH:** Miroslav Ondricek. **M:** J.S. Bach. Universal, 1972.
A man who has been captured by aliens constantly moves through various moments of his life, including his captivity in World War II and his survival of the allied bombing of Dresden. The film is often viewed as an allegory of Vietnam.

Small Circle of Friends, A. Rob Cohen. With Brad Davis, Karen Allen, Jameson Parker, Shelly Long. PROD: Tim Zinnemann (Small Circle of Friends Inc). W: Ezra Sacks. PH: Michael Butler. M: Jim Steinman. United Artists, 1980.
Harvard undergraduates experience the turmoil of the sixties.

Soldier Blue. Ralph Nelson. With Candice Bergen, Peter Strauss, Donald Pleasance. PROD: Harold Loeb, Gabriel Katzka (Katzka-Loeb). W: John Gay from Theodore V. Olson's novel *Arrow in the Sun*. PH: Robert Hauser. M: Roy Budd. Avco Embassy Films, 1970.
A cavalry soldier and a woman must travel across the wilderness after Indians massacre her military escort. Afterward, they witness the Sand Creek Indian Massacre. The film is often viewed as an allegory of Vietnam.

Soldier's Revenge. David Worth. With Nicolas Savage, Maria Socas, Edgardo Moreira. PROD: J. C. Crespo. W: Lee Stull and David Worth. PH: Leonard Solis. Continental Motion Pictures, 1984.
A war hero who deserted returns home to local anger. He flees with a South American woman who is running guns to revolutionaries because they are holding her father as a hostage.

Some Kind of Hero. Michael Pressman. With Richard Pryor, Margot Kidder, Ray Sharkey. PROD: Howard W. Koch. W: James Kirkwood and Robert Boris from the novel by James Kirkwood. PH: King Baggot. M: Patrick Williams. Paramount, 1982.
A returning Black POW finds that his wife wants to leave him, the army wants to forget him, and society wants to ignore him.

Some May Live.TVM Vernon Sewell. With Joseph Cotten, Martha Hyer, Peter Cushing. PROD: Philip N. Krasne (Foundation). W: David T. Chantler. PH: Ray Parslow. M: Cyril Ornadel. RKO, 1966.
An American intelligence officer discovers that a woman in his office is passing classified documents to her communist husband. Also known as In Saigon, Some May Live.

Southern Comfort. Walter Hill. With Keith Carradine, Powers Boothe, Fred Ward. PROD: David Giler (EMI/Phoenix/Cinema Group Venture). W: Michael Kane, Walter Hill, David Giler. PH: Andrew Laszlo. M: Ry Cooder. 20th Century-Fox, 1981.
A squad of National Guardsmen on maneuvers in a Louisiana swamp find themselves in hostile territory after they provoke a conflict with local Cajun fisherman.

Special Delivery. Paul Wendkos. With Bo Svenson, Cybil Shepherd. PROD: Dick Berg (Bing Crosby). **W**: Don Gazzaniga. **PH**: Harry Stradling, Jr. **M**: Lalo Schifrin. 20th Century-Fox, 1977.
Four veterans rob a bank using commando tactics, but three are caught while escaping and the fourth must fight to get the money back after he hides it in a mailbox.

Stanley. William Grefe. With Chris Robinson. 1972.
A veteran befriends snakes and uses them to kill his enemies.

Steele Justice. Robert Boris. With Martin Kove, Sela Ward. **PROD**: John Strong. **W**: Boris. **PH**: John M. Stephens. **M**: Misha Segal. Atlantic Releasing, 1987.
A veteran's investigation of the murder of a Vietnamese friend and his family leads him to a former Vietnamese general who is now a drug lord in America.

Stone Killer, The. Michael Winner. With Charles Bronson. **PROD**: Michael Winner (Dino DeLaurentiis). **W**: Gerald Wilson from John Gardner's novel *A Complete State of Death*. **PH**: Richard Moore. **M**: Roy Budd. Columbia, 1973.
A hard-nosed cop uncovers a plan to brainwash veterans for use in an underworld massacre.

Strawberry Statement, The. Stuart Hagmann. With Bruce Davison, Kim Darby, bud Cort. **PROD**: Robert Chartoff, Irwin Winkler. **W**: Israel Horovitz from the book by James Simon Kunen. **PH**: Ralph Woolsey. **M**: Ian Freebairn Smith. MGM, 1970.
A student becomes involved in the Columbia University antiwar revolts in order to meet a girl, but becomes committed to the cause when he witnesses the police brutality.

Streamers. Robert Altman. With Matthew Modine, Michael Wright, Mitchell Lichtenstein. **PROD**: Altman, Nick J. Mileti (Rank/Streamers International). **W**: David Rabe from his play. **PH**: Pierre Mignot. United Artists, 1983.
Four recruits wait in bootcamp for the call to go to Vietnam.

Stunt Man, The. Richard Rush. With Peter O'Toole, Barbara Hershey, Steve Railsback. **PROD**: Rush. **W**: Lawrence B. Marcus from novel by Paul Brodeur. **PH**: Mario Tosi. **M**: Dominic Frontière. 20th Century-Fox, 1980.
A Vietnam veteran running from the police is protected by a film director who wants to use him as an inspiration for the antiwar film he is making.

Summertree. Anthony Newley. With Michael Douglas, Jack Warden. PROD: Kirk Douglas (Bryna Company). W: Edward Hume, Stephen Yafa from the play by Ron Cowen. PH: Richard C. Glouner. M: David Shire. Columbia, 1971.
A music student opposes the war, but his father tricks him into enlisting; he dies in Vietnam.

Suspect. Peter Yates. With Cher, Dennis Quaid, Liam Neeson. PROD: Daniel A. Sherkow. W: Eric Roth. PH: Billy Williams. M: Michael Kamen. Tri-Star, 1987.
A mute veteran suffering from post traumatic stress lives on the streets and is accused of murder.

Taking Off. Milos Forman. With Lynn Carlin, Buck Henry. PROD: Alfred W. Crown, Michael Hausman (Forman-Crown-Hausman with Claude Berri). W: Forman, John Guare, Jean-Claude Carrière, John Klein. PH: Miroslav Ondricek. Universal, 1971.
When a young girl runs away, her parents pursue her through various sixties' experiences.

Targets. Peter Bogdanovich. With Boris Karloff, Tim O'Kelly, Nancy Hsueh. PROD: Bogdanovich (The Filmgroup). W: Bogdanovich. PH: Laszlo Kovacs. AIP, 1968.
A horror star decides to retire because the real world has become more violent than his films, and the point is driven home by a Vietnam veteran sniper at a drive-in showing the actor's films. Bogdanovich's directorial debut.

Taxi Driver. Martin Scorsese. With Robert De Niro, Cybill Shepherd, Jodie Foster. PROD: Michael and Julia Phillips (Italo-Judeo). W: Paul Schrader. PH: Michael Chapman. M: Bernard Herrman. Columbia, 1976.
A veteran takes a job as a taxi driver and becomes obsessed with the violence and corruption in New York City.

Tiger by the Tail. R.G. Springsteen. With Christopher George, Tippi Hedren, Dean Jagger. PROD: Francis D. Lyon. United Pictures, 1968.
When a war hero is accused of his brother's murder, he enlists the brother's socialite girlfriend to help him uncover the real killer.

To Heal a Nation.TVM Michael Pressman. With Eric Roberts, Glynnis O'Connor, Marshall Colt. PROD: Robert M. Sertner with Gordon Freedman, Ian Sander (Lionel Chetwynd, Orion TV and van Zerneck-Samuels). W: Chetwynd from the memoir by Jan C. Scruggs and Joel L. Swerdlow. PH: Denis Lewiston. M: Laurence Rosenthal. 1988.

The life of Jan Scruggs, who spearheaded the effort to build the Vietnam Veterans Memorial.

To Kill a Clown. (GB) George Bloomfield. With Alan Alda, Blythe Danner, Heath Lamberts. **Prod:** Theodore Sills (Palomar Pictures International). **W:** George Bloomfield, I.C. Rapoport from Algis Budry's novel *Master of the Hounds*. **Ph:** Walter Lassally. **M:** Richard Hill, John Hawkins. 20th Century-Fox, 1972.
A crippled, deranged Vietnam veteran traps a married couple in an isolated beachhouse and terrorizes them with his dogs.

To the Shores of Hell. Will Zens. With Marshall Thompson, Richard Jordahl, Kiva Lawrence. **Prod:** Will Zens (Robert Patrick). **W:** Robert McFadden, Will Zens. **Ph:** Leif Rise. **M:** William Schaeffer. Parade, 1965.
A soldier returns to Vietnam in search of a brother who the communists have kidnapped because of his medical skills.

Tour of Duty.тvм Bill L. Norton. With Terence Knox, Stephen Caffrey. **Prod:** Ronald L Schwary (Zev Braun, New World TV). **W:** Steve Duncan & L. Travis Clark. **Ph:** Stephen L. Posey. **M:** Joseph Conlan. CBS-TV, 1987.
A television series follows an infantry platoon in Vietnam in the late sixties. "The message...is that survival depends on cooperation among one another—but then how many series survive delivering a message?" (Variety).

Tracks. Henry Jaglom. With Dennis Hopper, Taryn Power, Dean Stockwell. **Prod:** Howard Zucker, Irving Cohen, Ted Shapiro (Camera One). **W:** Jaglom. **Ph:** Paul Glickman. **M:** Robert Ragland, Robert Rosene. Rainbow, 1976.
A slightly manic soldier escorts a military coffin on a train across the United States. Jaglom filmed nearly the entire film on an Amtrak train traveling back-and-forth between Los Angeles and San Diego, although he had not received permission.

Trained to Kill. Daniel J. Vance. With Steve Sandor, Rockne Tarkington, Heidi Vaughn. 1973.
A veteran confronts a gang of sadistic killers in his hometown. Also known as The No Mercy Man.

Trained to Kill (1988). H.K. Dyal. With Chuck Connors, Ron O'Neal. 1988.
Years after a soldier informs on a friend's drug running organization, the friend seeks revenge.

Trial of Billy Jack, The. T.C. Frank (Tom Laughlin). With Tom Laughlin, Delores Taylor. PROD: Joe Cramer (Taylor-Laughlin). **W:** T.C. Frank, Teresa Christina. PH: Jack A. Marta. **M:** Elmer Bernstein. Warner, 1974.
Billy Jack defends the Freedom School from more intolerance, but cannot protect them from a massacre by the National Guard.

Trial of the Catonsville Nine, The. Gordon Davidson. With Gwen Arner, Ed Flanders. PROD: Gregory Peck (Melville). **W:** Daniel Berrigan, Saul Levitt from Berrigan's play. PH: Haskell Wexler. **M:** Shelly Manne. Melville, 1972.
The nine men and woman who burned the draft records in Catonsville defend their action.

Twilight Zone: The Movie (Segment One). John Landis. With Vic Morrow. PROD: Steven Spielberg and John Landis. **W:** Landis. PH: Steven Larner. **M:** Jerry Goldsmith. Warner, 1983.
A racist is suddenly transported to Vietnam where he must rescue some Vietnamese children from the fighting. Vic Morrow and the two child actors died during the filming.

Twilight's Last Gleaming (U.S./West Germany). Robert Aldrich. With Burt Lancaster, Richard Widmark, Paul Winfield. PROD: Merv Adelson (Geria) **W:** Ronald M. Cohen, Edward Huebsch from the novel *Viper Three* by Walter Wager. PH: Robert Hauser. **M:** Jerry Goldsmith. Allied Artists, 1977.
A renegade officer escapes from death row, captures a nuclear missile silo, and threatens to start a nuclear war unless the President tells the truth about the Vietnam War to the American people.

Two. Charles Trieschmann. **W:** Charles Trieschmann. Colmar, 1974.

Two People. Robert Wise. With Peter Fonda, Lindsay Wagner. PROD: Robert Wise (Filmmakers Group). **W:** Richard DeRoy. PH: Henri Decae with Gerald Hirschfield (NY). **M:** David Shire. Universal, 1973.
A deserter returns to American justice despite the pleadings of a model he meets on the way.

Ugly American, The. George H. Englund. With Marlon Brando, Eiji Ukada, Pat Hingle. PROD: George Englund. **W:** Stewart Stern from the novel by William J. Lederer and Eugene Burdick. PH: Clifford Stine. **M:** Frank Skinner. Universal-International, 1963.
A new Ambassador to a Southeast Asian nation exacerbates the civil war there by insisting on supporting an unpopular, but anticommunist, regime.

Ulzana's Raid. Robert Aldrich. With Burt Lancaster, Bruce Davison, Jorge Luke. PROD: Carter deHaven, Aldrich. **W**: Alan Sharp. PH: Joseph Biroc. **M**: Frank deVol. Universal, 1972.
A young officer is sent to recapture or kill an Indian who has left the reservation and led his followers on a murderous rampage.

Uncommon Valor. Ted Kotcheff. With Gene Hackman, Robert Stack, Fred Ward, Patrick Swayze. PROD: John Milius and Buzz Feitshans. **W**: Joe Gayton. PH: Stephen H. Burum, Ric Waite **M**: James Horner. Paramount, 1983.
An American colonel brings together the surviving members of his son's platoon for an attempted POW rescue mission. Roughly from a true incident.

Universal Soldier. Roland Emmerich. With Jean-Claude Van Damme, Dolph Lundgren, Ally Walker. PROD: Allen Shapiro, Craig Baumgarten, Joel B. Michaels (Carolco International). **W**: Richard Rothstein, Christopher Leitch, Dean Devlin. PH: Karl Walter Lindenlaub. **M**: Christopher Franke. Guild, 1992.
Modern technology allows the military to re-vivify the corpses of Vietnam War casualties for use as a new type of super-soldier. The plans go wrong when one of the resurrected soldiers remembers his past.

Vanishing Point. Richard C. Sarafin. With Barry Newman, Cleavon Little, Dean Jagger. PROD: Norman Spencer (Cupid). **W**: Guillermo Cain. PH: John A. Alonzo. 20th Century-Fox, 1972.
A Vietnam veteran and former race car driver now returns rental cars between cities. When he runs foul of the speed cops, a disk-jockey turns him into a folk-hero as he races to the coast one last time.

Vietnam.TVM John Duigan, Chris Noonan. With Barry Otto, Veronica Lang, Nicholas Eadie. PROD: Terry Hayes, Doug Mitchell, George Miller (Kennedy-Miller). **W**: Terry Hayes, John Duigan, Chris Noonan. PH: Geoff Burton. **M**: Bill Motzing. Network Ten, Australia, 1987.
An Australian family survives the Australian involvement in the Vietnam War from November 1964 to December 1972.

Vietnam War Story.TVM Michael Toshiyuko Uno. With Tim Guinee, Wesley Snipes, William Frankfather. PROD: Garry Jossen (Home Box Office, Consolidated). **W**: Adam Rodman. PH: Stephen Lighthill. **M**: Jonathon Sheffer, Mark Snow. HBO-TV, 1988.
First in a series of half-hour stories about American soldiers in Vietnam, their allies, enemies, and their relatives. The series was later reproduced in a series of videos, each containing three stories.

Vietnam, Texas. Robert Ginty. With Robert Ginty, Haing S. Ngor. PROD: Ginty, Ron Joy (Epic). **W:** Tom Badal and C. Courtney Joyner (Epic). PH: Robert M. Baldwin, Jr. **M:** Richard Stone. 1990.
A priest's search for the Vietnamese woman he had abandoned in Vietnam leads him to a Vietnamese community in Texas, where the woman has married the local drug baron.

Visitors, The. Elia Kazan. With James Woods, Patrick McVey, Steve Railsback, Chico Martinez. PROD: Chris Kazan-Nick Proferes. **W:** Chris Kazan. PH: Nick Proferes. **M:** Johann Sebastian Bach. United Artists, 1972.
When two veterans are released from prison after serving time for the rape of a Vietnamese woman, they terrorize the veteran who put them there.

Volunteers. Nicholas Meyer. With Tom Hanks, Rita Wilson, John Candy. PROD: Richard Shepherd, Walter F. Parkes (HBO/Silver Screen). **W:** Ken Levine, David Isaacs from story by Keith Critchlow. PH: Ric Waite. **M:** James Horner. Tri-Star, 1985.
In the 1960s, a rich kid enlists in the Peace Corp to avoid bookies. Sent to a Southeast Asian nation, he is caught between extremist communist Asians and rabid anticommunist Americans.

Wanderers, The. (U.S./Netherlands) Philip Kaufman. With Ken Wahl, John Freiedrich, Karen Allen. PROD: Martin Ransohoff. **W:** Rose Kaufman, Philip Kaufman from the novel by Richard Price. PH: Michael Chapman. Orion, 1979.
In a story of street gangs in 1963, the meanest gang on the streets meets its undoing when a marine recruiter persuades them to enlist and go to Viet Nam.

Welcome Home. Franklin Schaffner. With Kris Kristofferson, Brian Keith, Jo Beth Williams. PROD: Martin Ransohoff (Rank). **W:** Maggie Kleinman. PH: Fred J. Koenekamp. Warner, 1989.
After seventeen years hiding from the Khmer in Cambodia, an American pilot has a new wife and two children, but he decides to return home to his first wife, who has now also remarried, and his teenage son.

Welcome Home, Johnny Bristol.TVM George McCowan. With Martin Landau, Brock Peters, Jane Alexander. PROD: Arthur Joel Katz (Cinema Center 100). **W:** Stanley R. Greenberg. PH: Robert L. Morrison. **M:** Lalo Schifrin. CBS-TV, 1971.
A POW's memories of his home in Charles, Vermont help him survive his captivity, but when he returns to America he learns that this hometown was just a fantasy. He actually lives at the corner of Charles and Vermont streets in a rundown section of Philadelphia.

Welcome Home, Soldier Boys. Richard Compton. With Joe Don Baker, Paul Koslo, Alan Vint. Prod: Marvin Schwartz. W: Guerdon Trueblood. Ph: Don Birnkrant. M: Ken Wannberg, Ronee Blakely. 20th Century-Fox, 1974.
A group of veterans destroys a western town before they are destroyed by the National Guard.

Whatever It Takes. Bob Demchuk. With Tom Mason. Prod: Demchuk. W: Chris Weatherhead, Demchuk. Ph: John Drake. M: Gary Sherman. Aquarius Films, 1986.

When Hell Was in Session. tvm Paul Krasny. With Hal Holbrook, Eva Marie Saint, Mako, Ronnie Cox. NBC, 1979.
Jeremiah Denton survives seven-and-a-half years as a POW in North Vietnam.

When You Comin' Back Red Ryder? Milton Katselas. With Marjoe Gortner, Lee Grant, Hal Linden. Prod: Marjoe Gartner. W: Mark Medoff from his play. Ph: Jules Brenner. M: Jack Nitzsche. Columbia, 1979.
A psychotic veteran terrorizes people in a diner.

White Nights. Taylor Hackford. With Mikhail Baryshnikov, Gregory Hines, Isabella Rossellini. Prod: Hackford, William S. Gilmore (New Visions/Delphi V). W: James Goldman, Eric Hughes. Ph: David Watkin. M: Michael Colombier. Columbia, 1985.
A black man who defected to Russia in protest against the Vietnam War has become disenchanted with the communist state and helps a Russian ballet dancer to defect to America.

Who'll Stop the Rain. Karel Reisz. With Nick Nolte, Tuesday Weld, Michael Moriarty, Richard Masur. Prod: Gabriel Katzka, Herb Jaffe (The Dog Soldiers Co.). W: Judith Roscoe, Robert Stone from Stone's novel *Dog Soldiers*. Ph: Richard H. Kline. M: Laurence Rosenthal. United Artists, 1978.
A veteran helps a journalist smuggle heroin into America, then must defend the drugs and the journalist's wife from corrupt narcotic agents. Also known as Dog Soldiers.

Windflowers: The Story of a Draft Dodger. Adolfas Mekas. With John Kramer, Pola Chapelle. Prod: Adolfas Mekas (Windflowers Company). W: Adolfas Mekas. Ph: Bruce Sparks. M: Mekas, Pola Chapelle. Filmmakers Distribution Center, 1968.
A draft dodger being hunted by the FBI dies when the local police mistake his walking stick for a gun.

Yank in Indo-China, A. Wallace A. Grissell. With John Archer, Douglas Dick, Jean Willes, Maura Murphy. Prod: Sam Katzman. W: Samuel Newman. Ph: William Whitley. M: Rossi diMaggio. Columbia, 1952.
American pilots run bombing raids against Chinese munitions dumps until they crash in Vietnam and must escape through the jungles. A woman in the group is pregnant and gives birth during the escape. Also known as Hidden Secrets.

Yank in Viet-Nam, A. Marshall Thompson. With Marshall Thomson, Enrique Magalona, Mario Bari. Prod: Wray Davis (Kingman). W: Jane Wardell, Jack Lewis from a story by Lewis. M: Richard Lasalle. Allied Artists, 1964.
A U.S. marine pilot is shot down over the Mekong Delta and joins forces with a guerrilla group to save a local doctor. During the rescue he manages to romance the doctor's daughter. Also known as Year of the Tiger.

Year of the Dragon. Michael Cimino. With Mickey Rourke, John Lone, Ariane. Prod: Dino De Laurentiis (Dino De Laurentiis Corp) W: Oliver Stone and Michael Cimino from the novel by Robert Daley. Ph: Alex Thomson. M: David Mansfield. MGM/UA, 1985.
A cynical Vietnam veteran, now the most highly decorated detective in New York, battles the heroin trade in Chinatown.

Youngblood. Noel Nosseck. With Lawrence-Hilton Jacobs, Bryan O'Dell, Ren Woods. Prod: Nick Grillo, Alan Riche. W: Paul Carter Harrison. Ph: Robbie Greenberg. American International, 1978.

Zabriskie Point. Michelangelo Antonioni. With Mark Frechette, Rod Taylor, Saria Halprin. Prod: Carlo Ponti. W: Antonioni, Fred Gardner, Sam Shephard, Tonino Guerra, Clare Peploe. Ph: Alfio Contini. M: The Pink Floyd. MGM, 1970.
Antonioni's version of the sixties' youth movement includes protest, racism, sexual liberation, capitalism, and violence.

Works Cited and General Bibliography

Adair, Gilbert. *Hollywood's Vietnam: From* The Green Berets *to* Apocalypse Now. New York: Proteus, 1981.

————. *Hollywood's Vietnam: From* The Green Berets *to* Full Metal Jacket. London: Heinemann, 1989.

Adler, Renata. Review of *The Green Berets. New York Times* 20 June 1968:49.

Anderegg, Michael, ed. *Inventing Vietnam: The War in Film and Television.* Philadelphia: Temple UP, 1991.

Appy, Christian. "Vietnam According to Oliver Stone: John Wayne Rides Again." *Commonweal* 23 March 1990: 187-89.

Auster, Albert and Leonard Quart. *How the War Was Remembered: Hollywood and Vietnam.* Westport, CT: Praeger, 1988.

Baker, Mark. *Nam.* New York: William Morrow, 1981.

Bates, Milton J. "Men, Women, and Vietnam." Gilman and Smith. 27-63.

Beck, Avent. "Mythic Structures in the Popular Vietnam Combat Movie." Master's thesis, Columbia University, 1990.

Beidler, Philip D. *American Literature and the Experience of Vietnam.* Athens: University of Georgia Press, 1982.

Bellamy, Michael. "Carnival and Carnage: Falling Like Rock Stars and Second Lieutenants." Gilman and Smith. 10-26.

Berg, Rick. "Losing Vietnam: Covering the War in an Age of Technology." Dittmar and Michaud. 41-68.

Blake, Richard A. "Mind and Heart." *America* 21 February 1987: 159, iii.

Brooke, Joshua. *Just a Little Inconvenience.* New York: Dell, 1978.

Brownlow, Kevin. *The War, The West, and the Wilderness.* New York: Knopf, 1979.

Bryan, C.D.B. *Friendly Fire.* New York: Putnam, 1976.

————. "Barely Suppressed Screams." *Harpers* June 1984: 67-72.

Burdick, Eugene and William J. Lederer. *The Ugly American*. New York: Norton, 1958.

Byron, Stuart. "I Can't Get Jimmy Carter to See My Movie." Interview with Robert Aldrich. *Film Comment* 13 (1977): 46-52.

Caputo, Philip. *A Rumor of War*. New York: Ballantine, 1977.

Cawley, Leo. "The War about the War: Vietnam Films and the American Myth." Dittmar and Michaud: 69-80.

Cocks, Jay. "Marrakech Local." *Time* 2 April 1973: 60.

Colby, William with James McCargar. *Lost Victory: A Firsthand Account of America's Sixteen-Year Involvement in Vietnam*. Chicago: Contemporary, 1989.

Coppola, Eleanor. *Notes*. New York: Simon and Schuster, 1979.

Corliss, Richard, et.al. "*Platoon*: Vietnam. The Way It Really Was, on Film." *Time* 26 January 1987: 54-61.

Cowie, Peter. *Coppola*. London: Faber & Faber, 1989.

Crowdus, Gary. "Personal Struggles and Political Issues: An Interview with Oliver Stone by Gary Crowdus." *Cineaste* 16 (1988):18-21.

Dean, Eric T. "The Myth of the Troubled and Scorned Vietnam Veteran." *Journal of American Studies* 26(1992)1: 52-74.

Denby, David. "Blood Brothers." *New York* 12 November 1984: 121-2, 125.

Dickstein, Morris. "Bringing It All Back Home." *Partisan Review* 45 (1978): 627-33.

Dittmar, Linda and Gene Michaud, eds. *From Hanoi to Hollywood: The Vietnam War in American Film*. New Brunswick, NJ: Rutgers UP, 1990.

Edelman, Rob. "A Second Look: *Go Tell the Spartans*." *Cineaste* 13 (1983): 18-19, 54.

Elshten, Jean Bethke. *Women and War*. New York: Basic, 1987.

Emerson, Gloria. *Winners and Losers*. New York: Random House, 1976.

Farber, Stephen. "End of the Road?" *Film Quarterly* 23 (Winter 1969): 3-10.

Fearing, Franklin. "Warriors Return: Normal or Neurotic." *Hollywood Quarterly* 1 (1945).

Fiedler, Leslie. "Mythicizing the Unspeakable." *Journal of American Folklore* 103 (1990): 390-399.

Film Review: Rogue's Regiment. *Time* 29 November 1948: 98.

Fitzgerald, Francis. *Fire in the Lake: The Vietnamese and the Americans in Vietnam*. Boston: Little, Brown, 1972.

Fore, Steven. "Kuntzel's Law and *Uncommon Valor* or, Reshaping the National Consciousness in Six Minutes Flat." *Wide Angle: A Film Quarterly of Theory, Criticism, and Practice* 7 (1985): 23-32.

Fox, Terry Curtis. "Stalking *The Deer Hunter*." *Film Comment* 15 (1979): 22-25.

Franklin, H. Bruce. "The POW/MIA Myth." *The Atlantic Monthly* December 1991: 45-81.

Galperin, William. "History into Allegory: *The Wild Bunch* as Vietnam Movie." *Western Humanities Review 35 (1981): 165-172.*

Garnham, Nicholas. *Samuel Fuller*. New York: Viking, 1971.

Gelb, Leslie and Richard K. Betts. *The Irony of Vietnam: The System Worked*. Washington, DC: Brookings, 1979.

Geng, Veronica. "Mistah Kurtz—He Dead." *New Yorker* 3 September 1979: 70.

Gilman, Owen W. Jr. and Lorrie Smith, eds. *America Rediscovered: Critical Essays on Literature and Film of the Vietnam War*. New York: Garland, 1990.

"Glory." *The New Yorker* 29 June 1968: 24-27.

Goldman, Peter et. al. "Rocky and Rambo." *Newsweek* 23 December 1985: 58-62.

Greenberg, Harvey R. "Dangerous Recuperations: *Red Dawn, Rambo,* and the New Decaturism." *Journal of Popular Film and Television* 15 (Summer 1987): 60-70.

Greene, Graham . *The Quiet American*. New York: Penguin, 1973.

Greil, Marcus. "Journey Up the River: An Interview with Francis Coppola." *Rolling Stone* 1 November 1979: 51-57.

Hagen, William M. *"Heart of Darkness* and the Process of *Apocalypse Now.*" *Conradiana* 13 (1981): 45-53.

Hallin, Daniel C. *The Uncensored War: The Media and Vietnam*. New York: Oxford UP, 1986.

Hatch, Robert. Review of *Getting Straight*. *The Nation* 8 June 1970: 700.

———. Review of *Rogue's Regiment*. *New Republic* 3 January 1949: 29.

Hayslip, Le Ly with James Hayslip. *Child of War, Woman of Peace: Heaven and Earth Part Two*. London: Pan Books, 1993.

——— with Jay Wurts. *When Heaven and Earth Changed Places: A Vietnamese Woman's Journey from War to Peace*. New York: Plume, 1989.

Hellman, John. "Vietnam and the Hollywood Genre Film: Inversions of American Mythology in *The Deer Hunter* and *Apocalypse Now.*" *American Quarterly* 34 (1982): 418-39.

Herr, Michael. *Dispatches*. New York: Avon, 1977.

Hoberman, J. "Film Review: *The Killing Fields.*" *The Village Voice* 3 November 1984: 57.

James, David. "Presence of Discourse/Discourse of Presence: Representing Vietnam." *Wide Angle: A Film Quarterly of Theory, Criticism, and Practice* 7 (1985): 41-51.

Jeffords, Susan. "Friendly Civilians: Images of Women and the Feminization of the Audience in Vietnam Films." *Wide Angle: A Film Quarterly of Theory, Criticism, and Practice* 7 (1985): 13-22.

———. "The New Vietnam War Films: Is the Movie Over?" *Journal of Popular Film and Television* 13 (Winter 1986): 186-194.

———. "'Things Worth Dying for': Gender and the Ideology of Collectivity in Vietnam Representation." *Cultural Critique* 8 (Winter 1987-88): 79-103.

———. *The Remasculinization of America: Gender and the Vietnam War.* Bloomington: Indiana UP, 1989.

Jensen-Stevenson, Monica and William Stevenson. *Kiss the Boys Goodbye: How the United States Betrayed Its Own POWs in Vietnam.* New York: Dutton, 1990.

Just, Ward. "Vietnam: Fiction and Fact." *TriQuarterly* 65 (Winter 1986): 215-220.

———. "Vietnam: The Camera Lies." *Atlantic* December 1979: 63-65.

Kael, Pauline. "Winging It." *The New Yorker* 27 November 1971.

———. "Shearing the Sheep." *The New Yorker* 25 November 1974: 180-183.

———. Film Review: *Platoon. The New Yorker* 12 January 1987: 94-96.

Kane, Kathryn. *Visions of War: Hollywood Combat Films of World War II.* Ann Arbor: University of Michigan, 1982.

———. "The World War II Combat Film." In *Handbook of American Film Genres.* Ed. Wes D. Gehring. Westport, CT: Greenwood, 1985: 85-102.

Karnow, Stanley. *Vietnam: A History.* New York: Viking, 1983.

Klein, Michael. "Historical Memory, Film, and the Vietnam Era." Dittmar and Michaud. 19-40.

Koppes, Clayton R. and Gregory D. Black. *Hollywood Goes to War: How Politics, Profits, and Propaganda Shaped World War II Movies.* New York: Free Press, 1987.

Kovic, Ron. *Born on the Fourth of July.* New York: Pocket, 1977.

Lang, Daniel. *Casualties of War.* New York: Pocket, 1989.

Lederer, William J. and Eugene Burdick. *The Ugly American.* Greenwich, CT: Fawcett Crest, 1958.

Lenihan, John. *Showdown: Confronting Modern America in the Western Film.* Urbana: University of Illinois, 1985.

Lewy, Guenter. *America in Vietnam.* New York: Oxford UP, 1978.

MacPherson, Myra. *Long Time Passing: Vietnam and the Haunted Generation.* New York: Doubleday, 1984.

McCarthy, Todd. "Milos Foreman Lets His Hair Down." *Film Comment* 15 (1979): 17-21.

McGilligan, Pat. "Point Man: Oliver Stone Interviewed by Pat McGilligan." *Film Comment* 23 (1987): 11-20, 60.

McInerney, Peter. "Apocalypse Then: Hollywood Looks Back at Vietnam." *Film Quarterly* 33 (Winter 1979-80): 21-32.

———. "'Straight' and 'Secret' History in Vietnam War Literature." *Contemporary Literature* 22 (1981): 187-204.

Miller, Mark Crispin. "How TV Covers War." In *New Challenges for Documentary*. Ed. Alan Rosenthal. Berkeley: University of California, 1988: 365-374.

Molesworth, Charles. "Rambo, Passion and Power." *Dissent* Winter 1986: 109-111.

Moore, Robin. *The Green Berets*. New York: Crown, 1965.

Morrow, Lance. "Viet Nam Comes Home." *Time* 23 April 1979: 22-28.

Muse, Eben. "From Lt. Calley to John Rambo: Repatriating the Vietnam War." *Journal of American Studies* 27 (April 1993): 88-92.

———. "The Land of Nam: Romance and Persecution in Brian DePalma's *Casualties of War*." *Literature/Film Quarterly* 20 (1992): 205-212.

———. "Romance, Power and the Vietnam War: Romantic Triangles in Three Vietnam War Films." *Durham University Journal* 86 (July 1994): 307-313.

Nguyen Phut Tan. *A Modern History of Viet-Nam (1802-1954)*. Saigon: Khai-Tri, 1964.

Nichols, Bill. *Ideology and the Image*. Bloomington: Indiana UP, 1981.

Nixon, Richard. *No More Vietnams*. New York: Arbor House, 1985.

Norden, Martin F. "The Disabled Vietnam Vet in Hollywood Films." *Journal of Popular Film and Television* 13 (1985): 15-23.

Page, Tim. *Page after Page*. London: Sidgwick & Jackson, 1988.

Pally, Marcia. "Red Faces." *Film Comment* February 1986: 32-37.

Paris, Barry. "Maximum Expression." Interview with Robert De Niro. *American Film* October 1989: 30-39, 54.

Paris, Michael. "The American Film Industry and Vietnam." *History Today* April 1987: 19-26.

Peary, Danny. *Guide for the Film Fanatic*. London: Simon and Schuster, 1987.

Phillips, Julia. *You'll Never Eat Lunch in This Town Again*. London: Heinemann, 1991.

Proffitt, Nicholas. "Pete Bravado's War and Peace." *New York Times Book Review*, 21 May 1989:7.

Rafferty, Terrence. "Remote Control." *Sight and Sound* 56 (1987): 256-59.

Rich, Adrienne. "Vietnam and Sexual Violence." In *On Lies, Secrets, and Silence: Selected Prose, 1966-78*. New York: Norton, 1979.

Rowe, John Carlos and Rick Berg, eds. *The Vietnam War and American Culture*. New York: Columbia UP, 1991.

Schanberg, Sydney H. "The Death and Life of Dith Pran." *The New York Times Magazine* 20 January 1980: 16-24, 35-38, 42-53, 64-65.

Sheehan, Neil. *A Great Shining Lie: John Paul Vann and America in Vietnam.* London: Jonathan Cape, 1989.

Slotkin, Richard. *Regeneration through Violence: The Mythology of the American Frontier, 1600-1860.* Middletown, CT: Wesleyan UP, 1973.

Smith, Julian. "Between Vermont and Violence: Film Portraits of Vietnam Veterans." *Film Quarterly* 26 (Summer 1973): 10-17.

———. *Looking Away: Hollywood and Vietnam.* New York: Scribners, 1975.

Spark, Alasdair. "The Soldier at the Heart of the War: The Myth of the Green Beret in the Popular Culture of the Vietnam Era." *Journal of American Studies* 18 (1984): 29-48.

Stone, Oliver. "One from the Heart." *American Film* 12 (January/February 1987): 17-19, 56.

Suid, Lawrence H. "Hollywood and Vietnam." *Film Comment* 15 (September/October 1979): 20-25.

———. "The Film Industry and the Vietnam War." Diss. Case Western Reserve University, 1980.

———. *Guts and Glory: Great American War Movies.* Reading, MA: Addisson, 1978.

Taki. "War Record." *The Spectator* 17 March 1990: 50.

Thompson, Lawrence, Richard Welch and James Stephens. "A Vietnam filmography." *Journal of Popular Film and Television* 9 (Spring 1981): 61-67.

Thompson, Richard. "Stoked." Interview with John Milius. *Film Comment* 12 (July-August 1976): 10-21.

Tuchman, Barbara. *The March of Folly: From Troy to Vietnam.* New York: Knopf, 1984.

Turan, Kenneth. "Pandering." *The Progressive* 39 (March 1975): 39-40.

Weber, Bruce. "Cool Head, Hot Images." *New York Times Magazine,* 21 May 1989.

White, Susan. "Male Bonding, Hollywood Orientalism, and the Repression of the Feminine in Kubrick's *Full Metal Jacket.*" *Arizona Quarterly* 44 (Autumn 1988): 120-144.

Williamson, Chilton, Jr. "Gang Narcissism." *National Review* 1975: 278.

Willis, John, ed. *Screen World Annual.* London: Frederick Muller.

Zimmerman, Paul D. "Bombs Away." *Newsweek* 20 July 1970: 77.

Film Index

283

About the Author

EBEN J. MUSE is a graduate of Boston College. He earned his Ph.D. from the State University of New York at Buffalo in 1992 and has since published several articles on Vietnam War movies. He currently lives in North Wales, where he is working on a study of the film villain.